LORDS OF

THE SAMURAI

THE LEGACY OF A DAIMYO FAMILY

by Yoko Woodson

With the Assistance of Melissa M. Rinne

Essays by Takeuchi Jun'ichi, Thomas Cleary, and Deborah Clearwaters

Additional Contributions from Abe Junko, Miyake Hidekazu, Jennifer Chen, and Natasha Reichle

Prefaces by Hosokawa Morihiro and Jay Xu

Translations by Thomas Cleary amd Melissa M. Rinne

ASIAN ASIAN ART MUSEUM – CHONG-MOON LEE CENTER FOR ASIAN ART AND CULTURE

ISBN: 978-0-939117-46-8 (cloth) / 978-0-939117-47-5 (paper)

The Asian Art Museum–Chong-Moon Lee Center for Asian Art and Culture is a public institution whose mission is to lead a diverse global audience in discovering the unique material, aesthetic, and intellectual achievements of Asian art and culture.

All images in the book are courtesy of the Eisei-Bunko Museum, Tokyo, except for the following. Thomas Cleary essay (p. 7): photography by Kazuhiro Tsuruta, except for fig. 4, from *Japanese Scroll Paintings: Ippen Hijiri-e* (Tokyo: Kadokawa); cat. nos. 138, 141, and 143: photo by Kanda Yoshiaki; and cat. nos. 157–164 and 166: Copyright © Shinchōsha Publishing Co., Ltd. Photo by Nonaka Akio..

Notes on the text:
Japanese romanization follows the system used in *Kenkyusha's New Japanese-English Dictionary*. Chinese follows the pinyin system. Korean follows the new government romanization system. East Asian names are written with the surname followed by the given name, unless the person in question is based in the West. Diacritical marks have been omitted from well-known geographic place names and from Japanese words that are now part of the English language. The death year for Hosokawa Tadaoki (aka Sansai) is given as 1646 instead of 1645 because Tadaoki died in the twelfth month of the old lunar calendar, which corresponds roughly to January of the following year by the modern calendar. A similar calculation was made for some other figures, such as Hakuin Ekaku.

Front cover: cat. no. 11
Back cover: cat. no. 138
Title page: cat. no. 21
Page V: cat. no. 139
Table of contents: cat. no. 76
Page XVIII: cat. nos. 109 – 121
Page 5: cat. no. 139
Page 6: cat. no. 92

1 3 5 7 9 8 6 4 2

FIRST PRINTING

This book was published on the occasion of the exhibition *Lords of the Samurai: Legacy of a Daimyo Family,* organized by the Asian Art Museum and the Eisei-Bunko Hosokawa Collection, Tokyo. The exhibition was presented in San Francisco at the Asian Art Museum from June 12 through September 20, 2009. The presentation was made possible by Carmen M. Christensen and the Henri and Tomoye Takahashi Charitable Foundation.

Support for this catalogue was generously provided by the Society for Asian Art.

This exhibition is supported by a grant from the National Endowment for the Arts.

NATIONAL
ENDOWMENT
FOR THE ARTS

The exhibition was curated by Yoko Woodson. Melissa Rinne provided considerable assistance in preparing the catalogue content. Production of the catalogue was overseen by Thomas Christensen. James Donnelly edited and proofread the text. The book was typeset in Adobe Garamond, Univers bold, and Trajan. Ron Shore of Shore Design in Brisbane, California designed and produced the book. It was printed in Hong Kong on 170gsm silk artpaper by Regal Printing, LTD.

HOSOKAWA FAMILY COLLECTION
The Eisei-Bunko Museum (永青文庫), Tokyo.

The art objects, historical documents, and books that the Hosokawa family collected and used are now owned by the Eisei-Bunko Museum, which was established in 1950 for the purpose of preserving the family's art and cultural objects and displaying them to the general public. Many works in the collection are designated by the Japanese government as National Treasures, Important Cultural Properties, or Important Art Objects.

The collection was named "Eisei-Bunko" by Marquis Hosokawa Moritatsu (1883–1970), then head of the family, who had been granted an aristocratic title. To name the collection he combined the "ei" of Eigen'an (永源庵), a subtemple of Kenninji in Kyoto, with the "sei" of Seiryūji (青龍寺), the residence of Hosokawa Fujitaka (Yūsai, 1534–1610), the founder of the Hosokawa family branch of the premodern period.

The Eisei-Bunko collection includes military armors, swords, paintings, calligraphy, tea utensils, Noh robes, and other art objects. Some these works are kept in the Kumamoto Prefectural Museum of Art. The books, clan records, and documents, and maps are kept in the Kumamoto University Library.

The Asian Art Museum is deeply indebted to the Eisei-Bunko and its staff for making this exhibition and publication possible.

CONTENTS

HOSOKAWA MORIHIRO | Chairman, Eisei-Bunko Museum

It is my great pleasure to commend the successful organization of the special exhibition *Lords of the Samurai: Legacy of a Daimyo Family*. This is first time that the Hosokawa family's heirloom arms and armor, paintings, and decorative and applied art objects have been shown in a comprehensive way in the United States. I am very grateful to the Asian Art Museum of San Francisco and all the others who have collaborated in this project for providing us with this valuable opportunity.

The Hosokawa family dates back to the Muromachi period (1392–1573); its lords served as military generals during the subsequent era of Warring States, after which it was awarded a fiefdom that produced 540,000 *koku* (more than 97 million liters) of rice annually in Higo province (now Kumamoto prefecture). It is a family whose lineage has continued uninterrupted for seven hundred years. Only the imperial family and several other daimyo families have histories extending over a few hundred years; among them, the Hosokawa family is especially noted for its tradition of placing high value not only on military skill but also on the pursuit of arts and culture.

Japanese generals have always had a high regard for the arts. They decorated their swords with elaborately ornamented mountings and went to battle in exquisitely designed armor. At their banquets, they performed dances from the Noh theater, and as they approached death they composed death verses of classical *waka* poetry. They are known to have rewarded success on the battlefield not with land or status but with prized utensils for the tea ceremony. There was a time when a single tea utensil could be valued as highly as the land comprising an entire province. Because they put their lives on the line in battle, these warriors cultivated a consciousness for living life as richly as possible, which in turn led to a deep reverence for the arts and for literature. The maneuvers of military generals were not constrained to wartime: together with rivals who tomorrow might turn into their enemies on the battlefront they held *renga* linked poetry competitions and *chanoyu* tea gatherings; it was not uncommon for them to use such occasions for the purpose of political negotiation. No matter how much military strength a general might have, he would not be able to live through those troublesome times without being thoroughly versed in literature and the Way of Tea.

One of Japan's military lords best known for his cultural accomplishments was Hosokawa Fujitaka (later known as Yūsai; 1534–1610), the first-generation lord of the Hosokawa family in the early modern period. Fujitaka was not only a warrior but also a highly refined scholar, famed for his achievements and patronage of Noh and music, as well as his devotion to the Way of Tea; he was also recognized as the greatest renga poet of the Warring States period. Fujitaka stayed close to each of the rapidly changing military leaders of the day—Ashikaga Yoshiaki, Oda Nobunaga, Toyotomi Hideyoshi, and finally Tokugawa Ieyasu—and his skills were highly regarded by each of them. When his life came into jeopardy on the battlefront, the emperor himself sent an imperial edict to suspend hostilities out of concern that the tradition of renga would die with this man.

The second-generation lord, Hosokawa Tadaoki (later known as Sansai; 1563–1646), is known not only as the most valiant general to fight in the Battle of Sekigahara—which opened the door to the Edo period—but also as a great practitioner of the Way of Tea and a leading disciple of chanoyu tea master Sen Rikyū (1522–1591). After a confrontation with Japan's ruler Toyotomi Hideyoshi, Rikyū was forced to commit suicide by *seppuku*; the person who saw Rikyū off from Kyoto when he left to kill himself was none other than Tadaoki himself. Tadaoki's wife Gracia (1563–1600) was a devout Christian who lived a pure existence amidst a tumultuous warring age. Her name appears in the records of Jesuit missionaries in Japan at the time as well as in chronologies of Japanese history. Generals of the Warring States era contributed to the infusion not only of Christianity but also of Western books into Japanese culture.

In the early Edo period, the Hosokawa became lords of the 540,000-koku domain of Higo Kumamoto, after which they continued their family tradition as great patrons of the visual and performing arts. Each successive generation of Hosokawa lords embraced Noh actors, tea masters, artists, and craftspeople in a variety of fields and strove to protect and foster their culture.

It is my profound hope that by showing the people of San Francisco and beyond the wide range of artworks that have been preserved and handed down within the Hosokawa family, we will be able to promote deeper understanding of Japanese culture and contribute to the friendship between our nations.

JAY XU | Director, Asian Art Museum

The Asian Art Museum is honored to present this groundbreaking exhibition of art from several generations of the notable Hosokawa family. It was our privilege to work closely with the Eisei-Bunko Museum, Tokyo, which houses the Hosokawa daimyo family collection, to develop an exhibition that would offer a full view of the lords of the samurai, or daimyo—those remarkable figures who combined martial prowess with cultivated artistic taste and ability.

It was our good fortune, as part of this show, to include several ceramic artworks by Hosokawa Morihiro, former prime minister of Japan and eighteenth-generation head of the Hosokawa family. Mr. Hosokawa will attend the opening of the exhibition and share his unique understanding of the daimyo tradition with our museum community.

Takeuchi Jun'ichi, director of the Eisei-Bunko Museum, has been an invaluable resource and contributed an essential essay to this catalogue. Special thanks must go to Eisei-Bunko curator Abe Junko, who was in charge of the exhibition on the Japan side, as well as curator Miyake Hidekazu. Both spent countless hours on the preparation of this publication and the organization of the exhibition. They were assisted by all of the other staff members of the

Eisei-Bunko, to whom we are sincerely grateful. We also thank Matsui Bunko, the staff of the Office of Hosokawa Morihiro, and others whose cooperation helped make this exhibition possible.

I would especially like to thank Carmen M. Christensen and her family, Mrs. Tomoye Takahashi and Mrs. Martha Suzuki through the Tomoye and Henri Takahashi Charitable Foundation, United Airlines, and the National Endowment for the Arts for their early and important support of the exhibition. We are also deeply grateful for the support of the Society of Asian Art toward the publication of this catalogue and the organization of a scholarly symposium on the exhibition.

Director emeritus Emily Sano's initial vision and leadership were instrumental in conceiving and bringing this exhibition to San Francisco. The development and execution of this vision was completed within an extremely short time span by Yoko Woodson, curator of Japanese art at the Asian Art Museum. Dr. Woodson worked tirelessly in choosing the works to bring to San Francisco, in organizing and arranging the exhibition, and in preparing this catalogue. Thanks are due to the Asia Foundation's Margaret F. Williams Memorial Fellowship in Asian Art, established with the generous support of Dr. F. Haydn Williams, for enabling Dr. Woodson to travel to Japan to work on the exhibition.

Melissa Rinne, assistant curator of Japanese art, went beyond the call of duty in providing assistance on the catalogue, working long hours; the book benefits immeasurably from her grace, care, and thoroughness. In the midst of numerous other responsibilities, director of Education Deborah Clearwaters greatly enriched this catalogue with both her background in Japanese art history and her personal knowledge of the Way of Tea.

I am grateful to Thomas Cleary for his masterful essay on the code of the samurai, and to Jennifer Chen and associate curator Natasha Reichle for their invaluable contributions to the catalogue. The catalogue's production was overseen by Thomas Christensen, the museum's unflappable and immensely talented director of Publications. It benefited from the sensitive editing and proofreading of James Donnelly. Asian Art Museum librarian John Stucky assembled a core bibliography and provided research assistance throughout. Skye Alexander prepared the index. Jason Jose lent his efficient and skillful graphics expertise. Finally, I would like to thank Ron Shore of Shore Design for producing such a beautiful book.

Numerous staff members of the Asian Art Museum applied their skill and talent to making the exhibition a success, among them director of Museum Services Robin Groesbeck and her assistant Nahry Tak; chief curator Forrest McGill and the rest of the museum's Curatorial staff; registrar Cathy Mano and her colleagues; conservator Shiho Sasaki and the Conservation staff; Photo Services manager Aino Tolme and photographer Kazuhiro Tsuruta; exhibition designer Stephen Penkowski and the Preparation team led by Brent Powell; Visitor Services manager Pauline Fong-Martinez; and too many more to name. All of their contributions are deeply appreciated.

We hope that this exhibition and catalogue will aid in understanding the samurai and their daimyo lords as more than just skillful military strategists and fighters. The one hundred sixty-six objects presented here demonstrate that they were also dedicated artists and patrons of the arts.

FOREWORD: WARRIORS AND THE LITERARY ARTS

TAKEUCHI JUN'ICHI | Translated by Melissa M. Rinne

How did members of the warrior class (*buke*) spend their time from day to day?

That is a simple question, but it is not one easily answered. What we think of as the "age of the samurai" extended over many centuries, beginning when Minamoto Yoritomo (1147–1199) established military government at the end of the twelfth century and continuing for the 150 years of the Kamakura period (1185–1333), into the early fourteenth century. It then carried on for the 180 years of the Muromachi period (1392–1573), from the end of the fourteenth century through the late sixteenth century. During the second half of the Muromachi period, in the late fifteenth century, struggles for hegemony erupted across the country, initiating a period of Warring States that was finally quelled by Oda Nobunaga (1534–1582) in 1573. Then during the Momoyama period (1573–1615), over a mere twenty-five years, from 1573 to 1598, the country was unified, first under Nobunaga and then under Toyotomi Hideyoshi (1536–1598). Finally, Tokugawa Ieyasu (1542–1616) seized control of the country in 1600, and his successors ruled until 1867, over the long 260 years of the Edo period (1615–1868).

These periods collectively make up the "age of the samurai." But what occupied these warriors over the centuries?

In the strife dividing historical periods or administrative regimes, a warrior's first job, as one would expect, was to fight using his martial skills. In his 1954 film *Seven Samurai,* director Kurosawa Akira "envisions" the waning years of the Warring States period—the "age of the mid-sixteenth century." But his is not a re-creation founded in the history of a particular battle in a particular part of Japan. Rather, it is an enactment of Kurosawa's "envisioned age" in cinematic form—one that *feels* real. Despite this, it is a superb film with dynamic battle scenes, and as a result it has popularized a certain image of "what a samurai was" throughout the world.

The first-generation lord of the Hosokawa clan in the early modern period was Hosokawa Yūsai (1534–1610). Alternatively known by his real name of Fujitaka, Yūsai was a member of the warrior class whose life spanned from the end of the Warring States era through the Momoyama period. He served all three rulers of the day: Nobunaga, Hideyoshi, and Ieyasu. Yūsai's adolescence includes the "envisioned age" of *Seven Samurai,* and his biography includes numerous battle experiences. He served Oda Nobunaga during that warlord's quest for domination of all Japan, fighting in eight major battles between 1568 and 1580 in attempts to gain control of the castles of enemies. Yūsai then served Toyotomi Hideyoshi after he came into power, participating in the conquest of the large southern island of Kyushu in 1587.

Hosokawa Yūsai is best known as a warrior for an event that occurred in 1600, when he successfully defended a particular castle in Western Japan. The castle was the

residence of his son Sansai, who was away at battle in eastern Japan in the service of Tokugawa Ieyasu. Beginning in the seventh month of the year (August by our modern calendar), Yūsai, with fewer than 500 soldiers at his disposal, protected the castle from an enormous enemy force of 15,000 troops over a period of two months.

Yūsai's son, Hosokawa Sansai (also known as Tadaoki, 1563–1646), also lived during the "envisioned age" of *Seven Samurai*. Sansai, too, engaged in six major battles in his lifetime, beginning with his debut on the battlefield in 1577 at the tender age of fourteen (fifteen as ages were counted then), when Nobunaga was mounting his conquest of the entire country. Sansai, like his father, served in turn under Nobunaga, Hideyoshi, and then Ieyasu.

Yūsai's defense of his son's castle ended in the ninth month of 1600 with an incident that would probably be unthinkable in any other country. This incident revolved around a particular *fear*—a fear felt not only by Yūsai's allied generals but also by the generals on the enemy side, as well as by courtiers in Kyoto, who had nothing to do with the battle. The fear was even felt by the emperor.

What about Yūsai's battle could possibly have caused so much distress among so many people? Hosokawa Yūsai was the sole possessor of a secretly transmitted literary work called the *Kokin denju*. The fear that was shared by so many was that if Yūsai died in battle, this important literary tradition would be lost forever.

Kokin denju (Secret Transmission on the *Kokin wakashū*) was essentially a means of analyzing and critiquing the *Kokin wakashū* (Collection of Poems Ancient and Modern; also known as the *Kokinshū*), the first imperial anthology of Japanese *waka* poetry. Compiled at the beginning of the tenth century, and containing 1,100 poems, it became the model for all classical poetry anthologies thereafter. The *Kokin denju* comprised not only commentaries on the poems, but also a concordance of its words together with their lost, secret meanings. Compiled in the fifteenth century by Tō Tsuneyori (c. 1401–1484), the *Kokin denju* made clear the true meaning and literary value of the *Kokin wakashū* verses. A portion of the concordance was handed down in written form, but most of the explanations were transmitted orally from master to disciple. Not just anyone was party to these teachings—the secrets would be imparted only to individuals who had fully mastered and memorized the *Kokin wakashū,* who had written numerous waka poems of their own, and who were considered the most advanced members of waka poetry groups.

Yūsai was the third person in history to have been taught the entire *Kokin denju.* His predecessors were a *renga* (linked verse) poet and an aristocrat; Yūsai was the first member of the warrior class to have received this honor. Because he was the only one alive at the time with mastery over the entire *Kokin denju* tradition, Yūsai's potential death provoked the fear of losing not only the *Kokin denju,* which had been transmitted for over a hundred years, but also the more than six-hundred-year tradition of the *Kokin wakashū* itself.

In the midst of defending the castle, Yūsai negotiated to have a portion of the *Kokin denju* that was written down sent to his poetry disciple, an imperial prince, by way of a specially dispatched "armistice envoy." He also gave the envoy manuscripts for more than twenty-one different imperial poetry anthologies—including the *Kokin wakashū.* Because the only manuscripts in existence were handwritten copies, Yūsai's superb library was of extraordinary importance. He also sent his manuscript of the great literary epic *The Tale of Genji* (*Genji monogatari*) out of the castle and through the battlefield to the capital. Together, these works must have amounted to an vast amount of material that would have required several oxen to carry. Having handed over his life work to the prince, who then handed them over to the emperor, Yūsai prepared himself for death.

One of the reasons that this battle may have lasted so long was that the conquering generals (including some of Yūsai's own poetry students) were also strongly gripped by this *fear*, moderating their thirst for battle. In the end, the emperor finally stepped in and issued an edict through which peace was enacted and the battle was ended, saving both Yūsai's life and the *Kokin denju.*

What does this incident tell us? Was it caused by unique literary gifts possessed only by Yūsai? Was it just a coincidence that he was so bookish and so deeply involved in poetry? Of course not!

From the time that they first took control of the government in the Kamakura period, military rulers studied the *Kokin wakashū* and all later imperial poetry anthologies; they composed waka, sang poems to one another, formed alliances to critique one another's work, and held poetry gatherings. Sometimes they would even compile their own poems into books. Reading and studying waka anthologies required enormous effort: the only way a manuscript could be obtained was by hand copying. Then the copied manuscripts had to be transported from Kyoto to the seat of the military government in Kamakura. Despite their distance from the cultural nexus of the capital, the warriors of the Kamakura shogunate overcame these difficulties in their efforts to study poetry collections.

The tradition of waka study among the samurai elite continued after the Kamakura period right up to the Edo period. It is probably safe to say that not a single provincial lord in Japan, no matter how small his domain, was without poetry anthologies in his library. During the Edo period, however, the study of Japanese poetry went underground, both for the shogunate and for the warriors of each provincial domain, as study of Chinese classics (*kangaku*) replaced it as the official area of scholarship. A factor contributing to this development was the reduced need for provincial clans to comprehend the culture of the capital as a result of the shogun's shift of the center of power from Kyoto to Edo (present-day Tokyo).

This look at the relationship between the warrior class and waka poetry leads us to two questions. First, why did warriors spend so much time reading waka? And second, since waka are meant to be poetic expressions of an individual's true sentiments, why would other people feel compelled to study them? Would it not be enough to read them casually, purely for enjoyment?

The first question might be answered as follows: The warrior's essential goal in life was to gain supremacy. Just because a lord might be based in a far-off province did not change the fact that if the chance arose, his goal would be to conquer the capital. The problem for these military lords was that, without understanding Kyoto's unique culture—a culture centered around the imperial court and the aristocracy—they would never be able to successfully rule over this city. For this reason warriors were vigilant about their study of waka poetry, a literary form tied to the courtier class.

Moreover, even among the members of the warrior class, waka poetry was used as an vehicle for achieving cohesion and exchange. Before a major battle, when they went to pray for victory to the Shinto deities and Buddhas, they would write waka to leave as offerings. So entrenched were poetic traditions in the lives of the samurai class that without knowing waka they would have been unable to carry on relations with other regions. If the samurai's role in life was to follow the Way of the Warrior (*bushidō*), then it was equally their role to follow the Way of Poetry. It is safe to say that there was not a samurai in Japan who was not able to recite waka poetry.

It was during the period of Warring States that the culture of the imperial court and the aristocracy spread most pervasively around the country, even into distant provinces. In order to escape the fighting, courtiers fled to remote regional destinations, where they would be wholeheartedly welcomed by the provincial lords. The local

daimyo would pay enormous amounts of gold to those aristocrats, not for copies of poetry anthologies but for teaching waka to them in person, and for editing their own efforts in poetry competitions. The existence today of well-established cultural centers in each region of Japan dates back to the cultural assimilation that occurred in the middle of the sixteenth century.

The answer to the second question—why poetry was studied instead of simply being enjoyed—underscores the greatest difference between waka and contemporary literature. Waka were composed after prototypes from previously compiled anthologies of poetry. By the rules of the genre, the subject of a poem was limited to the topics (*dai*) found in those approved collections. Another rule was that a waka must be based on a preexisting poem, with just enough innovation to make it fresh. If a completely original poem were composed from personal experiences that fell outside the prescribed topics, for example, it would be categorized as "informal" (*ke*) and would be dismissed by one and all. Waka were composed not by individuals but by groups of anywhere from a few people to as many as twenty. The group's leader would designate a topic, and the group would compose the poem. The new poem would then be critiqued and at times edited by the leader. Such groups, called *kadan* (poetry circles), were composed of warriors from every region, or Kyoto aristocrats, or both. Sometimes these poems would be composed in a public gathering called *utakai* (poetry gathering) or *utaawase* (poetry contest); the verses written during such poetry contests might be later edited, copied, and preserved for posterity in other regions.

All poets belonged to poetry circles, so there were no "lone poets" in the world of waka. This poetic form was clearly suited to military bands, which depended on group cohesion. Knowing these facts about waka poetry composition makes it easier to understand how Yūsai's status as the recipient of the secret *Kokin denju* teachings would have been a matter of common knowledge among members of the warrior class and the aristocracy.

Let us next touch on *The Tale of Genji* (*Genji monogatari*). This epic novel, written in the eleventh century by the court lady Murasaki Shikibu, was read by aristocrats and samurai alike through every age of Japanese history. *The Tale of Genji* is a narrative centered around poetry—every scene is punctuated by characters exchanging waka poems. These poems are sublimations of particular situations in the narrative. *The Tale of Genji* is the ultimate text for studying the relationship between situations and their sublimations as poetry. Warrior lords needed to understand this relationship because waka anthologies contain nothing but the results of such sublimations of particular situations.

At the same time, *The Tale of Genji* evokes like no other literary work the essence of imperial court life; indeed, it is itself an example of aristocratic culture. Members of the warrior class read it not as a romantic novel but for its examples of the culture of the capital. They also showed great interest in paintings representing scenes from the book, along with *rakuchū rakugai-zu* (Scenes in and around the Capital), which were screen paintings depicting birds-eye views of Kyoto landmarks and customs. The daimyos' interest in such paintings stemmed from their depictions of a world that one day might fall under their own control. There is a famous episode about how Nobunaga sent a pair of *rakuchū rakugai-zu* screens to a rival general during the Warring States period. Toyotomi Hideyoshi is known to have had women read *The Tale of Genji* out loud for him, a practice copied by Tokugawa Ieyasu. Yūsai was the recipient not only of the *Kokin denju* but also of the *Genji monogatari denju,* a secret transmission of keys for understanding this novel. The *Kokin wakashū* and *Genji monogatari* held equal literary value.

Today, among the artworks owned by the Eisei-Bunko Museum are a number of handscrolls from the Kamakura and Muromachi periods, when waka culture was synthesized. These came into the Hosokawa collection as a result of the literary environment in which Yūsai and his successors sought to continue the aristocratic culture. These were not collected but were transferred to the clan from an old family collection in the early modern period. The Hosokawa family's Momoyama period folding screens on which fan paintings depicting scenes from *The Tale of Genji* and other *monogatari*-related artworks were pasted probably have similar provenances. The Hosokawa collection is distinguished by its unparalleled treasury, almost a time capsule, of works exemplifying the relationship between the warrior class and the literary arts.

Sansai continued the literary ethos begun by his father, Yūsai, but because he happened to meet the tea master Sen Rikyū (1522–1591) as a young man, much of his own focus was on *chanoyu,* the Way of Tea, and he went on to become a renowned tea master in his own right. In the Edo period he was revered as a living witness who could speak about Rikyū, and as a result he received less attention than his father among literary circles. Sansai, however, received from Tokugawa Iemitsu (1604–1651) in 1639 a paper bearing calligraphy by both Fujiwara Shunzei (1114–1204) and Fujiwara Teika (1162–1241). Both of these legendary poets were forefathers of the Reizei house, the aristocratic family most closely associated with the waka tradition. Iemitsu, a warrior well versed in poetry, presented this extraordinary gift because he recognized particular literary ethos of the Hosokawa clan. The generations succeeding Sansai continued to distinguish themselves through literature, especially waka; but that subject goes beyond the scope of this essay.

The Edo period domain of the Hosokawa was in present day Kumamoto prefecture. Today, in the center of that territory in Kumamoto city is a large garden in which generations of Hosokawa lords sought relaxation over the centuries. In one corner of this garden is a rather small one-story wooden building with a medieval-style roof thatched with thin cypress wood shingles. This is called the Kokin Denju Room. It is still lovingly preserved today.

References:

Ogawa Takeo, *Bushi wa naze uta o yomu ka: Kamakura shōgun kara sengoku daimyō made.* Kadokawa sensho 40. (Tokyo: Kadokawa Shoten, 2008).

Mitamura Masako, *Kioku no naka no Genji monogatari.* (Tokyo: Shinchōsha, 2008).

THE EMERGENCE AND DEVELOPMENT OF SAMURAI WARRIORS AND THEIR GOVERNMENT

YOKO WOODSON

The origins, development, and eventual disappearance of samurai are the result of complex factors operating over a long time. Emerging early on as rural militias, samurai eventually achieved significant status, something those early warriors would not have imagined could have happened. They became deeply involved in Japan's politics and society, and they made substantial contributions in the areas of art and culture. Their powerful presence profoundly affected the course of Japanese history.

The samurai's energetic endeavors and heroic deeds, as well as the poignant and tragic events in which they were at times involved, inspired writers and poets to narrate their life stories and moved artists to glorify their deeds in colorful paintings. Americans have sometimes compared the Japanese warrior to the lone gunmen of the old West, but the samurai were not lone, stray men. Rather, they acted in bands, each individual performing a part clearly prescribed for the operational purposes of the group. The bands' numbers gradually swelled to avoid being overwhelmed by other groups. Each samurai's activities were not aimed at fulfilling his personal ideals and goals. Rather, the samurai found meaning and satisfaction in supporting ideals and goals set by the group's leaders.

ORIGINS OF THE SAMURAI

Early in Japan's history, the imperial court adopted Chinese ideals of public ownership of the land (*ritsuryōsei*); they maintained that system for several centuries. But during the eighth and ninth centuries, land holdings began to be privatized in the northern provinces of Honshu, the largest of the islands of the Japanese archipelago. The number of these privatized lands, called *shōen*, rapidly increased.

The growth in the number of privately controlled militias was the result of multiple factors. First, the imperial court in Kyoto was unable on its own to safeguard frontier regions from the Emishi (Ainu) people who were migrating from Sakhalin, an island farther north. Second, the northern regions are mountainous, with active volcanoes and steep hills. The weather is cold and harsh. As a result, their ties to the imperial court in Kyoto were fragile. Third, court-appointed nobles to provincial governors' positions were little inclined to leave the comfortable and cultured environment of the capital to take up administrative posts in a remote, unknown place. And the appointed court nobles who were willing to take up such posts were unprepared and unequipped for maintaining security and administering their regions.

Consequently, the court appointed deputies from among the local people—these men were forerunners of the samurai. They managed private landholdings, keeping them safe from thieves (while sometimes keeping a portion for themselves). To build power they sought to increase the number of members in their groups, known as "warrior bands."

Starting as little more than family organizations, warrior bands were initially recruited by chieftains from among their kinsmen and maintained only as long as necessary to carry out specific military campaigns. At the conclusion of the campaigns they would return to work their lands. But by the eleventh century the bands had developed a more feudal structure, based on lord-vassal ties among fighting men who were not necessarily connected through kinship. There was, however, a tendency to apply fictive kinship qualities to the groups: for example, vassals were designated as *kenin* (housemen) or *ienoko* (children of the house), and lords were viewed as fathers.

THE FIRST WARRIOR GOVERNMENT: THE KAMAKURA SHOGUNATE, 1185–1333

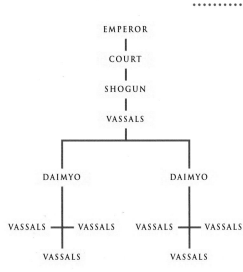

THEORETICAL HIERARCHY OF THE WARRIOR STATE

Though actually weilding more political power than the emperor, the shogun was in theory subservient to him. As well as maintaining his own vassals who reported to him directly, the shogun also oversaw other vassals throughout the state through their daimyo lords, who reported to him

During the eleventh century, the Genji (or Minamoto) clan distinguished itself in the northeastern region of Honshu by defeating several other powerful clans including the Abe and the Kiyohara. By the late eleventh century, the Genji was recognized as the most powerful clan in the region. In the mid twelfth century, the Genji fought with the Heike (or Taira) clan, who had conquered their rivals in the western region. In 1185, the two clans waged war, which resulted in the crushing defeat of the Heike. The victorious Genji established the Kamakura shogunate in Kamakura.

In 1185, Minamoto Yoritomo (1147–1199) was appointed shogun by the imperial court. He established a garrison government, known as the *bakufu*, in Kamakura in the northeastern region of Honshu. In that same year, Yoritomo was given imperial permission to appoint constables or military governors (*shugo*) and land stewards (*jitō*) to administer regional domains. Now equipped with officials who all were warriors, Yoritomo inaugurated the warrior government in Japan, which would continue until 1868 through four dynastic warrior governments: the Kamakura (1185–1333); Muromachi (1392–1573); Momoyama (1573–1615); and Tokugawa, or Edo (1615–1868).

The shogun's position established by Minamoto Yoritomo did not last long, because the Minamoto family produced no direct heirs. After the third shogun, Minamoto Sanetomo (1192–1219), the shogunal office was held by imperial princes sent from the court in Kyoto. But real power was held by shogunal regents from the family of Hojō Masakō (1156–1225), Yoritomo's wife. As a result, political relations between the warrior and imperial families became complicated, yet the warrior government established by Minamoto Yoritomo continued to be the basic model for governance over the next six hundred years.

This system was based on a complicated interaction among political leaders who were perceived in a hierarchical structure with the emperor holding the highest position, followed by the shogun and then the daimyo. While the location of the court of the emperor (*tennō*) might vary, he always laid claim to a sacerdotal sovereignty. Beneath the emperor in the hierarchy of authority were the shogun and the daimyo.

THE SHOGUN

The title *shogun* was originally held by an imperial prince. Under the warrior government it was applied to a leader of the warrior order who was delegated by the emperor to rule the country. The conferring of the title of *seii taishōgun*, or Great General

Who Quells the Barbarians, limited the shogun's authority to those military affairs that involved foreign invaders. Eventually the shoguns expanded their authority beyond the limited range conferred by the emperor. From that point on, the warrior class, led by the shogun, assumed the political, economic, and cultural leadership of Japan, paying token respect to the emperor and his court.

THE DAIMYO

The title *daimyō*, or "lords of the samurai," as used in this exhibition, derives from *dai,* "great," and *myō* (for *myoden*), meaning "named lands"; the two parts together mean "holders of the great named lands." The number of daimyo ranged from 50 to 250 at different times. They were appointed by the shogun and served as the leaders of bands of hereditary samurai vassals. They administered regional domains to which they were assigned.

It was within this political configuration that Minamoto Yoritomo established his warrior government. From that point on, the samurai ideal and the samurai culture began to develop vigorously. The ideal of the samurai viewed two important parts of the warrior ethos, *bun* and *bu*—roughly culture and arms—as integrated within the newly emerging warrior elite. Warriors and courtiers could share their distinct tastes in activities such as tea drinking and the appreciation of objects such as tea utensils.

THE SECOND WARRIOR GOVERNMENT: THE ASHIKAGA SHOGUNATE OF THE MUROMACHI PERIOD, 1338–1573

The Kamakura shogunate was overthrown in 1333 and succeeded by the Ashikaga shogunate (1338–1573). The samurai themselves were organized into lord-vassal hierarchies, and their feudal and military value system was strengthened, promoting the virtues of honor, loyalty, and manly demeanor, along with a sense of duty and service for the good of the collective unit of their bands.

As was the case under the Kamakura shogunate, the Ashikaga shoguns were supported by the lord-vassal relationships between the shogun and his direct vassals (*gokenin*) and the system of regional constables (*shugo* daimyo) and land stewards (*jitō*). The shugo daimyo were provincial lords with their own lands. They were appointed to one or more provinces to maintain order, administer justice, and ensure the delivery of taxes.

Japanese society during this period could be compared to the feudal society of medieval Europe. Peasants were bound to the land as laborers, and they paid harvest rent to samurai. The samurai themselves were organized into lord-vassal hierarchical relationships.

LATER MUROMACHI AND PERIOD OF WARRING STATES (1490– 1600): THREE UNIFIERS OF THE COUNTRY

During the second half of the Muromachi period, from 1490 through 1573, Japan experienced a series of wars. Called the Warring States (Sengoku) period, these years saw Japan without an effective central government. Into this vacuum stepped a new type of warrior, who sought to unify the country. The three most notable of these were Oda Nobunaga (1534–1582), Toyotomi Hideyoshi (1537–1598), and Tokugawa Ieyasu (1543–1616). Under these ambitious military leaders the scale and scope of samurai warfare were greatly expanded. In addition, battles became more deadly as a result of the introduction of Western-style rifles.

A fierce warrior and capable tactician, Oda Nobunaga had conquered about a third of the daimyo realms when he was assassinated in 1582. It fell to Toyotomi Hideyoshi to complete the unification of the country. Once in power, Hideyoshi instituted a number of reforms. Of special importance was the severing of the ties between the samurai and their rural village communities. Until the Warring States Period lower-ranking samurai vassals were part-time soldiers who also worked as farmers. This resulted in their home villages being heavily armed, with samurai proper and farmers maintaining close ties. In unsettled times members of powerful rural groups could reject the authority of their lords and aspire to become daimyo themselves. This process was called *gekokujō* ("the lower toppling the higher").

Hideyoshi himself had risen to power through the *gekokujō* process. As a result, he saw clearly the danger of keeping samurai in the villages. He decreed that samurai who remained in villages must disarm and be treated as farmers, thereby ending the long-standing ties between the samurai and their villages.

Though brilliant, Hideyoshi was considered ruthless, unpredictable, and unreasonable. On his death the daimyo regents he entrusted with promoting his son as a hereditary ruler rejected this plan. Instead, Tokugawa Ieyasu, a daimyo whom Hideyoshi had most entrusted with the care of his son, became the founder of the Third Warrior Government, the Tokugawa shogunate (1615–1868)

THE THIRD WARRIOR GOVERNMENT: TOKUGAWA SHOGUNATE OF THE EDO PERIOD, 1615–1868

In September of 1600, Ieyasu won an important battle on the plain of Sekigahara in Mino. This resulted in his appointment by the emperor as shogun, and the establishment of the Tokugawa shogunate, which was to continue for fifteen generations over more than two hundred sixty years, from 1600 to 1868. This unprecedented longevity of the regime was matched by an unprecedented degree of control over people of all classes, including the daimyo and their vassals. At the same time, the absence of warfare enabled the samurai class to devote more of their time to such traditional civil arts as painting, calligraphy, poetry, the tea ceremony, and the Noh and Kyōgen theaters.

Under the Tokugawa shogunate Japan was a centralized feudal state. Based on Hideyoshi's land survey, the Tokugawa regime assessed land in terms of its rice productivity (*kokudaka*). Land tax was based on that assessment, together with village size. This calculation determined the allotment of daimyo domains, and samurai stipends. In the Tokugawa system, there were about 260 daimyo domains, each with its own castle, that were served by samurai vassals. Each domain collected an annual land tax, which was paid by rice. While daimyo domains operated as semi-independent states, their distribution throughout the country was based on the central government's security considerations. The shogunal government held absolute power to control the daimyo. It could relieve them of office, transfer them at will to domains in any sizes or any location, or even confiscate all or part of their domains. The daimyo, though entrusted with governance of the land and people of their domains, held no authority independent of the central government.

The shogunal castle was located in Edo in the Kanto plain, strategically surrounded by hereditary (*fudai*) daimyo's domains. Nonhereditary (*tozama*) daimyo were assigned to outlying districts, creating a secure structure for the central government.

This is called *bakuhan* system, consisting of a combination of a central government (*bakufu*) and semi-autonomous daimyo domains (*han*).

THE SYSTEM OF ALTERNATE ATTENDANCE (SANKIN KŌTAI)

As another means to controlling the daimyo, the System of Alternate Attendance was instituted, which required daimyo to spend alternate years in Edo. On the years when the daimyo returned to their domains, they had to leave their close families in Edo—in effect as hostages. This system proved an effective means of monitoring and controlling the daimyos' activities. For the daimyo it was a costly one, as they had to make complex work arrangements for their retainers. They had to maintain grand mansions on their allotted land in Edo in order to maintain prestige. They had to enable their retainers to conduct duties both in Edo and in their home domains while they were away from them. An annual journey on foot to Edo in a grand procession of armed retainers was another feature of the system of alternate attendance that entailed considerable expense for the daimyo.

Besides enabling the central government to keep watch on the daimyo the system also ensured that they would be unable to accumulate the resources needed to wage war. In this respect the strategy worked perhaps too well. In the end many daimyo ran into extreme financial difficulties and could no longer fulfill their obligations. Toward the end of the Tokugawa period, many daimyo requested the shogunate to relax its demands, and the shogunate reluctantly compromised. But as a result it began to lose some of its control over the daimyo.

The shogunate also controlled the imperial court. The emperor was defined legally as a "cultural existence" (*kinchū narabini kuge shohatto*). While the shogunate enriched the court economically it also held it under firm control; the emperor possessed cultural authority but little political power.

RESTORATION OF IMPERIAL AUTHORITY AND THE END OF THE WARRIORS' AGE: MEIJI PERIOD (1868–1912)

The last era when the warriors remained somewhat active, at least in its early years, was the Meiji period, named for its emperor, who reigned from 1867 to1912. With the Meiji Restoration that ended the Tokugawa shogunate, the emperor once again assumed supreme authority, ending eight centuries of shogun rule.

The Meiji emperor moved the capital from Kyoto to Tokyo (formerly Edo). He outlined the new government's philosophy in the Charter Oath of 1868. A new constitution was enacted, and the Diet—modern Japan's first legislative body—was founded. In a few short years, Japan was transformed from a feudal warrior state to one under parliamentary government.

These changes spelled the end of the daimyo as a primary political force. Having helped to overthrow the Tokugawa shogunate and bring about the Meiji restoration, the samurai class found itself stripped of power and effectively dissolved. Some samurai leaders responded violently, gathering their troops and waging war against progovernment forces. But the final expression of samurai might—the Satsuma Rebellion—was put down in 1877, and Japan continued its tumultuous transition to the modern era.

BUSHIDŌ: THE CULTURE OF THE SAMURAI

THOMAS CLEARY

Evolving over many centuries, Japanese culture has drawn on many sources to produce a flexible and durable civilization. The intellectual and artistic expressions of Japanese culture, socially and historically layered, reflect elements of several systems of thought and ways of life.

Typically associated with or influenced by various schools of Shinto, Confucianism, Taoism, and Buddhism, the animating elements of Japanese culture may be expressed in classical forms or combined in novel ways. *Bushidō* (武士道; "way of the warrior") as a code of conduct for samurai succeeded centuries of cultural development in Japan, and each of these traditions sheds light on the spirit of Japanese civilization, the culture of the samurai, and the evolution of Japanese arts.

The samurai's emergence as a ruling class in medieval Japan produced profound cultural changes with the restructuring of political power. But this development did not erase the cultural legacy of the past. The new order absorbed and transformed its precedents, combining them with fresh ideas from both domestic and foreign sources, to produce new intellectual, religious, and artistic syntheses.

If the virtues of loyalty, duty, and courage composed the backbone of the ancient warrior orders, the samurai's expanding roles of civil leadership naturally enlarged those traditional values to encompass classical conceptions of social conscience and public interest. As rulers not only of armies but of society at large, the samurai understood their duty as extending to the whole body of the people. To meet this obligation required enhanced levels of sophistication in the overall operation of their civilization, including all branches of knowledge necessary to the economic, social, and moral order.

CULTURE AND ARMS

The foundations of Japanese civilization may be said to rest on two bases, called culture and arms, or *bun* (文) and *bu* (武) in Japanese. In general terms, bun and bu suggest the constructive and the destructive as reflections of elemental forces of nature. They can also represent qualities of gentleness and intensity, in domains as diverse as medicine, psychology, and social policy.

For the samurai as warrior, this basic conceptual construction defines the primary purpose of warfare: to protect the civil society. For the samurai as ruler and administrator, the combination of bun and bu implies the mitigating influence of culture on the aggressive element of instinct, preserving social order by means of education as well as legal sanction.

The ideal individual embodied in his personality the qualities of bun and bu in appropriate place and proportion. The ability to be warm and humane in social life, cold and fierce in combat, was particularly prized in the person of the *bushi* (武士)—the Japanese warrior-knight. Each aspect of the personality was thought to have its proper place, the cultural capacity balancing the martial and the martial protecting the cultural.

An example of this reasoning, and its role in political science, are outlined by a samurai scholar of the early eighteenth century. In his *Instructions for Japanese Men,* Izawa Nagahide wrote:

> Culture and arms are like the two wings of a bird, so just as it's impossible to fly with one wing missing, if you have culture but no arms, people will slight you without fear, while if you have arms but no culture, people will be alienated by fear. Therefore, when you learn and practice both culture and arms, both intimidation and generosity are there, so people are friendly but also intimidated, so they're obedient.

> In the present age, those who aspire to cultural learning speak of martial arts as lowly and do not cultivate them, while those who study martial arts think of cultural learning as soft and do not study it. Because of this, they either become timid and weak like women and girls, or they become coarse and rough like field hands. In either case they are one-sided, to be sure. Samurai should pay full attention to clarifying this.

Here compared to the wings of a bird, the complementary development of bun and bu in the samurai was also commonly compared to the wheels of a chariot. Both analogies are Buddhist symbols of wisdom and compassion as two essential aspects of enlightenment. Wisdom is commonly represented in Buddhist literature by martial metaphors, such as a sword, in the sense that it cuts through delusion, while anything evocative of existence itself, reflecting the beauty of life, may represent compassion.

Arms and culture were associated with wisdom and compassion in literature and visual art. Portrayed as distinct yet ideally inseparable, the two qualities also merge with one another: the arts may convey a sense of austerity, impermanence, or tragedy; arms may be used symbolically to show their subjection to civilization.

The importance of civilizing warriors was much emphasized by samurai scholars of the last feudal era, beginning in the seventeenth century, in response to the militarism that had developed during the prolonged civil wars of the fifteenth and sixteenth centuries. Their belief was that the savagery of this so-called Era of Warring States had produced distortions in the national self-awareness and historical consciousness of the samurai. Kani Ian (1705–1778) lamented in his *Necessary Knowledge for Military Families:*

> It is mistaken to say that our country has been governed militarily since the era of the deities, that our country is a martial state while China is a cultural state. Both our country and China focus on the military to quell disturbance, and focus on culture to govern society. In the beginning of our nation, there were people who didn't follow the regal sway, so arms were used in the main; but though there are sayings in reference to this that praise military might, nevertheless there is no indication of governance only by arms.

> Misunderstanding this point, as civil wars went on and on ever since the Ashikaga Era, causing alienation from culture and loss of justice, a lot of people have only valued arms in their lust to take territory. People must have heard of the manners of those times and thought this country has always been that way since antiquity.

FIG. 1.

The Buddhist deity Gōzanze Myōō, 1200–1300. Hanging scroll; ink and colors on silk. *Asian Art Museum, Gift and Purchase from the Harry G. C. Packard Collection Charitable Trust in honor of Dr. Shujiro Shimada; The Avery Brundage Collection,* 1991.57.

Wisdom may be represented in Buddhist art and literature through martial metaphors. The main figure in this painting, the Esoteric Buddhist deity Gōzanze Myōō (Sanskrit: Trailokyavijaya), while ferocious in appearance, uses his powers of magical knowledge to protect believers and help them overcome obstacles to their spiritual development.

There is also a theory that we should value arms alone because the martial spirit of the people of our nation is naturally robust. If it is a nation with a robust martial spirit, then it is all the more imperative to respect cultural studies; the cultural and martial should match. There's no reason to develop robust martial spirit alone.

In terms of the psychological and ethical structure of the samurai mentality, the qualities of bun and bu are often epitomized by the virtues of humanity and justice. Humanity, or benevolence (*jin;* 仁), is pictured as a warm and gentle quality, the epitome of culture; justice, or duty (*gi;* 義), as a cold and stern quality, the epitome of arms. Each has its place in human interaction, precisely as the parallel influences of reward and punishment are considered the cultural and martial bases of governance and social order.

The qualities directly or figuratively associated with bun and bu suffused the samurai's conceptual and aesthetic understanding of the world. Bun and bu were cultivated in various ways, supported by the rich, eclectic Japanese culture. While it is conventional to speak of a civilization as an entirety, this custom of convenience naturally operates in retrospect; in the context of ongoing historical change and development, the range of thought represented within the samurai caste alone reflects the remarkable diversity of adaptations produced by cultural evolution in Japan.

THE RISE OF THE SAMURAI

The emergence of the warrior caste from the matrix of the old aristocracy, the assumption of political rule by the samurai, and the accompanying evolution of the military profession are ably outlined by Hoshino Tsunetomi, a samurai scholar of the early nineteenth century. He begins with the legend of the first emperor of Yamato, the original Japan:

> The origins of the samurai may be traced back to when Emperor Jimmu had a sudden rise to power from Miyazaki in the province of Nikko; introducing civilization to primitives, he invaded territory to the east and killed Nagasunehiko. Establishing a capital in Kashiwara in the province of Yamato, he set up an imperial guard. Dividing the imperial militia into two bodies, he had Michiomi-no-Mikoto and Umashimaji-no-Mikoto command them.[1]

Emperor Jinmu (Divine Warrior) is a pivotal figure in the origin myth of Yamato. His "sudden rise to power" refers to what is known as his "eastern expedition" from the southern island of Kyushu to the main island, Honshu, where he came to rule over populations already established there. Michiomi-no-Mikoto and Umashimaji-no-Mikoto are Shinto deities, represented as chiefs of imperial militia during the prehistoric divine age.

In modern Japan, Nikko is located in Miyazaki prefecture in eastern Kyushu. Kashiwara in Yamato was in Nara prefecture, on Honshu. Eventually the city of Nara would become Japan's first permanent capital. Nagasunehiko is traditionally portrayed as a prehistoric chieftain in Yamato who opposed Jinmu's entry into this territory.

Hoshino's account of the historical development of the samurai class continues with a notice of militias attached to the imperial court. Some were from ancient warrior clans whose histories have lapsed into legend; other armies of officers and conscripts were organized on models imported from China.

> The militia commanded by Michiomi-no-Mikoto was called the Kumebe, while the militia commanded by Umashimaji-no-Mikoto was called the

Mononobe. The Kumebe waned away over the generations, and only the Mononobe flourished as the shield and citadel of the imperial court. The so-called Eighty Clansmen of the Mononobe mentioned later were these.

The *be* (部) of ancient Japan were groups of specialists attached to the establishment of the emperor or other aristocratic families. The Kumebe (久目部) is thought to have been a *tomobe* (伴部) or auxiliary organization of the Ōtomo clan (大伴氏)—the Great Retinue, devoted to the service of the emperor. Because occupations were normally hereditary, professional organizations such as these were also called clans or houses. The Mononobe (物部) specialized in military and police functions for the imperial court.

Hoshino moves on to the subsequent adaptation of the Chinese legal system and the transformation of the Japanese military:

> The recruitment and training of the militia up to around the fortieth generation of human emperors are not defined in histories of the nation, but in the forty-fourth generation, during the Yōrō era [717–724] of Emperor Gensei, Fujiwara Fuhito [659–720], following an imperial command, devised a legal system based on the six codes of Tang dynasty China. From this thorough provision was made for the organization of the court, to be the standard for following generations. The work of Mr. Fujiwara must be said to have been great. He was given the honorific title Lord of the Pale Sea; and is it not a result of his contribution that the critical offices of regency have been performed by members of his family generation after generation, even up till now?

The Fujiwara clan was among the major allies of the imperial house of Japan over the ages, providing empresses and learned advisers and regents to the emperors.

A golden age of cosmopolitan culture, the Tang dynasty of China (618–906) expanded and diversified facilities for study of the arts, technologies, and sciences of the time; these schools accepted students and teachers from all over greater Asia. The Tang dynasty code is the earliest surviving body of Chinese law, but it draws on many centuries of precedent. Hoshino describes the Japanese adaptation of the Chinese military system:

> Although there were minor revisions after that, the overall law was no different. The training and recruitment of soldiers can also be discerned in this connection. After this there were six divisions of imperial guards at court, plus the Hayato and Takiguchi, private bodyguards and swordsmen, no more than two or three thousand.

The Hayato and Takiguchi were organizations of armed men who served as palace patrols and security guards. Drawn from members of the Kumaso people that inhabited Kyushu before the Japanese, the Hayato are said to have performed their native dances at official ceremonies. According to Hoshino, apart from these specialized organizations, soldiers were drafted from the populace for military campaigns; these conscripts learned infantry or cavalry skills at regional training centers.

> Military garrisons were established at Dazaifu, Chinjufu, and a citadel in Akita. When there was to be a punitive expedition, they'd recruit brave and strong men from the farming populations to serve as soldiers, returning them to farming when there was no trouble. A group training officer was permanently stationed in every province to exercise and train farmers in their spare time. People who learned the principle of battle formation and served as soldiers were to that extent even forgiven taxes and corvée.

Ranches were also established here and there in every province where horses were raised and armed peasants skilled at riding were selected. ... Every ranch had to send a certain number of horses to the capital every year as tribute, while the rest were left to the armed peasants to select for use according to their own abilities. So these were not merely expert riders; the legend of 330,000 cavalry throughout Japan comes from this era.

Hoshino now tells of the consummation of the centralized imperial system, under which Japan was formally organized as a legally constituted bureaucratic state to supplant, surmount, or superintend the tribe and clan structures of antiquity. Continuing expansion eastward, and a concentration of proprietary interests over widely dispersed landholdings, fostered the development of both military and managerial specialties among the scions of successful families. Hoshino succinctly describes this stage of the samurai saga:

Clans such as the Minamoto, Taira, and Fujiwara flourished, and the children and descendants of those who received territory and became provincial governors, prefectural overseers, and so on, continued to reside in these places; while those who stayed in the city but were given manors and estates sent their sons and younger brothers to oversee tax collection. These types gradually produced more and more descendants, and the local people somehow became like their serfs. Having the serfs turn in just a little bit of tax to the provincial government, in spite of sharing the rest with the serfs there was no lack. So depending on the size of the territory, as they had also stored armaments, private militias emerged.

This de facto division of powers led to tensions between local and central authorities, as well as between the managers of different domains. As the imperial administration devolved to weaker and more diffuse offices, private militias assumed control of military power.

The imperial court let this go without thinking ahead, because it seemed convenient for defense to have more soldiers without extra expense. So it was that private militias grew year by year, while recruits for the official army gradually dwindled. With no soldiers going to the group training officers in the provinces, practice and training ceased and the office itself died out, leaving only the private militias of the warrior clans. So they settled on an order among the provinces to take turns every two or three years providing resident guards for the capital, which they called the Royal Watch. The place they were posted was called the place of the warrior, or the place of the samurai.

The samurai stepped into a void they had helped to create, acquiring provincial authority as the central government's influence waned.

Military clans ran [the provinces] generation after generation, and had a lot of serfs. Since the state officials were only in office for four-year terms, their power naturally weakened and their administrative orders were not implemented, so they were a government in name only. As long as they got through their four-year stint without incident, they didn't care what happened after that; so even if military clans killed people in private feuds, the state officials would generally pretend not to notice. Even if they had no choice but to notify the capital, requesting a judgment from the bureau of criminal law, they'd only get banished, by the opinion of the jurisprudent. Therefore the military clans took greater and greater liberties, scorning the weakness of state officials.

As they became established in the provinces over the centuries, the samurai took charge of local affairs. In the absence of either secure central authority or defensible independence, they formed their own clan associations and military alliances. Inevitably the most powerful of them came into conflict, impelled by the goal of overall supremacy. The Minamoto and Taira clans waged the Genpei war from 1180 to 1185, and the victorious Minamoto established the first *bakufu*, or central military government. Hoshino describes the emergence of this institution and the system it inaugurated as a historical watershed:

> In those days, security was found in affiliation with a military commander with a reputation, depending on his stature. This was the source of the Genpei War, something that didn't happen overnight. [Minamoto] Yoritomo [1144–1199], former lieutenant of the imperial Armed Guard of the Right, raised a volunteer army while in exile, overthrew the Taira clan, and rose to the rank of Shogun, in command of all the warriors in the land. Putting protectors in every province and land chiefs on the manors, he brought them all under his control. This was a major change in the system of our country.

Despite the ascendancy of the samurai as a class and the constitution of a *bakufu* of national standing, the imperial system was not abolished in theory or in fact, however diminished its outreach and authority may have been by the rise of the military clans. According to Hoshino, "there were still state officials in the provinces sending a certain amount of tax to the imperial court, so the imperial and military orders coexisted."

The reasons for this conservative policy might be found in diffusion of power preventing absolute domination by military means, or the residual influence of the original ethos of the samurai as guardians of civilization, as represented by the state.

Preservation of the imperial organization was also a potential source of enhanced power for samurai clans themselves, as a nexus of alliances and a means of mobilizing resources. Eventually civil warfare erupted in imperial opposition to the military government, and competing samurai clans supported different claimants to the imperial throne. Hoshino cites the two major civil wars of this era that had the effect of consolidating samurai rule as a system while weakening the dominant clan:

> After the rebellion of 1221 [when Emperor Go-Toba tried to topple the bakufu], and the war of 1331 [when Emperor Go-Daigo tried to bring down the bakufu], the system of state officers was stopped, leaving only the protectors, so the administration of government wound up distributed among the military clans.

The renewed fragmentation of political and military power ultimately led to the chaotic Era of Warring States (c. 1467–1573), when Japan was plunged into widespread civil war for more than a century. In recounting how the warriors who were settled on the land maintained themselves through these turbulent times, even in defeat, Hoshino explains the policy of the victorious overlord Toyotomi Hideyoshi (1537–1598). Hideyoshi was instrumental in politically reuniting Japan, disarming the peasants, and removing samurai from the land to settle them in cities.

> Even among the warriors, only the familiars and bannermen lived near the protectors, while the others all stayed in their own bailiwicks, making their serfs do the farming. Those with few serfs also farmed along with them, and as they became quite friendly with the peasants as a result of this, no matter how badly they might be beaten in a battle with a warlord, it wouldn't reach the point where their base citadel was taken over. Or even if it happened to be taken, in most cases their sons and grandsons wouldn't disperse from the territory but mixed in with the populace, hiding among the peasants, waiting for an opportunity to strike back and retake it.

FIG. 2.

Portrait of Toyotomi Hideyoshi, 1599, by Seishō Shōtai. *Hanging scroll, ink and colors on silk. Asian Art Museum, Gift and Purchase from the Harry G. C. Packard Collection Charitable Trust in honor of Dr. Shujiro Shimada; The Avery Brundage Collection,* 1991.61.

Toyotomi Hideyoshi (1537–1598) was instrumental in removing samurai from the land to settle them in cities.

Distinction between soldiery and farming became extreme with the warlord Toyotomi Hideyoshi. Having acquired the whole land by power, Hideyoshi began the practice of transferring local lords, fearing that if any of the lords in the provinces lived permanently on the land they'd be hard to uproot and eliminate if there was trouble. The fever of the Era of Warring States had not yet cooled off. When a domain was changed, because there was no solidarity with the peasants it was not feasible to distribute military forces, so the samurai were concentrated in castle towns. Even when sufficient time had passed that they could be settled on the land, because it was profitable and advantageous to keep them living in castle towns, things were left that way. So eventually the time came when samurai were city dwellers.

While this entire process unfolded over some seven centuries, the original warrior rulers of the twelfth and thirteenth centuries realized early on that to become a civil leader, to assume the role of social exemplar and political authority, the man of arms must embrace intellectual and artistic growth.

Innovations in religion, education, and art transformed the tone of Japanese culture under samurai rule. Spawning a synthesis of utility and beauty, intellect and emotion, defining standards of action and repose designed to foster feelings of admiration and awe. In the political philosophy of the warrior caste, these sentiments were supposed to serve as a fundamental psychological cement of society. Refinement of the outward manifestations of the warrior's life was therefore directed at overall development of personality and character in the context of human relations, as well as individual self-discipline. In his *Bushidō for Beginners* the samurai scholar Taira Shigesuke (1639–1730) summarizes the importance of cultural refinement for warriors in practical terms:

> While it goes without saying that an attitude of hardness and strength is considered foremost in the way of the warrior, if strength is all you have you will seem like a peasant turned samurai, and that will never do. You should acquire education as a matter of course, and it is desirable to learn such things as poetry and the tea ceremony, little by little, in your spare time. If you have no education, there is no way for you to understand the reasons of things past or present. Then, no matter how smart or cunning you may be, in actual practice dealing with events you will run into many obstacles.[2]

To understand the psychology of the samurai, therefore, it is necessary to look to the sources of Japanese civilization for formative influences on their cultural ethos and aesthetics.

SHINTO AND JAPANESE CIVILIZATION

Shinto, which may be translated as the Spirit Way, is a complex phenomenon. Customarily considered to be the original native tradition, and thus quintessentially Japanese, Shinto has analogies in many other cultures; these make possible an understanding somewhat broader than that afforded by framing Shinto solely in terms of a national cult, although even as a national cult imperial Shinto is not historically uncommon.

Typical features of Shinto cults, such as systems of taboo, ritual purity, sympathetic magic, purposive prayer, mystic revelation, and personification of natural forces, are part of a common conceptual language of human civilizations that have prevailed and adapted survived standard replacement in many modern cultures. Some of the basic attitudes of a Shinto world view have always underlain the essential aesthetic spirit of Japan.

The idea of the manifest human god (*arabitogami*) is one such ancient survival, typified by respect for hierarchy and authority. Deification of leaders, living or dead, was similarly associated with political rulership in ancient Mesopotamia, Egypt, China, Greece, India, and elsewhere; but there is also a prepolitical process of apotheosis associated with cultural contribution to society, notably technological innovation, from which social and political leadership were once held to derive their original legitimacy. Some evidence of this underlying idea may be found in the fact that "genius" is one well-attested classical and literary meaning of the ideogram used for *shin* (神) in *Shintō* (神道), the ideogram traditionally used in China, Korea, and Japan for deity or spirit, *kami* in Japanese. This ideogram may be used to refer to exceptional ability in any domain of endeavor.

One feature of the imperial arabitogami institution of ancient Japanese culture that distinguishes it from apotheosis of rulers in many other societies is the absence of graven images celebrating the deified individual. The implications of this policy in the realm of the arts can be seen in the naturalistic orientation and elegant austerity of the Shinto aesthetic. In its subliminal effects on mass psychology, this element of reserve in representation may have played a quietly significant role in the survival of a single imperial clan in Japan—an exceptional phenomenon in world history.

Instead of imposing figures of idealized men, Shinto distinguishes the imperial clan by certain sacred objects, heard of but never seen by the world at large: a jade, a mirror, and a sword. In explaining the symbolic significance of these items, the samurai scholar Izawa Nagahide represents primitive Shinto as embracing underlying ethical and sociopolitical conceptions of Confucianism and Buddhism.

> The origin of the warrior goes back to the divine age of antiquity when the central ruler of heaven, the Great Goddess Lighting the Sky, made a pact with her august descendant Ninigi-no-Mikoto, saying, "Let the emperor use artful subtlety like the curve of the sacred gem to govern the earthly administration; use clarity like the sacred mirror to oversee the mountains and rivers, seas and plains; and wield the sacred sword to pacify the earth and benefit the populace."[3]

The Great Goddess Lighting the Sky is Amaterasu-Ōmikami, the Sun goddess, center of the Shinto pantheon. Ninigi-no-Mikoto is the name of the god superintending the earth. These deities are ancestors of the imperial clan, and this image of a pact between the ruling spirits of heaven and earth summarizes the imperial brief.

Izawa explains the symbolism of the sacred jade with respect to the art of governance:

> The sacred gem symbolizes flexibility and accommodation. The government of the earth should be carried out with the warm, rich quality of humaneness represented by this object. Artful subtlety is expressed by its rounded curvature; the path is not a single fixed straight line, but adopts what is suitable to the time, in accord with the context. So it is a way of adapting to the time.

This basic principle of adaptation pervades many aspects of Japanese society, and may be fundamental to the imperial clan's survival, among other immemorial elements of Japanese culture associated with native Shinto; the centuries of turmoil might have been fatal to a more rigid system. The Buddhist practice of *upāya-kauśalya,* or skill in means (*hōben* in Japanese; 方便)—applicable to any domain of human activity, including the political and cultural—also embodies the idea of adaptation to the needs of the time. The Japanese amalgamation of Shinto and Buddhism, technically called the cultivated communion of spirits and buddhas (*shinbutsu shūgō;* 神仏修合), is a product of this practice. Izawa's explanation of the sacred mirror's symbolism reflects the melding of Buddhist and Shinto images and ideas:

The sacred mirror symbolizes honesty. A mirror doesn't retain anything, but reflects everything impartially, so right and wrong and good and bad features all show. Virtue is to respond sensitively to those features. This is the basis of honesty. For a mirror the essential feature is clarity. When the essence of mind is clear, compassion and decisiveness are therein. If observed with honest intelligence clear as a mirror, there will be no one corrupt at court, and no savant neglected in the countryside. With the operation of government honest, and good communication between superior and subordinates, all people will find their places.

A common symbol in Zen Buddhism, the mirror represents unbiased awareness free of distorting fixations. In traditional political science, impartiality is considered quintessential to successful leadership. Only through impartiality can justice be preserved, as the disciplinary and punitive function of government is normally rationalized and accepted on the premise of objectivity.

The sacred sword symbolizes decisiveness. It implies the imperative to take the side of absolute firmness and freedom from greed to destroy the internal mental enemies selfishness and treachery, and execute the external bandits crime and violence, being straightforward and uncorrupted in body and mind and government affairs as well, imbued with the commanding presence to overawe the world.

The sword is also common in Buddhism, especially Zen, representing the incisive insight to see through the subtlest deceptions, even within one's own mind, is essential to enlightenment; without it, understanding is inhibited by intellectual and emotional conditioning. As the political analogy of the sword, objective judgment implies authenticity in the exercise of authority.

The symbolism of the sacred regalia summarizes a traditional formula for responsive government, combining the qualities of bun and bu, the cultural and the martial:

If there is no accommodation, the people will be alienated, so it is good to be flexible. In the absence of dignity, subordinates will be contemptuous, so it is good to be firm. If you are desirous, your instructions won't be carried out, so it is good to be honest. Without being like this it is impossible to govern oneself, order the home, rule the country, and pacify the world.

In concluding his exposition of the imperial regalia's significance, Izawa addresses the original communicative and didactic functions of art; without understanding these, it is not possible to appreciate the subtleties of Japanese culture, in which the material and the spiritual are intimately intertwined.

In high antiquity there was no writing, so these three articles were made as lessons for the imperial descendants, that if they preserved the three virtues symbolized by the sacred objects, they would flourish as eternally as heaven and earth.

While the divine emperors and the apotheosized political leaders and cultural innovators are commonly figures of high antiquity, deification continued into historical times. A prime example from medieval Japan can be found in the *Ippen Hijiri-e* (一遍 聖絵), a popular pictorial biography of the thirteenth-century Japanese Buddhist saint Ippen. Combining literary and visual artistry, this remarkable work prefigures the modern graphic novel and illustrates the assimilation and synthesis that characterize the development of Japanese civilization.

The story has a distinctive Shinto matrix, depicting the Buddhist saint in intimate communication with native deities or spirits, the *kami*, who are often the sources of

FIG. 3.
The Buddhist deity Fudō Myōō, 1200–1300. Hanging scroll; ink and colors on silk. *Asian Art Museum*, B70D2
The sword is a common Buddhist symbol for incisive insight. Shown here is Fudō (Sanscrit: Achala Vidyaraja), one of the powerful Five Bright Kings of Japanese Esoteric Buddhism.

Scene from the Ippen Hijiri-e, 1299, by En-i (text by Shōkai). Handscroll; ink and colors on silk. *Kankikō-ji monastery, Kyoto.*

The *Ippen Hijiri-e,* a pictorial biography of the thirteenth-century Japanese Buddhist saint Ippen, illustrates the synthesis of elements that characterizes the development of Japanese civilization. Here Ippen retreats to a cave in Iyo province for meditation.

Ippen's most important revelations, insights, and inspirations. Dense with imagery of supernatural events that entwine the threads of diverse regions and religions, the *Ippen Hijirie* reflects the mutual accommodation of Shinto and other traditions, joining Japan with the wider world in cultural communion.

In an early episode of Ippen's story, there appear the figures of two men of earlier centuries who became, guardian spirits of hallowed ground on the Japanese island of Shikoku. One is depicted as a native Japanese, an ancient hunter turned Buddhist devotee. He is described as having inaugurated the cult of Kannon (観音), the supernal embodiment of compassion in Buddhist literature and iconography—a frequent subject of sacred art and a popular object of devotion.

The second figure, while similarly mythologized as a guardian spirit, seems more historically concrete because he is associated with a state structure. According to the story he was originally an ambassador from China, sent by the empress of the Sui dynasty. This was a time when Japanese cultural relations with China were expanded on a grand scale.

This revealing episode of the saint's biography begins with a retreat in a cave in the mountainous province of Iyo on Shikoku, Ippen's ancestral homeland:

> In the seventh month of 1273, Ippen went into seclusion at a place called the Reed-Grown Rock Room in the Ukena district of the province of Iyo. This place is a holy ground where Kannon has appeared, an ancient site where immortals have cultivated their practices.

The setup of this scene demonstrates in its simplicity the use of concentration in the art of allusive representation. It conveys something of the spirit of Shinto in the act of naming the ground; invokes the sense of the miraculous associated with Buddhism; and connects the cave cloister conceptually with the Taoist mountain cults of China, which like Shinto were intensely intimate with nature.

This amalgamation of associations, moreover, skillfully evokes the attitude and atmosphere of the ancient Japanese mountain men, the *yamabushi* (山伏), counterparts to Chinese immortalists. Combining elements of Shinto, Buddhism, and Taoism, yamabushi beliefs and practices ultimately gave rise to the Japanese religion known as Shugendō (修験道).

Having thus introduced the context, the biography goes on to relate something of the history of this sacred place, beginning with a prototypical yamabushi:

In ancient times, when Buddhism had not yet spread through Japan, a man from Aki province came to these mountains to hunt. Climbing up to a ridge to wait for prey, one night he shot an arrow into a dead tree, which then glowed with light all night long.

The next day he took a good look. There was an ancient tree, covered all over with moss, its form indistinct. Inside there was something golden, in the form of a human being. The hunter did not know the name or form of buddhas or bodhisattvas, but he intuitively realized that this was Kannon. Inspired with faith and devotion, he built a reed hut to enshrine the image, using his catalpa bow as a ridge pole and his sedge rain cloak for a roof.

After Buddhism was established as a state religion in Japan, hunting became an outcaste profession because of the Buddhist prohibition against taking life. The image of a hunter abandoning his weapons upon coming to a religious awakening is also found in Chinese and Indian Buddhist lore. Here, the hunter's use of his bow as the ridgepole of a shrine presents a particularly powerful version of the theme of spiritual and cultural evolution, while the reed hut and its sedge-cloak roof retain the elemental Shinto spirit in their unembellished intimacy with nature. The story goes on to evoke a characteristic confluence of time and timelessness:

The same hunter came to this place again two or three years later, but the reed hut had disintegrated so completely that he couldn't even find a trace of it as he looked for the spot where he had constructed the little shrine. Scaling the ridges and descending into the valleys as he searched, at length he came upon a strange place deep in the vegetation. Drawing near, he saw the icon there, shining bright amidst the profusely growing sedges sprouting from his old rain cloak. Delighted, he constructed a new sanctuary, decorated it, and named it Sedge Grown Temple. There he made his determination to take refuge in Buddhism; vowing to become the guardian spirit of this place, he came to be called the Luminary Spirit of the Field's Edge. He is still there.

Deftly bringing together Shinto and Buddhist themes, this scene subtly alludes to Japan's history as well. Its vivid image of natural growth overwhelming human construction, evocative of Taoist and Shinto conceptions of primal forces, also makes a veiled reference to the forceful Shinto resurgence that overwhelmed nascent Buddhism at the imperial Japanese court in the sixth century.

The survival of the statue after the original shrine's disintegration also has both historical and religious meanings. On the historical level it represents the survival of Buddhism in the mountains, without institutional housing, after ejection from court. On the religious plane it represents the perpetual mission of the Buddhist bodhisattva, to postpone final emancipation in order to remain in the world to work for universal welfare and liberation.

The scene's conclusion, with rediscovery, reconstruction, reconsecration, and perpetuation, likewise reflects the revival and institutionalization of Buddhism in Japan, including the adaptation of Shinto to the conceptual role of local forerunner and protector of a universal religion, with Shinto spirits becoming guardian deities of Buddhism, or even alternate personas of supernal Buddhist bodhisattvas.

The *Ippen Hijirie* progresses to diplomatic and cultural relations between Japan and Buddhist China, through which Japanese civilization was further connected to the cultural riches of Central Asia and India.

Some years later, during the reign of the Emperor Yōmei, an ambassador from China arrived with the news that the Empress of Emperor Wen of the Sui Dynasty had experienced a miraculous omen during her pregnancy, and had offered three precious treasures to this Icon of Kannon [in Japan]:

FIG. 5.

Prince Shōtoku, 1700–1868, by Jugo 1 Kansei Seibaigan Koji. Wood, lacquer, and gilding. *Asian Art Museum, the Avery Brundage Collection,* B62S65.

Prince Shōtoku (573–621), an icon of Japanese history, looked to China for political and religious inspiration. Under the governance of his father, emperor Yōmei (d. 587), Japan received increased cultural influences from mainland Asia.

boxes representing conduct, meditation, and wisdom; a bell; and a ringed staff. The Chinese ambassador subsequently remained in this place, acting as its guardian, appearing as the Great Luminary Spirit of White Mountain, dwelling to the south of the shrine hall.

Emperor Yōmei of Japan, who died in the year 587, was the father of the famous Prince Shōtoku (573–621), one of the most celebrated icons of Japanese history. The Sui Dynasty of China, though short-lived (lasting from about 581 to 618), is considered a watershed in Chinese history. Emperor Wen, founder of the Sui Dynasty, reunited long-divided north and south China and enacted important legal reforms. His empress was a woman of the Xianbei nation, a federation of tribes that had ruled northern China since the fourth century.

The Xianbei state had sponsored Buddhism in north China to such an extent that Emperor Wen of the reunifying Sui dynasty enacted a crackdown on monastic establishments in order to appropriate the statuary for the government, melting it down and converting the metal into secular forms such as coinage and weaponry. But Buddhism's intellectual and cultural prestige persisted in China. The ruling house of the superseding Tang dynasty, which was also intermarried with the old Xianbei aristocracy, generally sponsored Buddhism (but also found it profitable to confiscate material and manpower from monasteries in the ninth century).

Japan had inherited a well-established—if ambivalent—conception of state Buddhism by 607, when Yōmei's son Prince Shōtoku, to whom the first Japanese constitution is traditionally attributed, sent an official mission to Sui dynasty China. Saint Ippen's biography thus illustrates an earlier phase of international contact, accurately reflecting the historical fact that the Sui court was first to make diplomatic overtures to Japan.

Of special interest here, in terms of the artistic representation of complex concepts and the construction of social values through art, is Buddhism's role in integrating individual experience with values of national, transnational, and international scope. Evocation of the medium of dreaming is of particular note with respect to cultural confluence: dreaming is recognized as a potentially valid mode of perception in all shamanic traditions, including Japanese Shinto, as well as in the canon of Mahayana Buddhism.

Dream revelations from Shinto spirits are particularly prominent in the *Ippen Hijiri-e;* Ippen himself explained dream perceptions in terms of Buddhist psychology. While the interpretation of dreams may be distorted by subjective delusion or insidious suggestion, this is precisely the reason for the intense mental discipline of the adepts who employ it. In this context the constructive use of imagination in the form of dream vision illustrates the Buddhist rationale for the purposeful use of the arts in religion, education, and general psychological hygiene.

Quickly weakened and exhausted by warfare, the Sui Dynasty was soon supplanted by the Tang Dynasty, which was to last for nearly three hundred years, from 618 to 906. Cultural exchange between China and Japan continued under the Tang, and Confucianism and Buddhism were firmly established in Japanese civilization. Both traditions were blended with Shinto and with native customs to produce innovations in politics, religion, technology, and the arts.

CONFUCIANISM AND JAPANESE CIVILIZATION

Although traditional Chinese political philosophy covers a wide spectrum of thought, the dominant ideology has typically been characterized as Confucian. In practice this has always been mixed with Legalism (法家), the doctrine of governance by an impersonal rule of law. Like most native Chinese philosophies, Confucianism is essentially concerned with concepts of social order and requirements of good government.

The primary function of the arts in this connection has traditionally been to regulate the emotions in order to refine the personality and behavior of people in positions of leadership. Consequently, the arts were employed to discover and cultivate people with leadership potential. Music, poetry, visual art, and ritual were not just leisure class luxuries but means of training sensibilities, disposition, and manners in early preparation for social responsibility.

Confucius himself is widely quoted to illustrate the importance of character development in leadership. There are many famous axioms in the Analects (論語), the most popular collection of the discourses and sayings of Confucius and his disciples:

"If they are directed by government policy and made orderly by punishment, the people will try to evade these, and not even feel any shame about it. If they are guided by charisma and unified by courtesy, they will be conscientious and upright of character." (2:3)

"If leaders are courteous, their people will not dare to be disrespectful. If leaders are just, people will not dare to be intractable. If leaders are trustworthy, people will not dare to be dishonest." (13:4)

"When government is done by virtue, it is like the North Star abiding in its position, with all the other stars surrounding it." (2:1)

The Great Learning (大学), a classic Confucian tract particularly popular in Japan, sets forth the controlling concept of the continuity of individual and collective governance, and the consequent importance of study for personal development:

Those who wished to clarify enlightened virtue in the whole world in ancient times governed their countries first. Those who wished to govern their countries regulated their households first. Those who wished to regulate their households cultivated their persons first. Those who wished to cultivate their persons rectified their minds first. Those who wished to rectify their minds made their intentions sincere first. Those who wished to make their intentions sincere developed their knowledge first. Development of knowledge is a matter of investigating things.

Education was considered essential for samurai in civil life, particularly those in positions of responsibility and leadership; not only for the cultivation of practical knowledge, but also for the development of character and gravity appropriate to their role as personal exemplars to society at large. Book learning alone was never considered sufficient, even in highly scholastic schools of Confucianism, without the full engagement of the personality in the purposes for which education was established. Yamaga Sokō (1622–1685), a Japanese Confucian who has been called the de facto founder of Bushidō, articulates the role of education and art in the life of the samurai:

There are methods of development and education to teach knights. Development means improvement, capable cultivation. Education means learning and practice. There is physical cultivation and there is psychological cultivation. Education has knights establish their will, study literature and arts, master etiquette and harmony, speak correctly, regulate their appearance, and make their manners cordial.[4]

Confucius said, "If you can correct yourself, what trouble would you have in government? If you cannot correct yourself, what can you do about correcting others?" (13:13) This reflects a basic Confucian concept of personal example as intrinsic to the effective influence of formal leadership. The scholar Nakae Tōju (1608–1648) describes the relationship of this prestige to the enforcement of law:

> The root of government is the enlightenment of the mind and ethical conduct of the ruler defined as the model and mirror for the whole country. The individual stipulations of the laws are the branches and leaves of government. Since the preferences of the ruler are imitated by everyone all the way down the hierarchy, when the ruler's mind is enlightened and he acts ethically, then people's minds spontaneously become good, even without laws. All the more so when both root and branches are authentically and aptly effected, the nation thrives and survives forever.

> The difference between government by character and government by law should be well understood. Government by character means first correcting your own mind and then correcting the minds of others. This is like the plumb line and square of the carpenter, which when in proper condition correct warping. Government by law means trying to correct the minds of others without one's own mind being upright.[5]

In classical Confucian thought, government by character and leadership by example also implied active and effective interest in the welfare of the people. One of Confucius's senior disciples, as recorded in the *Analects*, characterized the master's doctrine as consisting solely of loyalty and reciprocity. These were considered both political and personal virtues, bases of cohesion for society and state.

Another well-known saying from the *Analects* illustrates the pivotal role of social conscience for both rulers and ruled in the Confucian conception of state. When a disciple asked Confucius if there was a word one could put into practice all one's life, Confucius replied, "Perhaps that would be 'reciprocity.' What you don't want yourself, don't do to others." The original form of the Golden Rule, this axiom is understood to apply vertically as well as horizontally. An ancient Confucian commentary embedded in the *Book of Changes* (易経) says, "Noble people comfort others and urge reciprocity."

In this context, the technical term for *duty* thus also means *justice:* if the duty of the people is to conform to the laws of the government, the duty of the government is to render justice to the people. Confucius said, "To guide a state, be serious and faithful in its affairs; be economical and love the people, employing the citizens in season" and "It is beautiful to make humaneness one's home. If you do not choose to dwell in humaneness, how can you attain knowledge?"

Mencius, conventionally cited as the second great philosopher in the Confucian tradition, was a monumental humanitarian thinker who believed in the essential goodness of human nature. He emphasized the idea of the state as the protector of the people's welfare. In the famous book that bears his name, he exemplifies this concept with a reference to King Wen, a founder of the classical Zhou dynasty of China and an embodiment of personal and political virtue in Confucian doctrine:

> The elderly without wives are called widowers, the elderly without husbands are called widows, the elderly without children are called alone, the young without fathers are called orphans. These four are the destitute people of the world, without anyone to resort to. King Wen enacted policies of humane government, always giving priority to these four. The Classic of Poetry says, "How excellent that a man of wealth takes pity on these who are all alone!"

The famous Japanese Zen master Hakuin Ekaku evoked this fundamental principle of socially responsible government even in his meditation instructions for Confucian samurai. Here he uses a traditional analogy of the body to the state,

common to Taoism and Legalism, to incorporate the mental posture and personal discipline of the samurai leader into the structure of political policy:

> Spirit is like the ruler, vitality is like the ministers, and energy is like the people. Now then, caring for the people is the means of keeping the country intact. To be sparing of your energy is the means of keeping your body intact. When the people flee, the country perishes; when energy runs out, the body dies. For this reason, a sage ruler always focuses his mind below, while a mediocre ruler always indulges his heart on high. When the heart is indulged on high, the nobles rely on personal favor, the officials are arrogant with power; they never pay attention to hardship among the people, while importunate ministers greedily skim and cruel officers deprive by deception. There may be plenty of vegetables in the fields, yet people are collapsing from starvation in the countryside. The intelligent and the good go into hiding, ministers and commoners are angry and resentful, the masses of people are ultimately reduced to abject misery, and so the pulse of the nation dies out forever.

> When the mind is focused below, never forgetting the toil of the people, the populace is well nourished and the state is strong; no ministers or commoners violate the law, while no enemy states invade the domain. So it is with the human body. The perfect people always have mental energy filling below, so the emotions do not act within, while the material world cannot invade from without. With the camp guard fully supplied, the mental spirit is strong. Ultimately the body doesn't know the sting of acupuncture or moxibustion, just as the people of a powerful nation don't hear cries of alarm.[6]

Caring for the populace implies understanding their conditions, problems, and needs. The internal Taoistic Zen exercise, here recommended to a samurai—the focusing of mental energy below the navel—is not only an analogy for the political practice of focusing attention on the populace; it is a meditative method for clearing the mind of internal and external influences in order to make perception more unselfish and objective. Personal development is represented as essential to the samurai's political acumen and efficiency as a leader. This idea is consistent with Confucianism and Taoism, and typical of Zen advice to samurai, for self-improvement as well as superior statecraft. The samurai scholar Takayama Kentei emphasizes the cultivation of the practical knowledge necessary for good government, which psychological stabilization is supposed to support:

> Governing a nation is principally a matter of governing people. Governing people is in knowing their dispositions. Knowing their dispositions is in distinguishing provincial customs.

Humans are the most intelligent of beings. Though the people of all nations are not different, according to the provincial characteristics of the places they were born their temperaments are not the same. As these become habitual, they differ in their strengths and weaknesses.

When you distinguish their differences accurately and make use of their strengths without attacking their shortcomings, people are all useful to the nation. If you neglect their strengths because you hate their shortcomings, then people do harm to the nation instead.

Distinguishing provincial customs is key to governing people.[7]

For the samurai, gaining practical knowledge of the conditions, the lives, of the populations under their authority was a prerequisite for effective administration; but it was also part of the warrior's process of total mental and physical training. This involved getting to know the land as well as the people, incorporating a program of familiarization into the fabric of military exercises. The practice is outlined by Yamaga Sokō in his *Primer of Martial Education:*

The way to be a knight involves knowing the lay of the land, the defiles and dangers, distances, mountains and rivers; surveying the varieties of customs, popular songs, and local opinion; personally going into the marshes and forests wielding bow and arrow, gun, sword, and spear, becoming nimble of hand and foot, training your body; considering the abilities of your knights and soldiers, and reviewing the warriors' exercises.[8]

For the shogun and the daimyo in particular, as leaders in both military and civil spheres, the role of warfare in governance and social order was of signal concern. The underlying need for solidarity made the concept of just war not only an ethical issue but a matter of strategy and social policy. The famous Confucian Kaibara Ekken (1630–1714), who was also trained in medicine and military science, examined the confluence of moral and military matters in the samurai's transition to civil government:

Brave and fierce men of old who were excellent commanders may have been successful in war and founded states, but without wisdom it is impossible to preserve culture, keep secure, and hand on the legacy to posterity. Therefore a warrior leader considers wisdom first; courage is next to that.[9]

The regime of the samurai was called military rule—but not martial law, which referred specifically to extraordinary measures in wartime; thus the importance placed on cultivation of civil consciousness in the samurai class. Still prominent in the minds of scholars of Kaibara's time, the medieval *sengoku jidai* (Era of Warring States) had proved that military prowess and martial law, however necessary in emergencies, were inadequate foundations for a successful state. Yet the security of the state, including the organs of civilization that support its existence, depended upon the soundness of the defense system.

Kaibara emphasized the importance of order in the military:

A man of old said, "Victory in war is a matter of cohesion, not numbers." This means that winning in warfare is a matter of officers and soldiers obeying the commander, so orders are not disregarded, all join forces together as one, and they fight selflessly.

Cohesion is also central to civil society, but the consequences of its absence are felt more immediately and acutely in combat. For samurai, the analogy illustrated the power of unity in a particularly practical way.

An army is not to be relied upon just because it is big. If the officers and soldiers do not take to the commander but disobey and desert, since they don't work together and unite as one, even with a million men an army can't win.

For those in positions of leadership, this also suggests that political ambitions are better framed in terms of social integrity rather than in territorial dimensions. Leadership in war requires the same basic qualities of character that Confucian doctrine calls for in civil leadership.

In the use of arms, martial dignity is certainly important. Without humaneness and justice, however, the hearts of the men won't go along. Then it is impossible to mobilize warriors.

"Martial dignity" here implies that while subordinates must be afraid to disobey superiors, humaneness and justice are not only ethical but necessary: superiors cannot afford to alienate subordinates. This applies both to relations within a military organization and to the purpose for which it is mobilized. Even if well paid and well treated, warriors sent into strategic blunders by inept commanders were unlikely to remain loyal for long. Therefore, when Kaibara maintains that good leadership requires just and humane treatment of subordinates, that is not solely a statement of moral ideology; it also implies practical, tactical sophistication in choosing only intelligent operations:

The battles of a good general are well planned and carefully thought out; [such generals] win when it is easy to win. Therefore not a lot of officers and soldiers get killed. Ignorant generals and benighted leaders, not knowing this principle, delight in large numbers of deaths on both sides. This is not only inhumane, it is due to stupidity in military procedure.

Kaibara supports this point, essential to civil as well as military leadership, with the prestige of ancient tradition, alluding to Chinese classics of military science and Taoism, Sun Tzu's *The Art of War* and Lao Tzu's *Tao Te Ching:*

Superior warriors consider it best to win without fighting. If a fight is unavoidable, a good commander is skilled in the ways of war and has strategy, so he doesn't get a lot of people killed, whether enemies or allies.

A man of old said, "After three generations of generals, a family will have no posterity." The meaning of this is that the Way of Heaven hates inhumanity and does not like killing. Since everyone under heaven is a child of heaven, as it hates the killing of its children, if you like to kill people your own posterity dies out.

Even if they become generals, humane men do not kill a lot of people. If so, what would be the harm in generations of generals? As for men who are inhumane and have killed a lot of people, it doesn't necessarily take three generations—there are a lot of examples past and present of men who became generals and whose posterity ended in one generation. This is how it can be known that the Way of Heaven detests inhumanity.

This concept of minimalism in warfare implies consideration of the future, in view of the constructive purpose requisite to an ethically permissible conflict. As the *Tao Te Ching says,* "When you reconcile bitter enemies yet resentment is sure to linger, how can that be called good?" When wars prompted by political ambitions create popular hardships and hatreds, the resulting distortion of ordinary norms can imperil the entire fabric of society. Thus another argument for minimalism advanced by Kaibara, drawing on the immortal Sun Tzu, addresses the practical problem of backlash:

> When battling opponents, if you are excessive in beating them, they'll lash back and fight powerfully. So stop at the first victory. This may seem lax, but there will be no disaster in the aftermath.

> Even in an argument between ordinary men, if one vilifies the other too much and is excessive in beating him down, he'll wind up the loser if the other man can't put up with it and retaliates vehemently.

> The art of war of good commanders of ancient times involved no massive victory and no massive defeat. This is a good commander's art of war. Commanders who don't know the art of war may score tremendous victories by luck, but they also incur many huge losses. This is the not the way a good commander employs a military force.

Returning to the traditional analogy of mental and physical phenomena on large and small scales, Kaibara translates this minimalist martial strategy into equivalent social grace befitting the samurai as civic models and leaders:

> When an argument turns into a fight, it always comes from contention. Contention means rebuking another's excessive words and discourtesy, refusing to tolerate them. If you tolerate them, there is no contention, no enemy, and no disgrace. When dealing with people, it is imperative to be polite in speech and manner, avoiding discourtesy.

The question of when to contend and when to forbear is at once ethical and strategic; the concept of justice in warfare is therefore essential to all the issues Kaibara raises for samurai rule: the energetic advantages of unity and integrity, the political and economic morality of minimalism, and the pragmatic requirements of precision in understanding and action in pursuit of justice:

> When you start a war, you have to examine whether it is just or unjust. If your military order is organized and your army is strong, you are sure to beat your opponent, but if the adversary is not one that ought to be attacked, then it is unjust to start a war. War should not be instigated. This means making justice the substance. Among five kinds of warfare, war for justice and war for defense are used by noble men. War out of anger, war out of pride, and war out of greed are not used by noble men; they are used by small men. Military action ought to be undertaken on the basis of humanity and justice. This means employing cultured warriors. If you make war unsupported by cultured warriors, you can't avoid making men into bandits.

> Ordinarily, making war is contrary to the benevolent heart of the universe that gives birth to beings. Sages use arms only when unavoidable. This is implementation of the principle of nature. The warfare of sages is an exercise in justice; humaneness is therein.

> Good commanders in ancient times did not excel only in bravery, ferocity, strategy, and tactics. They used both culture and arms, exercised both leniency and ferocity. Humane and loving, they pardoned minor errors, forgot old injuries, listened carefully to criticism and put it to use. They were generous in rewarding merit, without boasting of themselves. Therefore the officers and soldiers united in harmony, enabling them to achieve success.

In order to develop the moral backbone and intellectual acumen to exercise justice in war as well as peace, Confucian practice included study of oneself and the world through observation and experience as well as book learning. A manual for samurai called *Essential Endeavors,* composed by Udono Chōkai, a knight of the central military command, makes this point: "Those who study the path should first acquire real learning and simply resolve to understand the way of human ethics in everyday activities, practicing them personally."

Association with elders served several functions, cementing the continuity of generations and traditions and providing not only a forum for transmission of information and practice in decorum, but also an opportunity for unspoken observation and introspection. Listening to the elders' stories was always an important part of a warrior's upbringing; so it was the leader's responsibility, as head of household or head of state, to assess and employ people appropriate not only for their primary duties but as exemplars and mentors to the young.

Another avenue of education involved introspective exercises. As the warrior leader's awareness had to encompass external conditions to an extraordinary degree, an objective understanding of self and subjective psychology was essential to the achievement of internal autonomy combined with mastery of outward personal manifestations, such as emotions and desires, in the course of interactions with others.

Dignity in bearing and deftness of response in private and professional bearing and conduct were considered essential: the warrior leader's influence was understood to be secured by the respect and admiration of his subordinates. Without this element of esteem, the performance of duties would be perfunctory at best, and the integrity of the administration and the social system would decay.

The introspective and contemplative exercises practiced by samurai were typically drawn from the repertoire of Zen Buddhism and its neo-Confucian heirs. The social and political advantage of neo-Confucianism for samurai as civil leaders was the integration of individual developmental principles and practices from Buddhism and Taoism into state-centered Confucian doctrines.

The meditations prescribed for samurai took many forms, but they can be grouped in two main categories. One addressed the development of mental stability; the other focused on moral, psychological, and intellectual improvement. Ideally, the combination would produce a balanced personality capable of dealing as effectively with emergencies as with ordinary events, and a mind habitually composed and poised, in command of itself, aware of its own workings, master of the moment at hand.

BUDDHISM AND JAPANESE CULTURE

Japan is remarkable in the Buddhist world for its institutional preservation of many diverse schools and sects. In principle, these are distinguished by focus on different scriptures, treatises, doctrines, and methods; in practice there is considerable overlap in all of these areas. Depending on the particular emphasis or approach of a given school or individual teacher, moreover, elements of other philosophies, such as Shinto, Taoism, and Confucianism, as well as sundry arts and sciences, might be newly interpreted or incorporated into a specific projection of Buddhism. The full spectrum of traditions of thought, both native and naturalized, formed part of the samurai's cultural heritage, informing the thinkers who constructed the intellectual and moral foundations of Bushidō.

Buddhist schools normally include what are known as the Three Studies: conduct, concentration, and insight. Differences among schools and sects are, typically, differences in rules of conduct, methods of concentration, and modes of insight. The Three Studies were originally formulated for religious and spiritual education, but each could also serve specific functions in secular society. Monastic orders cultivated discipline in their populations to a degree envied by imperial courts, and their morality was often considered a model for lawmakers; meditation and concentration were prized for their effects on workers, artists, and intellectuals; and rulers had long sought out spiritual advisors for psychological and strategic insights as well as for religious enlightenment.

Conduct is one of the spheres of discipline of all Buddhist schools, but in Japan a special school of regulations called the Risshū (律宗) formed during the crucial Nara period (710–784) and centered on study of monastic regulationsgovernance. (There was no such school in India, where various bodies of rules had evolved in diverse communities; but early Buddhists in China, Korea, and Japan were confronted with an accumulation of these canonical developments, as well as with significant contextual differences between Indian civilization and their own.)

Many distinctions of detail developed in Buddhist codes of conduct as Buddhism adapted to conditions in different cultural environments. In general terms, the aim of Buddhist discipline is to attain inner autonomy by learning to control the body through the mind and the mind through the body. In this sense, discipline in Buddhism is analogous to Confucian rituals for cultivating mood, attitude, and awareness in human interaction. The distinguished Confucian scholar and military scientist Yamaga Sokō also studied Zen Buddhism; he explains the resonance of mind and body as the underlying principle of rites:

> Appearances are the substance of the vessel into which nature and mind are placed by the natural order. When inner thoughts are improper, appearance is influenced by them, with their manifestation becoming outwardly evident. If you want to rectify your appearance, you have to correct and clarify what you think inside. With thoughts inside, facial expressions appear outwardly; since the inside and the outside, the external and the internal, the root and the branches, are a natural continuum, you cannot consider them separately.[10]

The disciplines of restraint and ritual were incorporated into Zen, and both modes of training were essential to the ways of warriors. The concentration and mental focus of Buddhist meditation, meanwhile, were valued for the degree of discipline they enabled.

Expressed in the arts, an object's elegance becomes an emblem of the artist's discipline, an expression of meaning, and a medium for cultivating the beholder's sensibility. Similarly, the language of movement, posture, and gesture in theater and dance reflects the same principle as the rules and rites of Buddhism and Confucianism: mental and physical awareness are organized so as to intensify and refine each other, guiding perception and feeling in specific, meaningful ways. Yamaga Sokō offers an example of this sophisticated interplay of art, ritual, and physical and psychological training in his treatment of an ancient court custom:

> Regarding the practicing of hanging jades from the belt, the *Records of Manners* says, "Noble men of ancient times always wore jades. On the right side they wore jades sounding the notes *cheng* [sol] and *jiao* [mi], on the left *gong* [do] and *yu* [la]. They ran with the rhythm of the music *Gathering Herbs* and walked with the rhythm of the music *Relaxing in Summer*. They turned like a compass, cornered like a square. When they stepped forward it brought them together, when they withdrew it made them move; then the jades rang like music. So when a noble man is in a vehicle, the sound of gold bells is heard; when he walks, it causes his belt jades to jingle. In this way perverse thoughts don't enter the mind." This is a system whereby the sounds made by the jades worn on the left and right are harmonized in standing, sitting, and walking, without the slightest lapse of attention, to

FIG. 7.

Kabuki scene with samurai holding a man down, approx. 1820–1830, by Shunshōsai Hokuchō. Woodblock print; ink and colors on paper. *Asian Art Museum, Gift of Toshiro Nakayama,* F2005.42.88.

The language of movement, posture, and gesture in Japanese theater expresses an intensified and refined mental and physical awareness.

prevent unrestrained activity. If movements are at variance with courtesies, the sounds of the belt-jades do not harmonize. Having belt-jades hanging from the waist is used for correcting appearances and manners, as these may be likened to virtues. Putting bells on vehicles and harmonizing their sounds corrects the manners of the drivers, alerting against inward negligence, calming their minds. In sum, the intention is that one's manners become correct through the use of the jades hung from the belt to the left and the right.[11]

Rules and rituals fostered precise awareness of mind and body, so important in the life of the samurai for practical purposes and personal cultivation, and the blending of traditions in the production of these forms was already in progress in China when Buddhism and Confucianism were transmitted to Japan. In his *Essentials of the School of Precepts,* the medieval Japanese monk Gyōnen explains the formative function of discipline in Buddhism in terms of external and the internal resonance:

> The great canon of discipline, containing myriad principles, is beyond measure. The extensive practice of morality, concentrating a million measures, is unfathomable. Stagnant delusive feelings are wiped out all at once by disciplined conduct; the suffocating trap of death is forever broken by precepts. This is a precious raft to cross the river of attachment, a spiritual army to cross the mountains of resentment, an immediate cause of entry into the capital city of awakening, a direct road to the state of buddhahood.

As this passage illustrates, symbolism was a significant medium for linking mental and physical disciplines, formally connecting the inner domain of mind to the outer realm of the senses by means of both concrete and abstract art. This can be seen in the arrangement of a place of practice for a purification ceremony known as a repentance in the Tendai (天台) school of Buddhism, a powerful forerunner of Zen. *Stopping and Seeing,* the main manual of Tendai meditation, outlines the symbolic analogues of the configuration, offering a glimpse of the ancient understanding of art's role in the cultivation of spiritual sensitivity, intelligence, and insight.

According to this classic work, the whole place of practice represents the sphere of purity, while perfumed oils represent noble conduct. A multicolored canopy covers the place, symbolizing attainment of liberation by analysis of the body-mind complex and developing compassion covering the universe. There is a round altar, representing the immutable ground of reality, with streamers and pennants symbolizing the overthrowing of illusions and awakening of understanding that inspire emancipation. Incense and lamps represent discipline and knowledge; the high seat of the preceptor stands for the emptiness of all things.

The text draws on scriptural sources to elaborate this process of symbolic association to cement the total experience of the rite. Going even further than the Tendai school in employing the arts in rituals designed for discipline and meditation, esoteric Shingon (真言) Buddhism used very complex sensual aids to focus concentration. This approach to religious experience appealed to ancient Japanese aristocrats, who developed a correspondingly sensuous culture that concealed its spiritual depths.

The phase of Japanese civilization associated with the supremacy of the Tendai and Shingon sects continued for some four centuries before it was superseded by the martial culture of the samurai, and it never died out entirely, despite adverse conditions. One reason for this may be that sound social principles of purposeful behavior, suitable in some form for any leadership sector, underlay the color and drama of ritual-based Buddhist disciplines.

The general outlines of these practical principles are summarized in the older Kegon (華厳) school, one of the first Buddhist dispensations formally established in

Japan. The first principle, called "subtle function according to conditions without convention," makes clear that a moral response to a situation may not necessarily be predefined by principle or precedent, so direct independent insight is indispensable to conscientious conduct.

The second general category of conduct is called "dignified, regulated, exemplary conduct." This refers to customary patterns of personal deportment: the way people carry themselves, the standards according to which they behave, and the consequent impacts, impressions, and influences on others. The manners and courtesies of Confucianism and the normative precepts and dignities of Buddhism are examples of this domain of discipline, which was considered particularly important in the persons of rulers and commanders, such as the shōgun and the daimyō.

The third type of practical virtue is expressed in terms of treating people gently and harmoniously, yet straightforwardly. The difficulty of blending truthfulness and tact, requiring the first two types of discipline, highlights the utility of artfulness in human interaction, both individual and collective, from the outward courtesies of personal conduct to the entire range of communication facilitated by the refinements of civilization.

The fourth category of virtue is described as "accepting suffering in place of all beings." This is a general statement of the life of the bodhisattva of mainstream Mahayana Buddhism, who willingly forgoes personal peace in order to work for the sake of the welfare and liberation of the whole world. The broad Buddhist contribution to social welfare in such endeavors as relief for the destitute, ailing, and orphaned is a manifestation of this spirit of sacrifice for altruistic ends.

The Kegon scripture repeatedly emphasizes the significance of social and cultural service in the practice of Buddhism; work in the world is explicitly linked with perfection of meditation, preventing the development of a one-sided personality through excessive abstraction:

> The bodhisattvas, thus engaged, develop people by means of charity, kind speech, beneficial action, and cooperation. They develop people by showing forms, by revelation of enlightening action, by making clear the greatness of the enlightened, by showing the ills of the mundane whirl, by lauding the knowledge of Buddhas, and by production of great spiritual manifestations and application to various practices and works. The bodhisattvas, thus engaged in the development of sentient beings, with minds continually following enlightened knowledge, engaged in goodness without regression, intent on the search for supreme truth, practice *whatever in the world* would benefit sentient beings, such as writing, teaching, mathematics, physical sciences, and medical sciences; prevention of consumption, epilepsy, and possession; warding off poison, zombies, and witchcraft; song and dance, drama, music, storytelling, and entertainment; the construction of villages, cities, parks, canals, reservoirs, ponds abounding in lotuses, groves producing flowers, fruits, and medicines; the discovery of gold, jewels, and other precious substances. ... [12]

The Great Buddha (大仏) statue in Nara, Japan's first permanent capital, depicts the principal icon of this Kegon scripture: an immortal work of art silently memorializing the constructive contribution of Buddhism to Japanese civilization, at once secular and sacred. This monumental icon depicts the primal Buddha Vairocana (Illuminator; translated in Chinese and Japanese as the Great Sun Buddha 大日如来). Vairocana's icon is found as distantly as Borobodur in Indonesia and Bamiyan in Afghanistan, testifying to the immense reach of this kind of Buddhism. The deliberate acceleration of cultural and technological development in Japan and other parts

of Asia through entry into the Buddhist world abundantly exemplifies the expansive role of religion conveyed in the scripture:

> Bodhisattvas' various methods and techniques adapt to worldly conditions to liberate people. Just like lotus blossoms, to which water does not adhere, in the same way they are in the world provoking deep faith. With extraordinary thoughts and profound talent, as cultural kings, song and dance, and conversation admired by the masses, like magicians they manifest all the various arts and crafts of the world. Some become grandees, city chiefs; some become merchants, caravan leaders; some become physicians and scientists, some become kings and ministers. … If they see a world just come into being, where the people don't yet have the tools for livelihood, bodhisattvas become craftsmen and teach them various skills.[13]

The great master Kūkai (空海), founder of the Shingon sect, is an eminent example of the historical Japanese bodhisattva. Commonly known as Kōbō Daishi (弘法大師), the Great Teacher Who Spread Religion, Kūkai is an immortalized Buddhist saint and a paradigmatic culture hero whose name is known to all Japanese people.

According to his own account, Kūkai studied with the native yamabushi and also imbibed the doctrines of Confucianism, Taoism, and Buddhism. Then he traveled to China, where he met a rare master of the mystical rites, received esoteric initiations, and acquired a number of special texts, including a new translation of the concluding book of the seminal Kegon scripture. Even the invention of Dual Shintō (両部神道) synthesizing Buddhism and Shinto, among his most distinguished contributions to Japanese culture, is a type of expedient technique of bodhisattvas explicitly described in the Kegon scripture and historically employed in some manner everywhere Buddhists went.

The genius of Kūkai's Shingon Buddhism influenced the evolution of the Tendai school, from which emerged specialized sects of Pure Land, Nichiren, and Zen Buddhism. The Zen sect is commonly associated with the samurai class, patronized as it was by the Shoguns, and certain elements of this historical context reflect qualities severity and asceticism, such as might mark the life of the warrior as well as that of the Zen monk.

Something of the pivotal role Zen might play in the life of samurai may be glimpsed in dialogues with Zen masters. The shogun Ashikaga Yoshimitsu is said to have put this matter to the Zen master Myōō: "The realm of complete awakening does not admit the calculations of the errant mind. Now, my everyday activities all use the errant mind—please instruct me." This request alludes to a fundamental problem in the unification of consciousness, critical in Mahayana Buddhism and typically expressed as being torn between aloofness and involvement.

The master replied, "What's the problem? Scripture says: 'If you know illusion as such, you are detached from it; when you're detached from illusion, then you're awakened.' Since you are indeed cognizant of the errant mind, then dealing with myriad events is all complete awakening. Don't forget: 'The word *knowing* is the gateway of myriad marvels.'" Such a way of bridging the conceptual and experiential gap between the mundane and the spiritual, fairly typical of Zen teaching at this level, provides many means of apprehending and expressing the transcendent within the ordinary.

A famous dialogue between Yoshimitsu's successor, the shogun Ashikaga Yoshimochi, and a Zen master named Dōshū illustrates this essential attitude in a little more detail. The inquiry outlines the essential quandary: how to approach spiritual liberation while simultaneously fulfilling social responsibilities. To a military and civil authority, this psychological and practical ambivalence has a moral and ethical aspect. "I have believed deeply in Zen since youth," said the shogun. "But I have been prevented by worldly duties from attaining unalloyed unity. Also, my job impels me to command armed forces and administer punishment, so I may be accumulating causes of damnation. How can I escape?"

The master's reply evokes an ideal of integrating social values and spiritual enlightenment, fulfilling external responsibility fortified by internal independence:

> Zen is in the mind, not in things; concentration depends on oneself, not on others. You have already become the reliance of the people, riding the wheels of your vows: when you enact a policy, the populace is pleased; when you utter a word, the officials all agree. Censuring wrong and representing right, you encourage good and indict evil; penalties are applied only to the guilty, punishment isn't inflicted on the innocent. Each day that you maintain the general peace, multitudes of people enjoy effortlessness. All of this flows from your heart; none of it comes from anyone else. Buddha said, "As one mind is pure, the minds of the multitudes are pure; the world and the lands of buddhas are all completely pure."

In the context of leadership, the Zen theme of individual autonomy is consistent with the Confucian concept of social responsibility: autonomy implies the ability to reason and act independently of internal or external compulsion. The Zen master went on to explain to the shogun that meditation does not require quietism, as true transcendence can be realized in the process of engagement:

> An ancient teacher said, "All times, past and present, of self and others, are not apart from the immediate moment of thought; infinite lands, of self and others, are not separated by so much as a hair." This is your meditation in the midst of daily affairs as a minister of state. Would you only consider it concentration if you close your eyes, still your thoughts, and shut off your senses? What is important is not obscuring true cause and not losing great potential. That is why Devadatta felt as blissful as in the third meditation heaven even while in hell, because he had great potential. Now you've always had that potential—how can you fear the pains of hell?

Devadatta is a stock villain of Buddhist scripture, a cousin of Buddha who is traditionally depicted has having attempted to assassinate him. Zen lore typically turns the image of "assassination of Buddha" into a positive metaphor for transcending the peace of nirvana to return to the ordinary world and consciously carry out vows for the welfare of society. This attitude was particularly important for lay practitioners, the more so the greater their worldly responsibilities, but the confusion of quietism with meditation was a perennial problem. Centuries later, the famed Zen master Hakuin was still warning samurai of the dangers of dualism:

> If you think dead sitting in silent awareness is enough, you'll waste your life and deviate greatly from the way of enlightenment. Not only will you deviate from the way of enlightenment, you'll neglect worldly truth too. Why? If the lords and grandees gave up government to sit deathlike in silent awareness, if the warriors ignored archery and horsemanship and forgot martial arts to sit deathlike in silent awareness, if the merchants closed up shop and broke their abacuses to sit deathlike in silent awareness, if the farmers threw down their plows and hoes and stopped tilling and weeding to sit deathlike in silent awareness, if carpenters discarded their plumb lines and tossed away their planes to sit deathlike in silent awareness, the nation would wither, the people would weary, robbers would rise up repeatedly and the state would be in peril. Then the people would say indignantly that Zen is extremely inauspicious.

For the Japanese founders of the sect, as for many of their Chinese predecessors, Zen was in effect a graduate school of Buddhism, integrating the essentials of the other sects and adapting them to the needs of the time, place, and person. Zen's primary emphasis on the mind provided a ready rationale for this approach, as well as a direct avenue of intuition into the subtler functions of art. The dynamic element of Zen method, aimed at integrating enlightenment with action in the ordinary world, also brings the arts into play as means of orienting and articulating attention to induce specific effects on the mind. In Kegon Buddhism—highly influential in Song dynasty Chinese Chan, the precursor of Japanese Zen—this intentional use of art as a medium of instruction, at once a method and a means of meditation, is called an "entryway to mysteries using objects to illustrate teachings."

In Shingon Buddhism, which like Kegon teachings makes extensive use of art for concentration, this mode of practice is explained as addressing a technical requirement of Buddhist education, a means to produce a complete cognitive effect that can be attained only by apprehending certain principles simultaneously, in particular relation to one another.

Within the context of literary art, this level of presentation is commonly encountered in the structures of poetry and the Zen koan. It is by nature as elastic as awareness, and it assumes many forms in the applied and fine arts, from the austere aesthetics of age in utensils to the emblematic articulations of the mind-altering mandalas used in Tantric and Pure Land Buddhism.

A wide range of representative materials, from items of everyday life to mystic meditation maps, bear the hallmarks of Japanese art and speak to the rich synthesis of Japanese culture: a reverent intimacy with the forms and textures of nature, redolent of Shinto and Taoism; a Confucian consciousness of harmony and order; Zen-like understatement and intrigue; and the Tantric flair for energy and color. Perhaps the essence of Japanese art, from the perspective of the samurai charged with the protection and preservation of society, is its inseparability from life as a whole.

Even art that is assumed to operate only on an aesthetic level may be considered practical or applied art, for it is intended to educate, refine, and uplift the human spirit. Individually and collectively, the arts provide a medium of communication, a method of focusing minds and facilitating communion of consciousness—in short, an active ingredient of the essence of human society. That is why patronage of the arts has always been more than a polite pastime in Japanese history. The arts played their roles in diplomacy, international trade, and economic and cultural development; and so their patronage has been an integral aspect of political science: indeed, of political morality.

NOTES

1. Hoshino's work is cited from *Training the Samurai Mind* by Thomas Cleary. Boston: Shambhala Publications, 2008.
2. From *Code of the Samurai* by Thomas Cleary. Boston: Tuttle Publishing, 1999.
3. Izawa's work is cited from *Training the Samurai Mind*, op. cit.
4. *Samurai Wisdom* by Thomas Cleary. Boston: Tuttle Publications, 2009.
5. *Training the Samurai Mind.*
6. *Training the Samurai Mind.*
7. *Training the Samurai Mind.*
8. *Samurai Wisdom.*
9. This and following citations from Kaibara are from *Training the Samurai Mind.*
10. *Samurai Wisdom.*
11. *Samurai Wisdom.*
12. *The Flower Ornament Scripture*, translated by Thomas Cleary. Boston: Shambhala Publications, 1993.
13. *The Flower Ornament Scripture.*

INTRODUCTION TO THE CATALOGUE

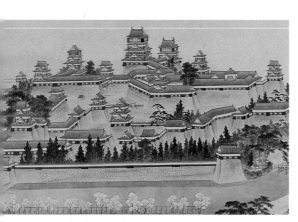

DEBORAH CLEARWATERS

The Hosokawa is one of Japan's most elite and enduring samurai clans, with origins that can be traced to a Japanese emperor (Seiwa, 850–880) as well as to the Ashikaga family of warriors, who ruled Japan under imperial aegis during the Muromachi period (1392–1573). Like many of the great daimyo families, the Hosokawas collected a variety of fine art—paintings, calligraphy, metal weaponry, armor, ceramics, lacquer, textiles, and bamboo. Much of the collection, amassed over more than six hundred years, is now housed at the Eisei-Bunko Museum located in Tokyo on the property where the Hosokawa family lived while in attendance to the shogun in Edo—as Tokyo was called when it was the seat of the Tokugawa military government from 1615 to 1868. Most of the objects in this exhibition are drawn from this renowned collection, as well as from the Matsui Bunko on Kyushu Island, the seat of the Higo domain formerly ruled by the Hosokawa daimyos (figure 1).

Most objects in this exhibition were either commissioned, purchased, or received as a gift by a member of the Hosokawa family. Some of the artworks were created or designed by a member of this clan. As will be seen in the following catalog entries, several family members mastered literary and artistic skills in addition to developing the political and military savvy that was essential for the daimyo. Examining the collection, it becomes clear that the Hosokawa family consciously strove to embody the ideal characteristics of the warrior elite discussed in Thomas Cleary's essay in this book, "Bushidō: The Culture of the Samurai"—as he points out, "the foundations of Japanese civilization may be said to rest on two bases, called culture and arms, or *bun* (文) and *bu* (武) in Japanese." The acts of collecting art and preserving family lore were ways for daimyo families like the Hosokawas to express their erudition and nobility.

The samurai of medieval Japan felt vulnerable to being characterized as class upstarts, usurping political power from the imperial family and struggling amongst themselves for hegemony. Not wishing to be seen as mere strongmen, upwardly mobile samurai knew that they should present an image of strength, erudition, and spiritual purity in order to achieve long-lasting legitimacy as rulers. The arts aided in this quest for authority. With the gradual cessation of warfare beginning in the early 1600s, the primary responsibilities of the samurai became less military and more administrative; as a result, more time could be devoted to educational and artistic pursuits for pure pleasure.

Samurai lords also felt compelled to patronize the arts as a consequence of explicit and implicit rules of conduct and sumptuary laws that were designed to keep the social classes visually distinct. As Yoko Woodson observes in her essay in this

book, during the Edo period (1615–1868) the shogun required his lords to alternate attendance (*sankin kōtai*) between their domains and the capital city of Edo. Their social stature required them to furnish impressive residences in both locations, lest the merchant classes, who were quickly becoming rich, upstage the samurai. By requiring each of his regional lords to make these costly journeys, and maintain multiple households, the shogun ensured that his vassals were kept too busy and strapped for funds to mount any kind of insurgency (figure 2). Families of the lords were required to reside in Edo as insurance against any attempts at treason. A building boom of new villas in Edo pumped resources into the arts economy. Wood carvers, masons, tile makers, screen painters, and metal workers thrived and the arts flourished.

Although some less urbane warriors found themselves unprepared for new roles as "the highest social stratum of the land," this was not the plight of the Hosokawa family, who already had a strong cultural pedigree at the dawn of the Tokugawa era (the era takes its name from the shogun family that ruled from 1615 through 1868).[1] The Hosokawas' fine collection survives to the present day because this multitalented clan survived and thrived. They won battles, and lost some, but perhaps more importantly, they made good choices in political allies, particularly through the battle-torn years of the 1500s, which ensured they were often on the winning side.

Typical of Japan's great families, many heirloom objects are marked with the nine-planet Hosokawa family crest. For example, the crest is the main design on battle flags such as the one shown in figure 3, a Western-style bronze bell (cat. no. 8), and it was painted onto a set of lacquer bowls associated with Hosokawa Gracia (born Akechi Tama, 1563–1600; cat. no. 102).[2] The crest, serving a dual role as a design motif and as a symbol of family pride, adorns robes worn in family portraits (cat. nos. 12–14, for example), military garments (cat. nos. 70 and 73), armor (on the body armor of cat. no. 21), and textiles used in the mountings of many of the hanging scrolls, particularly as the thin strip of fine brocade silk fabric bordering the top and bottom of the image called *ichimonji.*

The collection includes what might be termed decorative arts, or items beautifully made for practical purposes. A distinction between art made for art's sake and functional crafts is not emphasized in the Japanese tradition. Most of the furnishings of a daimyo family's everyday life, such as arms and armor, food serving items, clothing, writing accessories, games, and the like, were made by skilled artisans. Almost anything (see figure 4) could be decorated, and was.

FIG. 4.
Incense ceremony box and implements with design of nine planet family crest, 1800–1868. Japan; Edo period (1615–1868). 127 parts, lacquered wood with sprinkled metalic powder (*makie*) decoration. *Eisei-Bunko Museum*, 2161, cat. no. 112.

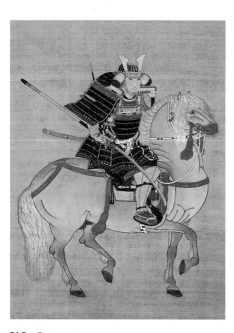

FIG. 5.
Portrait (detail) of Hosokawa Sumimoto (1489–1520), 1507, by Kanō Motonobu (1476–1559), inscription by Keijo Shūrin (1440–1518). Muromachi period (1392–1573). Hanging scroll, ink and colors on silk. *Eisei-Bunko Museum*, 466, cat. no. 3.

The Hosokawa's collection of paintings gives perhaps the broadest impression of the different interests held by this daimyo family. Formats include hanging scrolls used in the alcove of a traditional Japanese room, folding screens used as room decoration or to demarcate space within larger rooms, handscrolls that were examined in one's hands, and albums containing several images, also intended for private or small group viewing. The subject matter of the paintings is equally diverse, varying from works that served formal display and historicizing functions, such as paintings of the family's castle and portraits (of which twelve are included in this exhibition) to paintings that were intended for casual enjoyment or individual study, such as literary handscrolls (cat. no. 90) or Zen paintings (cat. nos. 95–100).

The portraits hold fascination today for what they seem to express about the personalities of their subjects. They appear to convey a likeness of the actual person and provide information about how various garments were worn. Inscriptions indicated how the subjects wished to be memorialized. Inscriptions on some of the family portraits appear to emphasize the sophistication of this illustrious bloodline. On the oldest portrait included in the exhibition, Hosokawa Sumimoto (1489–1520; cat. no. 3, figure 5), is described as the ideal samurai lord: "Hosokawa Sumimoto, a great archer and horseman, is far above other humans. He is also versed in Japanese poetry (*waka*) and appreciates the moon and the wind…"

Although pictured as a formidable warrior in full armor, astride an impressive steed, halberd in hand, sword at his belt, the inscription (dated 1507 at the peak of Sumimoto's career) attests to the equally important, cultured side of this man. He possesses the education and sensitivity to write poetry about the austere beauty of the wind and moon, two phenomena much examined in Japanese literature for their bittersweet evocations of transient beauty. However, this portrait, like many paintings of historical people, is also a tool for self-mythologizing—it tells the story desired by the person commissioning it. Recent historians have not been so kind, calling Sumimoto a "puppet, manipulated by a Hosokawa vassal …"

The inscription on Hosokawa Yūsai's (1534–1610) portrait (cat. no. 6) posthumously lauds the subject's cultural accomplishments even more emphatically:

> Renowned for his elegant pursuits, he is a complete man combining arts [*bun*] and arms [*bu*]. A man of nobility, a descendant of the sixth grandson of the emperor Seiwa, he was a ruler endowed with awesome dignity and inspiring decorum…. He built a splendid castle, which was majestic, beautiful and high…. He discussed Chinese poetic styles and recited by heart the secret teachings of Japanese poetry….[5]

The claims for Yūsai's poetic skills are unquestioned—several poems written in his hand remain in the Eisei-Bunko collection.[6] He wrote a commentary on Japan's *One Hundred Poems by One Hundred Poets, Hyakunin Isshu,* and left an anthology of his own poems, *Shūmyōshū.*[7] Both portraits amplify the seeming contradiction in terms—the artistic and sensitive, yet lethal and disciplined, warrior—which make the mythology of the samurai class so alluring to the present day.

ARMS AND ARMOR

While the most iconic weapon employed by the samurai, the sword was by no means his only weapon. The sword was used in close combat and one-on-one duels, but a variety of other weapons was also used—foot soldiers wielded lances, mounted

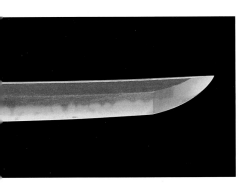

FIG. 6.

Ceremonial long sword (*tachi*) blade (detail), 13th century, signed "Moriie tsukuru" (made by Moriie). Kamakura period (1185–1333). Forged and tempered steel. *Eisei-Bunko Museum,* 1784, cat. no. 34.

FIG. 7.

Dōmaru gusoku–type armor (detail), 18th century, worn by Hosokawa Nobunori (1676–1732). Edo period (1615–1868), iron, gilt bronze, metal, tooled leather, lacquer, silk embroidery, braided silk, fur, feathers. *Eisei-Bunko Museum,* 4098, cat. no. 21.

samurai carried spears, bows and arrows, and swords, and archers and, later, gunners were strategically positioned to fire on approaching troops. The matchlock gun (cat. no. 58) was introduced onto the scene in the mid 1500s. It changed armor and castle architecture, as both now required stronger fortifications to defend against the new firepower.

The sword was famously likened to the samurai's soul by Tokugawa Ieyasu (1543–1616):

> The Way of letters and of arms, of archery and of horsemanship, must be culti- vated with all the heart and mind. In times of order we cannot forget disorder; how then can we relax our military training? The sword is the soul of the warrior. If any forget or lose it he will not be excused.[8]

Ieyasu, building on the efforts of his predecessors Nobunaga and Hideyoshi, ushered in the beginning of nearly 250 years of peace in Japan, yet he still urged samurai to hone their traditional fighting skills. By Ieyasu's time in the early 1600s, gunfire decided many battles; nonetheless, the sword became an even more potent symbol of honor because un- like the gun, with which anyone could easily learn to kill in a short time, swordsmanship required years of training and discipline to master. Elite samurai shunned firearms, and left guns to be fired by the lower classes of soldier. Swords have held special value in Japan since its earliest history, when a sword was one of three sacred symbols of the imperial regalia. (The other two were a comma-shaped jewel and a bronze mirror, and all three continue to be passed down within Japan's imperial family.) As Thomas Cleary observes in his essay in this book, "Wisdom is commonly represented in Buddhist literature by martial metaphors, such as a sword, in the sense that it cuts through delusion." As a result the sword enjoyed a prestige that firearms did not share.

Of the six blades included in this exhibition, the oldest (figure 6, cat. no. 34) dates from the early 1300s and is signed "Made by Moriie." Categorized by the Japanese government as an Important Cultural Property, this exemplifies the finest of Japan's famous sword craft. Also included are sword accessories, such as five finely lacquered and wrapped mount- ings. The pairing of short (*wakizashi*) and long (*katana*) swords, known as "the great and the small" (*daishō*), became the standard blades worn by samurai by the end of the Muro machi period (1392–1573) through the Edo (1615–1868). Also included are twelve sword guards (*tsuba*) in a range of intriguing designs, many of them incorporating symbolically meaningful motifs that make poetic reference to the transience of life. Two of these are Important Cultural Properties and one is an Important Art Object.[9] There are also a pair of wooden training swords (cat. no. 89) made by one of Japan's most famous swordsmen, Miyamoto Musashi (1584–1645), who is said to have preferred his wooden swords over steel one.[10] Musashi served the Hosokawa towards the end of his life. His *Book of Five Rings* is still popular reading today among students of sword-based martial arts—as well as business students seeking strategic insights. A set of handscrolls containing this text transcribed by one of Musashi's students is included in this exhibition (cat. no. 90).

Armor, such as the examples in this exhibition, served a crucial public relations func- tion. The dramatic helmets and face covers proclaim an almost superhuman image of power (figure 7, cat. no. 21). Exquisite silk braiding and fine decorations in lacquer ensure that the warrior could go to his death in style. Warriors slain in battle were often buried in the armor they were wearing at the time.

As might be expected, armor construction changed as a result of developments in weaponry. At first ingeniously designed using lightweight interlocking plates for mobil- ity, armor with heavier, more solid plates of metal meant to protect against bullet fire became more common following the introduction of firearms.

In addition to armor, this exhibition includes other articles of clothing that were worn for formal occasions by Hosokawa men (cat. nos. 18 and 19), as well as collectable textiles such as Noh and Kyōgen costumes (cat. nos. 138–145 and 148–151).

The official daily wear of a daimyo, while elegant, could be quite simple in color and design (figure 8, cat. no. 18). The warrior's battle garb, including the jacket worn over his armor (cat. nos. 70–73), in contrast, was often boldly decorated in bright colors.

Performed on the same simple stage, Noh (literally "ability" or "skill") and Kyōgen (literally "wild speech") are closely related theatrical arts originally associated with temples and shrines. Noh is a highly stylized form of chanted dance-drama. Its stories evoke themes from classical literature and history, and examine the inner feelings of real, living characters or portray more fantastical stories about ghosts, demons, or deities.[11] Kyōgen developed alongside Noh, and is a farcical, slapstick-infused theater. The Kyōgen actors performed during interludes between Noh performances, providing comic relief. In both, major figures might wear masks, which also became precious collectable artworks (see cat. nos. 138–153 for examples of Noh and Kyōgen costumes and masks).

These dramatic forms have been highly favored by the samurai elite since at least the Ashikaga shogunate in the fourteenth century. During the Edo period, Noh became an art form exclusively for the samurai class. A major category of the Noh repertoire features stories about warrior heroes (*shuramono*) that must have resonated with the real-life warriors.[12] Some members of the Hosokawa family avidly studied Noh theater. Hosokawa Fujitaka (1534–1610) and Hosokawa Shigekata (1720–1785) both published Noh chant scripts called *utaibon*. These books are composed of written text with a complex system of interpretation indicated in red alongside the text. Hosokawa Tadatoshi (1586–1641) wrote several Noh plays.

Noh costumes are often made of lavishly decorated, high-quality silk fabrics. Kyōgen costumes are usually of humbler material, such as hemp, and feature bold, graphic designs. The designs reflect the contrast of these two dramatic forms— the Noh costumes are formal and refined, featuring multiple weaving, dyeing, and embroidery techniques in one multicolored silk extravaganza. The Kyōgen robes have large, often playful graphic designs using fewer decorative techniques.

TEA IMPLEMENTS AND OTHER HOUSEHOLD ACCESSORIES

Over the generations, several Hosokawa family members have played major roles in shaping the history of *Chanoyu*, the Way of Tea.[13] Hosokawa Fujitaka (Yūsai, 1534–1610) and his son Hosokawa Tadaoki (Sansai, 1564–1646) founded the renowned family collection of tea paraphernalia and learned the Way of Tea from the great masters of their day. They appear prominently in well-known anecdotes about the foundational history of tea. Former prime minister Hosokawa Morihiro (born 1938) continues this family legacy. Now retired from political life, Hosokawa Morihiro dedicates his time to writing calligraphy and making ceramic art primarily for use in the tea room.

The samurai lord asserted his power and authority in battle and through brokering political alliances; he showed his sophistication and nobility by collecting prized tea

FIG. 9.

Verses of precepts of the seven Buddhas, 15ᵗʰ century, by Ikkyū Sōjun (1394–1481). Muromachi period (1392–1573). Hanging scroll; ink on paper. *Eisei-Bunko Museum,* 1076, cat. no. 85.

utensils, mastering the literary arts, and aligning himself with the leading tea masters of his time. It was important to samurai scholars of the Edo period (1615–1868) that they embody an ideal balance of the qualities of civilized culture and military might.

The pursuit of culture was also important to samurai lords of earlier times. Ashikaga Yoshinori (d. 1441), the sixth shogun of the Muromachi period, had reception rooms in his mansion for appreciating Chinese art objects and enjoying tea. As *kanrei,* or deputy shoguns, under the Ashikaga, members of the Hosokawa family undoubtedly enjoyed hospitality within these rooms. Ashikaga Yoshimasa (d. 1490), the eighth shogun of Muromachi, built what is thought to be the earliest extant tea room, named Dōjinsai, in his Higashiyama Villa. The celebrated tea master Sen Rikyū (1522–1591) built a teahouse called Taian in Kyoto at the order of the warlord Toyotomi Hideyoshi (1536–1598) in 1582; five years later, Hideyoshi ordered tea masters from all over Japan to participate in his Grand Kitano Tea Gathering. (Hideyoshi is infamous in the history of tea for ordering Rikyū to commit ritual suicide in 1591.) Hosokawa Tadaoki (Sansai) is reported to have built as many as ten tea houses, including the extant Shōkō-ken (松向軒, "pine-facing arbor") a two-and-three-quarter tatami mat room attached to the formal study room of Kōtō-in, a sub-temple of Daitoku-ji, the large Buddhist monastery in Kyoto.[14]

Rikyū's influence on the Way of Tea, as it has been passed down to the present day, is monumental. Three of the most prominent tea traditions—Omotesenke, Urasenke, and Mushakōjisenke—trace their blood lineage and teachings to Rikyū and his style of rustic tea (*wabicha*). Hideyoshi's patronage of Rikyū enhanced the tea master's influence, and the drama surrounding the end of their relationship contributed to elevating Rikyū's profile. His fame has eclipsed the important role played by other tea practitioners of his day.

The practice of drinking powdered green tea was introduced to Japan by monks returning from China in the thirteenth century. Seen initially as a medicine, tea wasn't drunk as a social and aesthetic beverage until the fifteenth century. At this time, wealthy warlords were amassing impressive collections of art, mostly from China, such as the Chinese tea bowls in this exhibition (cat. nos 115 and 116). Lavish tea parties allowed the lord to show his collections; tea was a luxury drink served in formal halls. Beginning in the late fifteenth century, a succession of tea masters simplified tea practices, infusing the environment in which they prepared tea for their guests with Zen Buddhist philosophy, locally made utensils (cat. no. 126, for example), and an austerely pared-down, rustic aesthetic.

The value and importance of a utensil was not determined just by its origin, the artist's skill, or the intrinsic value of its materials, but also by its pedigree and history of ownership. Some tea utensils were given poetic names; if a piece was named by a revered Zen priest, tea master, or samurai lord, its value increased, especially if such a person inscribed the box with the name of the object, along with his signature or seal (see the tea scoops, cat. nos. 132–135). These named, pedigreed objects, no matter how unassuming they may appear, are priceless today, and they thrill people who are lucky enough to see and handle them in a tea gathering.

Many of the utensils required to host a tea are on view in this exhibition. In preparation for a gathering, the host considers his guests' interests; he tries to use objects that will resonate with them and that also reflect the season, the time of day, and the occasion for the tea, such as a farewell, memorial, or new year's celebration. In the tearoom's alcove (*tokonoma*), the host usually hangs a calligraphy scroll written by a Zen monk—perhaps with pictorial imagery, such as in figure 9, cat. no. 81, as

NOTES

1. Nishiyama Matsunosuke, *Edo Culture: Daily Life and Diversions in Urban Japan, 1600–1868,* translated and edited by Gerald Groemer (Honolulu, HI: University of Hawai'i Press, 1997), 33.

2. Jared Lubarsky, *Noble Heritage: Five Centuries of Portraits from the Hosokawa Family* (Washington, DC: Smithsonian Institution Press for the National Portrait Gallery, 1992), 64–65.

3. Translation adapted from Miyajima Shin'ichi in Yoshiaki Shimizu, ed. *Japan: The Shaping of Daimyo Culture 1185–1868* (Washington, DC: National Gallery of Art, 1988), 61.

4. George Bailey Sansom, *A History of Japan, 1334–1615* (Stanford, CA: Stanford University Press, 1961), 233. H. Mack Horton provides background on Sumimoto's battles, saying that Sumimoto "was backed by the real holder of power in Awa, Miyoshi Yukinaga" (died 1520) in the notes to his translation of *The Journal of Sōchō* (Stanford, CA: Stanford University Press, 2002), 298.

5. Translation adapted from Miyajima Shin'ichi in Yoshiaki Shimizu, ed. *Japan: The Shaping of Daimyo Culture 1185–1868* (Washington, DC: National Gallery of Art, 1988), 78.

6. Such as catalog numbers 64 and 66 in Yoshiaki Shimizu, ed. *Japan: The Shaping of Daimyo Culture 1185–1868* (Washington, DC: National Gallery of Art, 1988), 116–118.

7. Earl Miner, Hiroko Odagiri, and Robert E. Morrell, *The Princeton Companion to Classical Japanese Literature* (Princeton, NJ: Princeton University Press, 1988), 166.

8. Gregory Irvine, *The Japanese Sword: The Soul of the Samurai* (Trumbull, CT: Weatherhill, Inc. by special arrangement with The Victoria and Albert Museum), 71.

9. Under the Law for the Protection of Cultural Properties, the Japanese government identifies rare and important cultural objects, and once listed, there are restrictions on alteration, repairs, and export. Ministry of Cultural Affairs' website http://www.bunka.go.jp/english/pdf/chapter_04.pdf

10. Richard Cohen, *By the Sword: A History of Gladiators, Musketeers, Samurai, Swashbucklers, and Olympic Champions* (New York: Modern Library, 2002), 148.

11. Japan Arts Council, "Noh and Kyogen: An Introduction of Noh and Kyogen," (Japan Arts Council, 2004), http://www2.ntj.jac.go.jp/unesco/noh/en/index.html

12. Donald Keene, Keizō Kaneko, *Nō and Bunraku: Two Forms of Japanese Theatre* (New York: Columbia University Press, 1990), 21.

13. "*Chanoyu*" (茶の湯) literally means "hot water for tea" but has come to denote "The Way of Tea" or *chadō* (茶道) in modern usage. The Way of Tea refers to the art of preparing tea in which students learn the precise choreographed procedures of making a bowl of tea and also study a vast range of related arts such as the history of ceramics, poetry, etiquette, and cuisine. For many tea practitioners the popular usage of the English phrase "tea ceremony" is problematic because of the rigidity and religious tone it implies, which is not representative of their experience of tea.

14. Robin Noel Walker, *Shōkō-ken: A Late Medieval Daime Sukiya Style Japanese Tea-house* (Routledge, 2002), 41.

15. Charles Whipple and Morihiro Hosokawa, *Seeing Japan* (Tokyo: Kodansha International, 2005), 6.

16. Tokugawa Yoshinobu, "A Daimyo's Possessions" in *The Shogun Age Exhibition* (Tokyo: The Shogun Age Exhibition Committee, 1982), 28–31.

well as cat. nos. 84–88, 91–92, and 95–100. The scroll is a focal point in the gathering—it is carefully examined by the guests and may be the center of discussion, particularly if its words are enigmatic, as Zen phrases often are. Flowers are also usually placed in the tokonoma, in flower containers of bronze, ceramic (cat. no. 162), or bamboo. A full tea gathering includes a light meal, which is served using lacquer tableware such as the set of bowls with the Hosokawa crest (cat. nos. 103 and 104).

A teabowl, the vessel in which the beverage is prepared and drunk, is, of course, an essential utensil. This exhibition's examples range from imported Chinese objects used in only the most formal of tea gatherings—such as the *tenmoku* bowl (cat. no. 118), which would be supported in a fine Chinese lacquer stand (cat. no. 117)—to more rustic tea bowls made in Japan (cat. nos. 125–127). Iron kettles (cat. nos. 136 and 137), tea containers, either lacquered (cat. nos. 130 and 131) or ceramic (cat. nos. 128 and 129), bamboo tea scoops (cat. nos. 132–135), and jars for cold water to replenish the kettle (cat. nos. 124 and 158) are among the other tea implements on view in this exhibition. Together they open a door to the tea gathering, an intimate environment in which to enjoy many Japanese arts—poetry, calligraphy, lacquer, ceramics, bamboo, metalwork, architecture—in a tactile and experiential way.

Hosokawa Morihiro exemplifies in his life and writing his high regard for the Way of Tea in Japanese culture. After serving in Japanese politics, Morihiro turned to a life of studious, quiet retirement, following a long tradition expressed by literati poets in Chinese and Japanese history. About his life after politics, Morihiro has written:

> Pottery occupies an important place. . . . What has fascinated me personally is that it allows me to experience what I think is the essential spirit of what it means to be Japanese. That spirit can be found specifically in the making of utensils for the Japanese tea ceremony, and I myself have found it in making tea bowls.[15]

The oldest items included here are a teabowl from China dated between 1100–1300 (cat. no. 115) and a ceremonial long sword from the thirteenth century by the Japanese artist Moriie (cat. no. 34). The most recent items are the tea wares made by Hosokawa Morihiro (b. 1938) from 2003 through 2007 (cat. nos. 158–166) and the porcelain wares painted by his father Hosokawa Morisada (1912–2005) in the 1960s (cat. nos. 154–157). These oldest and newest items from the collection aptly evoke the depth and personality of the Hosokawa daimyo aesthetic, showing a profound appreciation for Chinese culture, honoring of heirloom Japanese weaponry, and the discipline to develop oneself as a highly-skilled amateur artist.

The possessions of a daimyo family are often divided into two main categories according to their intended use and audience. Official articles (*omote dōgu,* literally "front article") include arms and armor; decorative items for formal reception halls and tea huts, such as calligraphy by renowned Zen masters, flower vases, and tea implements; Noh costumes and accessories; and library materials required for the daimyo's education. Private articles (*oku-dōgu,* literally "inner article") include objects used for personal enjoyment or private study, such as letter boxes, garment and cosmetic boxes, board games, clothing, musical instruments, genre or narrative painting, and calligraphy and paintings by members of the household.[16] Now these possessions fulfill a different role. They provide an intimate glimpse into the public and private lives of a daimyo family through its storied history.

安南 壽ノ字

偸閑

大呂

念八

青江

山櫻

澁紙菴

大挽

芝山

浪華

神風

野田

Sketches of tea containers and teabowls, 18th century. Edo period (1615–1868).
Accordian album, ink and colors on paper. H. 28.2 cm x W. 21.8 cm.
Eisei-Bunko Museum. Some objects here appear in the exhibition, but most,
like the sketch itself, are not included.

1 ◀

赤星閑意筆　熊本城之図

KUMAMOTO CASTLE

By Akahoshi Kan'i (1835–1888)

Japan; Meiji period (1868–1912), 19th century

Hanging scroll; ink and colors on paper

H. 63.0 cm x W. 112.0 cm (image); 135 cm x 122.4 cm (overall)

Eisei-Bunko Museum, 29-aka215

2 ▼

伝赤星閑意筆　熊本城之図

KUMAMOTO CASTLE

Attributed to Akahoshi Kan'i (1835–1888)

Japan; Meiji period (1868–1912), 19th century

Hanging scroll; ink and colors on paper

H. 62.6 cm x W. 111.5 cm (image); 146 x 123.1 cm (overall)

Eisei-Bunko Museum, 1028

Hosokawa family records indicate that the painting at upper left was executed by Akahoshi Kan'i (1835–1888), the family's painter in residence. The painting beneath it is attributed to Akahoshi as well, given the works' very strong similarities. They can be dated to approximately 1872–1877.

These paintings depict a grand view of Kumamoto Castle as it stood before 1877. Generations of Hosokawa lords administered their Higo domain from the castle between 1632 and 1868, when feudal rule ended.

Katō Kiyomasa (1562–1611), a daimyo warrior originally from Owari province—and an excellent castle architect—began to build Kumamoto Castle in 1601. Construction of the major portion was accomplished by 1607. Kiyomasa died a few years later, and his son Katō Tadahiro (1586–1641) succeeded his father as lord of Higo and moved into the castle. Perhaps as a result of his youth and inexperience, Tadahiro was unable to manage the domain; the shogun removed him from power and ordered that he live in seclusion.

Katō Tadahiro's misfortune was good fortune for the Hosokawa family. Hosokawa Tadatoshi (1586–1641), then the daimyo of the smaller Buzen domain, was named lord of Higo. In 1633 he took up residence in Kumamoto Castle, which became the Hosokawa clan's headquarters for more than two hundred years.

Surrounded by moats and walls, two donjons—one six stories high, the other half that—soared into the sky. They must have stood out clearly at a great distance. There were forty-nine turrets (*yagura*), eighteen turret gates, and twenty-nine other gates. Open spaces within the compound were bounded by stone walls topped with tiled parapets. The winding mazelike configuration was designed to disorient any unwanted invaders.

Castles are structures built for defense: their purpose is to endure warfare in the long term. If besieged and cut off from supplies, the inhabitants of this castle would have been able to survive on stored food and on water from the castle's more than 120 wells. Abundant trees within the castle compound gave shade as well as fruits and nuts.

One of the most beautiful castles in Japan, Kumamoto Castle endured throughout the feudal age and into the early imperial Meiji period. It was sacked, however, in the civil strife of the Satsuma Rebellion (Seinan no Eki): in 1877, troops led by the disaffected samurai Saigō Takamori attacked the castle and burned both donjons and the surrounding buildings.

The castle has been largely restored, and now houses a museum. —YW

3

重要文化財

狩野元信筆　景徐周麟賛　細川澄元像

IMPORTANT CULTURAL PROPERTY

PORTRAIT OF HOSOKAWA SUMIMOTO (1489–1520)

By Kanō Motonobu (1476–1559); inscription by Keijo Shūrin (1440–1518)

Japan; Muromachi period (1392–1573), 1507

Hanging scroll; ink and colors on silk

H. 119.7 cm x W. 59.7 cm (image); 209 cm x 65.8 cm (overall)

Eisei-Bunko Museum, 466

Hosokawa Sumimoto, a distant ancestor of the Hosokawa lineage proper, exemplifies a warrior who experienced continual intrigue and conflict, and who was frequently engaged in war, throughout his short life.

The Warring States (Sengoku) period (late fifteenth and sixteenth centuries) was the most turbulent, bloody, and brutal time in which a Japanese warrior could live or die. Consumed by ambition, suspicion, or jealousy, many members of the distinguished warrior families fought even with their own family members.

Adoption featured among many warrior families; Sumimoto was adopted into the line of Hosokawa shogunal deputies. Sumimoto's adoptive father, Hosokawa Masamoto (1466–1507), had already adopted another son, Sumiyuki, from the powerful Kujō family. The adopted sons quarreled over succession to the Hosakawa line; in 1507 one of Sumiyuki's supporters murdered Masamoto. An attempt was made on Sumimoto's life as well, but he fled Kyoto for Ōmi province. There he remained until a family associate raised troops and ended Sumiyuki's bid for primacy in the Hosokawa house. Sumimoto returned to govern his branch of the Hosokawa—but only briefly: he was unseated in 1508. Sumimoto attempted more than once to regain his power; but in the end he died, disappointed, in Awa on the island of Shikoku.

In this equestrian portrait, Sumimoto, aged nineteen, wears *haramaki* armor (see cat. no. 22) and a helmet with a horn-like crest (*kuwagata*). His sword (*tachi*) mounting is slung at his left side; he holds a halberd (*naginata*), blade up, and a whip in his right hand, the reins in his left hand. A short sword is tucked into his belt.

For a warrior of Sumimoto's time, a horse was an essential possession. The country-side was often mountainous and thickly forested; to travel on foot in heavy armor was impractical. Warriors put serious effort and expense into buying and maintaining vigorous, well-built horses.

Keijo Shūrin (1444–1518), abbot of Nanzenji temple in Kyoto, added the inscription above the figure, which dates the portrait to 1507. It reads, in part:

Long ago the Genji clan subjugated the east of the capital. Military leaders rose in the eastern provinces. From Hosokawa Yoriharu to his son Yoriyuki, they were first called kanrei [deputy shoguns]. …

Hosokawa Sumimoto, a great archer and horseman, is far above other humans. He is also versed in *waka* [Japanese poetry] and appreciates the moon and the wind. …

Outside the citadel he takes bows and arrows; in meditation and reading of sacred books he protects Buddhism. Inside and outside, pledging to the mountains and rivers for the sake of the rulers and vassals, always with propriety and benevolence, he attains saintly wisdom.

[On] an auspicious day in the tenth month of the fourth year of Eisei [1507], Keijo Shūrin was ordered to add, and respectfully added, this inscription.

—Keijo [tripod-shaped relief seal] Shūrin [square intaglio seal][1]

—YW

1. Translation adapted from Yoshiaki Shimizu, ed., *Japan: The Shaping of Daimyo Culture 1185–1868* (Washington, D.C.: National Gallery of Art, 1988), 64.

源公澄元甲冑壽容

日照金鞍倚馬上定天下光揚寶劍射斗間出匣中其
提來也驅使豐城令其騎出也嘆起隆準公亂臣賊子
雖在蕭墻内覇氣輙掃敵陣空慶宴安未志死生
辭道貴介如優曇跋臨戰場不變神色笑他大丈夫求山
鞠窮所聞　尊民甲冑留像復覿　卬君盈岡命工昔
源氏奴洛右為諸將起關東自　頼春至　頼之始稱
菅領宗漁文章近傳明國徒　寶勝及　寶光繼封讚
州蕭何父子共輔漢官一門桃李相耀四海車書混同
故京兆擇彼支子孫賢者厥家眷為之大民族英宗匪
當射御離倫絕類亦能和歌評月品養賢如養花眇
觀齊人三千客在德不在險下視秦關百二重所祈弐
騰于五百冥靈之城秀出於十九少年之莘坒令都國
盡作曾恭卓茂出使朝家再致宋璟姚崇民間移風易
俗養外籠矢橐弓于教護佛法於内外為君為臣
琢曰山河者始終以規心祝達于聖聰
永正丁卯十月吉日　冥竹老衲景徐同麟壽命謹讚

4
細川頼有像
PORTRAIT OF HOSOKAWA
YORIARI (1332–1391)
Japan; Muromachi period (1392–1573)
16th century
Hanging scroll; ink and colors on silk
H. 79.2 cm x W. 39.4 cm (image);
166.3 cm x 60.7 cm (overall)
Eisei-Bunko Museum, 3355

The history of the Hosokawa family in a sense begins with Hosokawa Yoriari, from whom the family line descends to Hosakawa Morihiro, the present head of the family. The younger brother of Hosokawa Yoriyuki, the *kanrei* (deputy) of the Muromachi shogunate, and a fierce warrior, Yoriari fought and survived many campaigns—as did his son Yorinaga, the *shugo daimyo* (military lord) of Izumi province. Yoriari is seen as an early Hosokawa lord who relayed the bloodline to the present-day family, and is therefore revered as a distant ancestor.

In this formal portrait, which was executed more than a century after its subject's death, Yoriari sits on a tatami dressed in a black samurai hat (*eboshi*) and black *hitatare* outfit (see cat. no. 19). A short sword (*koshigatana*) is tucked in his sash; he holds a closed fan in his right hand. The inscription at top right reads *Shōmyōin dono shinei*—"portrait of the Lord Shōmyōin" (perhaps Yoriari's Buddhist name).

A suggestion of the degree to which later Hosokawa clan venerated Yoriari may be found in cat. nos. 20, 30, and 31—respectively, a nineteenth-century reproduction of his armor and helmet and two cavalry banners, each with the character *ari* (有), part of his name. —YW

5
画 田代等甫筆　色紙 細川幽斎筆
細川幽斎像

PORTRAIT OF HOSOKAWA YŪSAI (aka Fujitaka, 1534–1610)
Painting by Tashiro Tōho; poetry by Hosokawa Yūsai
Japan; Momoyama period (1573–1615), 1612
Hanging scroll; ink and colors on silk
H. 104.4 cm x W. 51.3 cm (image) H. 173.3 cm x W. 89 cm (overall)
Eisei-Bunko Museum, 3910

A key figure in the alliances that would reunite war-torn Japan for centuries, Hosokawa Fujitaka (1534–1610; also known by his later name, Yūsai) was a courageous warrior, a well-known poet in the classical *waka* form, and a scholar of ancient poetry. In the seventh month of 1600, Fujitaka's Tanabe Castle, then seat of the Hosokawa domain, was besieged by 15,000 enemies. Fujitaka and followers numbering fewer than five hundred—soldiers, women, and children—defended Tanabe for sixty days. His wife wore armor and attended to people in the castle. Believing that his death was inevitable, Fujitaka feared that his life's work, a study of the *Kokin wakashū*,[1] would perish as well. Through his arrangements, a delegation from the imperial court was permitted to pass through the siege to obtain Fujitaka's work.

Fujitaka composed the following poem for the emperor.

Inishie mo	In the world that remains,
Ima mo kawaranu	Past and present
Yo no naka ni	Unchanged,
Kokoro no tane wo	I leave these words:
Nokosu koto no ha	Seeds of my spirit.

Upon receiving the poem, Emperor Goyōzei (1571–1617) ordered an end to the siege on Tanabe Castle, and the lives of those within were saved. It was the only episode in Japanese history when literature trumped considerations of politics or war.[2]

In this portrait, (overleaf) Fujitaka/Yūsai, dressed informally and holding a fan, sits on a tatami mat; three of his poems appear above.[3] According to the record *Hanfu benran* (藩譜便覧), in 1612 Fujitaka's wife ordered the painter Tashiro Tōho to paint her husband's portrait. Portraits of Hosokawa family heads were often made to commemorate their lives. —YW

1. *Kokin wakashū* (Collection of Poems Ancient and Modern), also called *Kokinshū,* is a poetry anthology compiled in the early tenth century. It is notoriously difficult for its numerous references to Chinese poetry and multiple levels of meaning. Fujitaka was among the few scholars of his time to decode and teach these poems.
2. Okuda Bōyō, "Hosokawa Yūsai: Uta no kokoro," in *Eisei Bunko,* (Spring 2008), 11
3. Yatsushiro Shiritsu Hakubutsukan and Kita Kyushu Shiritsu Inochi no Tabi Hakubutsukan, eds., *Daimyō Hosokawa ke: Bun to bu no kiseki.* (Yatsushiro, Kumamoto: Yatsushiro Shiritsu Hakubutsukan Mirai no Mori Museum, 2005), 14–15.

6
細川幽斎像

PORTRAIT OF HOSOKAWA YŪSAI (aka Fujitaka, 1534–1610)
Japan; Edo period (1615–1868)
17th century
Hanging scroll; ink and colors on silk
H. 102.8 cm x W. 49.8 cm (image); 200 cm x 73.5 cm (overall)
Eisei-Bunko Museum, 3290-1

This portrait is identical, in the subject's clothing and posture, to an Important Cultural Property–designated painting of Fujitaka in the collection of Tenjuan temple, Kyoto. It depicts the daimyo Hosokawa Fujitaka (1534–1610) in a relaxed pose with a round Chinese-style fan in his right hand and a sword at his side. His bearing expresses a lofty state of mind. The Tenjuan painting was inscribed by the Zen priest Ishin Sūden, abbot of Nanzeji, in the fifth month of 1612:

> Renowned for his elegant pursuits, he was a cultivated man whose nature embraces *bun* (literary arts) and *bu* (martial arts). A man of nobility, a descendant of the sixth grandson of the emperor Seiwa, he ruled with awesome dignity and inspiring decorum. … He lectured on *The Tale of Genji.* … He discussed Chinese poetic style and recited by heart the secret teachings of Japanese poetry—*Kokinshū* (Collection of Poems Ancient and Modern), *Manyōshū* (Collection of Ten Thousand Leaves). … He recited sitting down or walking. …
>
> The round fan in his hand sweeps away the muggy heat. The sharp sword he wears at his waist severs human passions and ties. … Hosokawa Yūsai passed away suddenly on the twentieth day of the eighth month of the fifteenth year of Keichō [1610], aged seventy-seven. His bereaved wife, Kōjuin, commissioned an artist to paint a portrait of his benign face, and asked me to write an inscription. My refusal was unheeded, so I have written useless words and wasted statements. … [1]

—YW

1. Translation adapted from Yoshiaki Shiazu, ed., *Japan: The Shaping of Daimyo Culture, 1185–1868* (Washington: National Gallery of Art, 1989), 78.

7 ▼

細川忠興像

PORTRAIT OF HOSOKAWA TADAOKI

(aka Sansai, 1563–1646*)

Japan; Edo period (1615–1868), 17th century

Hanging scroll; ink and colors on silk

H. 110.0 cm x W. 50.5 cm (image)

H. 205.5 cm x W. 67 cm (overall)

Eisei-Bunko Museum, 3294

Hosokawa Tadaoki (also known as Sansai) was the oldest son of Hosokawa Fujitaka (1534–1615). Of all of the Hosokawa warriors, Tadaoki lived in one of the most turbulent, unstable ages: the Momoyama (1573–1615) and early (1615–1650) Edo periods. He managed not only to survive but also to play an important role in establishing the Hosokawa line.

An astute and loyal vassal, Tadaoki served, in succession, three military hegemons in their quest to unify Japan: Oda Nobunaga (1534–1582), Toyotomi Hideyoshi (1537–1898), and Tokugawa Ieyasu (1543–1616). A minor lapse of judgment in choosing whom he would support, and when, could have ended his life and his family lineage. In fact, Tadaoki lost his wife of many years, Gracia, to the struggle for power. A Christian, Gracia nevertheless took her own life to nullify her value as a hostage.

Gracia (née Tama) was a daughter of Nobunaga's assassin, Akechi Mitsuhide. Before the battle of Sekigahara (1600), in which her husband supported Tokugawa Ieyasu, Gracia was captured by the leader of the opposing force. To preserve her husband from wavering in loyalty to Ieyasu out of concern for her safety, Gracia ordered her servant to kill her. Following his victory in the battle, Tokugawa Ieyasu (who became the first shogun of the Tokugawa line) rewarded Tadaoki for his loyalty and military support by making him lord of the Buzen domain, in Kyushu.

When peace finally came, Tadaoki built a Christian temple in Buzen to honor his wife. He ordered a large bell for the temple. But a new shogun adopted an anti-Christian policy; persecution began, and the temple was destroyed. No one knew what had become of the temple bell. Three hundred years later, a large bell (see cat. no. 8) with the nine-planet Hosokawa crest was discovered hidden in a small turret in Tadaoki's castle. This bell is believed to be the one made in Gracia's memory.

In this portrait, Tadaoki, dressed in an aristocratic formal black robe, is seated on a tatami mat. His right hand holds a scepter (*shaku*); his left, a long ceremonial sword (*tachi*). The black banner behind him, hung from crossed bamboo poles, displays two diagonal white lines; it is the Hosokawa's early war banner. The design later changed to white with the nine-planet crest in black (see cat. nos. 32, 33) —YW

*Hosokawa Tadaoki's death year is commonly given as 1645. He died in the twelfth month of Shoho 2, which is equivalent to January 18, 1646.

8 ▶

南蛮寺鐘

WESTERN-STYLE BELL

with nine-planet family crest

Japan; Momoyama period (1573–1615), approx. 1607

Cast bronze

H. 80.0 cm x Diam. 71.0 cm, Weight 210 kg

Eisei-Bunko Museum, 7271

The Hosokawa family believes that this bell, with its nine-planet crests, was cast for Hosokawa Tadaoki (1563–1645), lord of Kokura Castle, in Kyushu, in honor of his wife, Hosokawa Gracia (1563–1600), one of Japan's early Christians. Tadaoki apparently intended to present the bell to a church located near his castle. In 1613, however, the shogunate banned Christianity; a year later, the church was destroyed. Its whereabouts unknown for many years, the bell was later discovered hidden away in a corner of the castle's tower. —YW

9

沢庵宗彭賛　細川忠利像

PORTRAIT OF HOSOKAWA TADATOSHI (1586–1641)

Inscription by Takuan Sōhō
(1573–1645)
Japan; Edo period (1615–1868), 1641
Hanging scroll; ink and colors on silk
H. 93.5 cm x W. 51 cm (image)
182 x 74.7 cm (overall)
Eisei-Bunko Museum, 3296-1

Hosokawa Tadatoshi was born to Tadaoki and Lady Gracia. In 1620, Tadatoshi became the heir to Tadaoki's Kokura Castle and Buzen domain in northern Kyushu. His father passed down the family leadership to him in 1632; that same year, Ieyasu, the founding Tokugawa shogun, removed Katō Hidetada from the lordship of the Higo domain and appointed Tadatoshi to replace him. Higo was then among the three largest domains in Japan.

The Hosokawa were strangers in their new domain, and Higo was notoriously hard on strangers. But Tadatoshi—a highly cultured man who practiced the Way of Tea, performed Noh theater, and played music—turned out also to be a careful and compassionate lord; he won the people's trust, and his administrative ability earned him the shogun's trust as well.

With Tadatoshi, the Hosokawa became top-level administrators of important holdings. The family's glory would continue until 1868, when the feudal *bakuhan* political system was abolished and shogunate Japan became imperial Japan.

In this portrait Tadatoshi is seated on a tatami mat, dressed in a courtly black formal robe and headdress, with a ceremonial scepter (*shaku*) in his right hand and a sword (*tachi*) slung from his belt on his left. The portrait's inscription, dated 1641, was written by the renowned Zen monk Takuan Sōhō. —YW

10

天柱義雪賛　細川綱利像

PORTRAIT OF HOSOKAWA
TSUNATOSHI (1643–1714)

Inscription by Tenchū Gisetsu
(1663?–1727)

Japan; Edo period (1615–1868), 1715

Hanging scroll; ink and colors on silk

H. 91.0 cm x W. 49.5 cm (image)

179.2 cm x 75 cm (overall)

Eisei-Bunko Museum, 3305

Tsunatoshi was very young when his father, Mitsunao (1619–1649), died—too young to inherit his father's position as daimyo under shogunal law. His chief steward, Ogasawara Tadazane, governed Kumamoto until 1661.

Tsunatoshi may best be remembered for the episode known as the Forty-Seven Loyal Retainers. In 1701 a young lord named Asano, from the province of Akō, was serving his term of duty at the shogun's court. After a humiliating incident, Lord Asano attacked Kira Yoshinaka, his tutor and a ranking official of the Shogunate. Yoshinaka did not die—not then—but Asano was sentenced to death.

Oishi Kuranosuke, the chief adviser to Asano's clan, led forty-six other retainers in avenging their dead master. On the night of December 14, 1702, they stormed Kira's villa in Edo and beheaded him.

They were arrested. While the shogun deliberated about what to do with them—for while they had broken the law, they had behaved in accordance with samurai honor—three daimyo were asked to house them. A third of them were placed in the custody of Hosokawa Tsunatoshi. Eventually the retainers were sentenced to death but allowed to commit *seppuku*, samurai fashion, rather than being executed like common criminals. They ended their lives in the garden of Tsunatoshi's villa.

This painting is inscribed by Tenchū Gisetsu, the 285th head of the large Zen temple complex of Daitokuji in Kyoto.
—YW

11

竹原玄路筆　秀山宗騏賛　細川重賢像

PORTRAIT OF HOSOKAWA SHIGEKATA (1720–1785)

By Takehara Harumichi; inscription by Shūzan Sōki (1754?–1807)

Japan; Edo period (1615–1868), 1786

Hanging scroll; ink and colors on silk

H. 93.5 cm x W. 49.3 cm (image); 179.3 cm x 72.8 cm (overall)

Eisei-Bunko Museum, 3314

To sit for his portrait may have made Shigekata impatient: noted for his energy and industry, he would probably have preferred to be out studying or painting the insects, marine animals, or botanical subjects that fascinated him. Indeed, he possessed encyclopedic knowledge on those subjects. As with many portraits of the Hosokawa lords, he is seated on a tatami and dressed in a formal robe. He holds a *shaku*, a wooden ceremonial scepter, and wears a ceremonial *tachi* sword slung from his belt. His black hat is embellished with *oikake*, fanlike decorations, over the ears. This is regalia of a type worn by bodyguards in the imperial court's army, suggesting that his tastes tended to the plain and simple. The portrait is inscribed by Shūzan Sōki, the 416th head abbot of Daitokuji temple in Kyoto.

Shigekata is remembered as a visionary social reformer. When he became lord of Kumamoto (Higo), in 1747, he inherited a financial mess that had been growing for years. His domain was deeply in debt; the Osaka bankers refused to lend any more money (unsurprisingly, as there was no con-crete policy of repaying loans). Shigekata emphasized that while his samurai might be poor, honor obliged them to endure hard-ship and behave as role models for the people. To reform their attitude and develop good character, he built a school, called Jishūkan. He also built a teaching hospital whose services were open to samurai and commoners alike (if they could afford treatment). This school is the ancestor of today's Kumamoto Medical University.

Shigekata's administration of justice was equally enlightened. The law as he found it punished major crimes with death and lesser offenses with exile; he created Japan's first modern penal system, modeled in part on Chinese civil law. Long before the concept emerged in the West, his system was designed to be corrective; penalties were codified, and convicted criminals were imprisoned for specified periods. While serving their time they were taught to be productive, and money they earned as prisoners was invested and returned to them upon their release. —YW

前德禅秀山宗騏敬賛

天明六丙午春三月十五日

感徹無邊自在身

靈威千仭高翔德

嘉聲誰掩木然真

不假丹青文鳳質

兼越州太守徹巌宗印大居士肖像

靈感院殿故肥後藩主前羽林次将

12 ◄

五姓田芳柳筆　平木柳静（政次）助筆
細川韶邦像

PORTRAIT OF HOSOKAWA
YOSHIKUNI (1835–1876)
By Goseda Hōryū (1827–1892) assisted
by Hiraki Masatsugu (1859–1943)
Japan; Meiji period (1868–1912), 1878
Hanging scroll; ink and colors on silk
H. 75.8 cm x W. 44.0 cm (image);
117.9 cm x 62.0 cm (overall)
Eisei-Bunko Museum, 3331

13 ►

五姓田芳柳筆　細川韶邦像
PORTRAIT OF HOSOKAWA
YOSHIKUNI (1835–1876)
By Goseda Hōryū (1827–1892)
Japan; Meiji period (1868–1912), 1878
Hanging scroll; ink and colors on silk
H. 94.4 cm x W. 44.0 cm (image); H.
178.5 cm x W. 62.3 cm (overall)
Eisei-Bunko Museum, 3333

These paintings by Goseda Hōryū—the
first with the assistance of his student Hiraki
Masatsugu (aka Ryūsei)—depict the last
Hosokawa daimyo of the Edo period,
Hosokawa Yoshikuni. He is seated, dressed
in a kimono and *haori* jacket with the nine-
planet family crest on his sleeve, his sword
in his belt. But these scrolls reveal a major
change in portraiture from the style in which
his antecedents were depicted: the artist's
use of shading and perspective produced a
much more realistic effect.

Yoshikuni's drawn, sober face also hints
at a great change that had occurred, in his
life and those of all Japanese. The feudal
system, in which the Hosokawa clan had
played such an important role, had collapsed:
the Meiji emperor assumed sole authority
in 1868, and Japan became: imperial Japan.

The change took its toll on Yoshikuni.
Never robust, he exhausted his strength in
futile efforts to mediate between rival court
and shogunal factions. The Hosokawa fiefdom
became the province of Kumamoto, and
Yoshikuni was appointed its first governor.
In failing health, he resigned in 1870; retir-
ing as head of the family at the same time,
he passed both roles to his younger brother
Morihisa. Yoshikuni died in 1876. —YW

14

狩野伊圭弘信筆　細川希姫像
PORTRAIT OF PRINCESS HOSOKAWA KŌ
(aka Baishuin; 1823–1826)
By Kanō Ikei Hironobu
Japan; Edo period (1615–1868), 1826
Hanging scroll; ink and colors on silk
H. 95.0 cm x W. 52.5 cm (image);
185.5 cm x 74 (overall)
Eisei-Bunko Museum, 3344

One of six daughters of the lord Hosokawa Narishige, the little Princess Kō was a child of a late second marriage; she was adopted by Narishige's oldest son, Naritatsu. Kō died when she was only three years old; the whole family grieved to lose her, and her adoptive father, devastated by her death, commissioned a number of memorial portraits of Kō to hang in temples under Hosokawa patronage.

The portraits are all much the same. With her hair in two rings on top of her head and in short bangs on her forehead, Princess Kō is seated on a thick cushion. A black obi secures her lovely kimono, of a light and dark checker pattern. Over this she wears a red *haori* jacket patterned in white with the nine-planet family crest.

The portraitist, Kanō Ikei Hironbu, also painted the Hosokawa lords Narishige (1759–1836) and Naritatsu (1789–1826). Hironobu studied painting in Edo under Kanō Seisen'in Osanobu (1796–1846).
—YW

15

細川益姫像

PORTRAIT OF PRINCESS HOSOKAWA MASU

(aka Kenkōin; 1806–1875)

Japan; Edo period (1615–1868)

19th century

Hanging scroll; ink and colors on silk

H. 114.8 cm x W. 54.8 cm (image)

H. 203 cm x W. 80.8 cm (overall)

Eisei-Bunko Museum, 3329-2

Princess Hosokawa Masu (Masuhime) was born the daughter of daimyo Asano Narikata (1773–1831), the eighth-generation lord of the Hiroshima domain. She married the tenth-generation Hosokawa lord, Narimori (1804–1860; see also cat. nos. 22, 63) and gave birth to three daughters. Though the first two died in infancy, her third child, Tokiko (aka Isahime), grew up to marry Matsudaira Yoshinaga, the last daimyo of the powerful Echizen Fukui domain at the end of the Edo period.

Princess Masu kneels on a tatami for this portrait. While her high, painted eyebrows and pale complexion give her face an aristo-cratic look, her garments clearly distinguish her as a woman from a powerful daimyo family. She wears a white *kosode,* heavily dyed and embroidered with swallows, wisteria, chrysanthemums, and flowing water—motifs suggesting late spring and early autumn. Her dark brown outer *uchikake* robe, worn loosely over the shoulders, is embroidered with undulating lines, water wheels, bouquets, flowers, and butterflies.[1] Textiles with this kind of ornate decoration and extensive embroidery were typically reserved for women from the elite echelons of the warrior class. —MR

1. The combination of a dark brown outer robe over a white underrobe is visually similar to the most formal midsummer outfit for daimyo family women: a dark brown, heavily embroidered silk *koshimaki* ("waist-wrap") worn over a linen-like ramie *katabira* with exten-sive small dyed (sometimes embroidered) patterns of flora, fauna, and landscapes. Because the robes in this portrait appear to have padded hems and red linings, and because the outer robe is worn over the shoulders instead of around the waist, these garments probably represent silk robes worn just before or just after the summer season.

Detail

16 (this page)
細川公御船入港図巻
SHIP OF LORD HOSOKAWA
COMING INTO PORT
Japan; Meiji period (1868–1912), 1882
Handscroll; ink and colors on paper
H. 63.3 cm x W. 432 (image)
Eisei-Bunko Museum, 3761

17 (overleaf)
橋本又左衛門筆　御船賦之図
FLEET OF SHIPS
By Hashimoto Matazaemon
Japan; Edo period (1615–1868) or
Meiji period (1868–1912), 19th century
Handscroll; ink and colors on paper
H. 39.3 cm x W. 702.3 cm (image)
Eisei-Bunko Museum, 3760

These handscrolls (cat. nos. 16–17) depict
the fleet of Hosokawa Yoshikuni (still known
at the time as Yoshiyuki, 1835–1876), who
became the last feudal lord of his family's
Higo domain. The fleet is entering the port
of Tsurusaki, in Higo province.

The son of Hosokawa Narimori (1804–
1860), Yoshikuni was born in Edo; this
was his first visit to his father's domain.
He departed Edo on the thirteenth day of
the ninth month of 1860 and followed the

Tōkaidō highway to Osaka, where he took
ship for Tsurusaki. Landing there, he traveled
on the Bungo Highway, arriving at Kumamoto Castle on the twenty-fourth day of
the tenth month. The whole trip took one
month and eleven days.

The fleet consists of numerous vessels,
each of which is labeled in a small cartouche.
Most carry banners bearing the nine-planet
Hosokawa family crest. There are small
craft for carrying messages, supply ships,
and passenger ships; the largest ship, depicted
in the middle of the handscroll, is Yoshikuni's
double-decked flagship, *Naminashi Maru*
("Ship of Calm Water"). Its main deck is
furnished like a large room, with painted
sliding-door panels (see below).

Cat. no. 16 has a colophon dated May
30, Meiji 15 (1882). The wooden storage
box for cat. no. 17 is inscribed "One scroll;
Fleet of Ships, by Hashimoto Matazaemon";
accompanying papers record the ships' officers' names and titles. (On some occasions
one or more painters would accompany a
lord on his travels).

These handscrolls are valuable evidence
of the means by which the Hosokawa lords
traveled between Edo, the shogun's capital,
and their domains. The journey to Edo was
not optional. In 1635 the shogunate created
the policy of *sankin kōtai,* which required all
provincial lords to observe "alternate attendance" at court. They had to live in Edo,
the seat of the shogun, for a full year; the
following year, they could return to their
province; and again the next year they

returned to Edo. Each lord's wife and children
had to reside permanently in Edo; effectively,
they were kept hostage. Furthermore, each
lord had to maintain three houses in the
capital—one for himself, one for his wife
and children, and one for the vassals and
attendants who accompanied him to Edo
every other year. The daimyo's multiple
residences, lavishly maintained, and frequent
travel, undertaken in full ceremonial panoply,
proved extremely expensive.

Because of the *sankin kōtai* system, Hosokawa Yoshikuni had never before visited
Kumamoto Castle, to which he would suc-
ceed when his father retired or died. This
was his first experience of travel by sea,
and his first view of the domain he was to
govern. For nearly all the people of Higo
province, it was the first time they would
see their future lord. —YW

Interior of ship *Naminashi Maru*

Detail

17

橋本又左衛門筆　御船賦之図

FLEET OF SHIPS
By Hashimoto Matazaemon
Japan; Edo period (1615–1868) or Meiji
period (1868–1912), 19th century
Handscroll; ink and colors on paper
H. 39.3 cm x W. 702.3 cm (image)
Eisei-Bunko Museum, 3760

18

藍麻地小紋九曜紋付裃 細川忠利所用

SAMURAI MAN'S FORMAL VEST AND TROUSERS
(KAMISHIMO)

with miniature pattern and nine-planet crests
Worn by Hosokawa Tadatoshi (1586–1641)
Japan; Edo period (1615–1868), 17th century
Ramie tabby with stenciled paste-resist dyeing (*komon katazome*)
L. 67.5 cm x W. 62 cm (jacket); L. 96.5 cm x W. 36.4 cm (trouser)
Eisei-Bunko Museum, 6964

The *kamishimo* is a two-part ensemble identified with the warrior class. The word *kamishimo*—literally, "upper and lower"—originally referred to any two-piece outfit made from the same fabric; over time, it came to refer specifically to the combination of a vest with open front and sides (*kataginu*) and pleated, skirtlike trousers (*hakama*), which are tied around the waist with ties extending from the waistbands at the front and the back. Though its roots were in commoner dress, this outfit, like the *hitatare* (cat. no. 19), rose in status to the extent that, in the Muromachi period, Hosokawa Harumoto (1514–1563) wore one for an audience with the shogun Ashikaga Yoshiharu (reigned 1521–1546).[1]

In the Edo period, the kamishimo—worn over a kimono-like *kosode*—became the standard costume for daimyo and their retainers, functioning as informal wear for

the former and formal official wear for the latter. There are two lengths of trouser, short (*hanbakama*) and long (*nagabakama*). This hakama is the short type, thought to have been worn for administrative duties and internal visits,[2] while longer trousers were reserved for more ceremonial occasions. The form of the kataginu vest changed over time; this vest has a narrower width and softer rounded shoulders,[3] while later vests had wider silhouettes whose prominently extended shoulders were often reinforced with whale baleen.

As in this example, kamishimo were commonly made from finely woven ramie, a crisp plant fiber similar to the flax used to make linen. The cloth was then stencil paste-resist dyed in indigo with an intricate *komon* ("miniature pattern") diaper, leaving space for the Hosokawa family crests adorning the front of each shoulder and the center

of the back. The type of komon used could also indicate rank or family. This very rare early kamishimo is known to have been worn by the daimyo Hosokawa Tadatoshi (1563–1645), whose portrait and helmet are also included in this catalogue (cat. nos. 9 and 27). —MR

1. *Zoku Ōnin ki* (1711), quoted in Maruyama Nobuhiko, "Buke no fukushoku." *Nihon no bijutsu* 9, no. 340 (Tokyo: Shibundō, 1994), 48.
2. Tokugawa Bijutsukan, ed., *Tokugawa Bijutsukan no meihō.* (Nagoya: Tokugawa Bijutsukan, 2000), 64–65.
3. In an essay, the Confucianist Dazai Shundai (1680–1747) noted that "men's kataginu in the past were made of ramie cloth 8 sun (30.3 cm, or 11.9 in.) in width, but since the Jōkyō (1684–1687) or Genroku (1688–1703) eras, they have extended to widths of 1 *shaku* (37.9 cm or 14.9 in.)." Quoted in Maruyama (1994), 61. The width of each panel in this Hosokawa family kataginu is 31.7 cm, excluding the central hem allowance.

19

紅梅精好地直垂　細川慶順（後十三代韶邦）着用

HIGH-RANKING DAIMYO'S FORMAL JACKET AND TROUSERS (HITATARE)

Worn by Hosokawa Yoshiyuki (aka Yoshikuni, 1835–1876)
Japan; Edo period (1615–1868), 1853
Silk tabby (*seigō*) with degummed warps and thick raw-silk wefts; braided silk cord
L. 66.5 cm x W. 152 cm (jacket); L. 144 cm x W. 38.7 cm (trouser)
Eisei-Bunko Museum, 8817, 8818

A costume closely associated with the upper echelons of the warrior class, the *hitatare* comprises a jacket (*uwagi*) with double-panel sleeves and a V-neckline—in contrast to the round neck of Chinese-influenced aristocratic garments—and trousers (*hakama*). Its prototype was worn by commoners and low-ranking samurai of the Heian period (794–1185); remnants of those practical roots can be found in the ties at the chest (originally to keep the front flaps from coming undone) and the draw cords through the ends of the sleeves (to facilitate movement), though in this garment they are essentially decorative. In the medieval age, the costume evolved into everyday wear for high-ranking members of the warrior class as well as for the aristocracy, who wore an unlined version. Under the Tokugawa shogunate, in the Edo period, the hitatare was elevated to official ceremonial dress for daimyo with status of fourth-rank chamberlain (*shii shijū*) and above.[1] When worn by a daimyo lord, it would be paired with a black hat of folded and heavily lacquered paper (*ori eboshi*), another marker of class and rank.

This costume is made from a specific type of stiff silk tabby (*seigō*), which uses different colors for the degummed silk warps and for the thicker raw-silk wefts. Its shade, described as red plum (*kōbai*), was woven from red warps and white wefts; the red safflower dye has now faded to yellow. (An ensemble's color indicated the rank of its wearer: only the shogun wore purple, only the top two Tokugawa daimyo families wore scarlet, and other top daimyo wore a variety of alternate colors.[2])

The original paper wrapping in which this outfit is still stored has an ink inscription telling us that it was worn on two occasions: first for an official visit to the shogun's Edo castle on the second day of the first month of 1853 (Kaei 6), and for a visit to the shogun's family temple of Kan'eiji in the Ueno district of Edo on the fourteenth day of the same month and year. Because we know that Hosokawa Narimori (1806–1860), the head of the family at the time, was then in Kumamoto for the New Year, this outfit is thought to have been worn by his nineteen-year-old son Yoshiyuki, who was later renamed Yoshikuni when he became the thirteenth-generation Hosokawa daimyo. Yoshiyuki had been appointed to fourth-rank lower chamberlain in 1851, and he had his coming-of-age-ceremony (*genpuku*) in the twelfth month of the following year, one month before he would have worn this hitatare.[3] —MR

1. Maruyama Nobuhiko, *Buke no fukushoku*. Nihon no bijutsu 9, no. 340 (Tokyo: Shibundo, 1994): 56.
2. Hachijō Tadamoto, *Subarashii shōzoku no sekai: Ima ni kikiru sennen no fasshon*. (Tokyo: Seibundō Shinkosha, 2006): 62.
3. Entry on this work by Yamazaki Setsu, in Yatsushiro Shiritsu Hakubutsukan Mirai no Mori Myūjiamu and Kitakyūshū Shiritsu Inochi no Tabi Hakubutsukan, eds., *Daimyō Hosokawa ke: Bun to bu no kiseki*. (Yatsushiro: Yatsushiro Shiritsu Hakubutsukan Mirai no Mori Myūjiamu and Kitakyūshū Shiritsu Inochi no Tabi Hakubutsukan, 2005), 44.
• See also Hinonishi Sukenori, *Fukushoku*. Nihon no bijutsu 6, no. 26 (Tokyo: Shibundō, 1968).

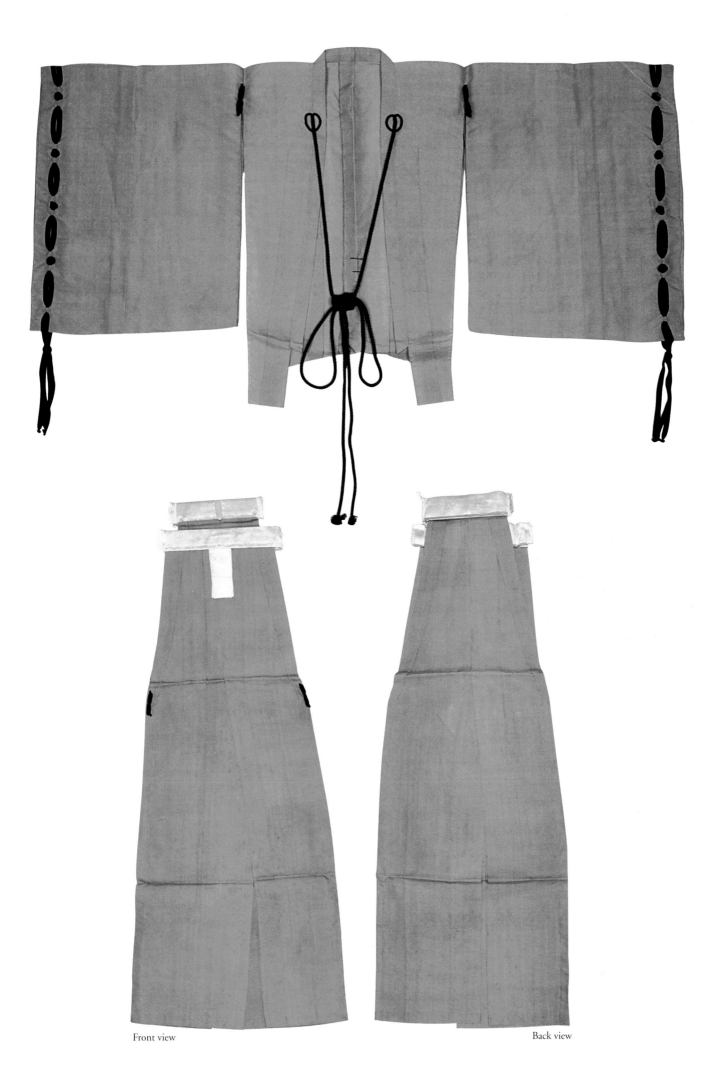

Front view

Back view

20

白糸威褄取大鎧（写し）

ŌYOROI-TYPE ARMOR

White cord lacing with diagonal corner accents (*tsumadori*)
Replica of a suit worn by Hosokawa Yoriari (1332–1391)
Japan, Edo period, 1829 (after 14th century original)
Iron, gilt bronze, metal, tooled leather, lacquer, braided silk, fur
Cuirass front H. 54 cm, tasset L. 29.4 cm, shoulder guard W. 36.8 cm, total weight 21.0 kg
Eisei-Bunko Museum, 4082

Ōyoroi is a type of armor comprising a helmet (*kabuto*), cuirass (*dō*), tassets (*kusazuri;* laced overlapping lames) to protect the hips, and shoulder guards (*sode*), among other pieces. It was used primarily from the late Heian period (794–1185) to the Kamakura period (1185–1333), when one-on-one mounted combat was the primary mode of warfare. Because a warrior's armor became his funeral attire if he was defeated, a great deal of attention was paid to decorative details such as the color of the lacing and the ornamentation of the metal fixtures. For that reason ōyoroi armor is not only heavy and showy, but often has high aesthetic value.

This suit of armor is a reproduction of the famous ōyoroi worn by the founder of the Hosokawa clan, Hosokawa Yoriari (1331–1390), in the battle of Kyoto in 1358. This authentic reproduction was made at the order of the eleventh-generation daimyo, Hosokawa Naritatsu (1789–1826), during a time when the revivalist Kokugaku (literally, "national studies") movement was in vogue, and it had become fashionable to reproduce famous suits of armor. Begun in 1824, the reproduction of Yoriari's ōyoroi took five years to complete.

Armor's lacing (*odoshi*) may incorporate leathers or braided silk cords of various colors, which are the primary distinguishing elements. The name of a suit of armor will usually contain a reference to material and color, such as "red cord lacing" or "purple leather lacing"; this suit, with its keynote of white braided silk, is known as an ōyoroi with white cord lacing. The diagonal accents of multicolored lacing in the corners of the shoulder guards and tassets are called *tsumadori*. The combination of white lacing with such tsumadori accents was very popular in Yoriari's time for its refined, austere beauty. This armor's hoe-shaped helmet crest (*kuwagata*) and right breastplate (*sentan ita*), the originals of which were missing, are fashioned after those on an ōyoroi armor in Itsukushima shrine in present-day Hiroshima prefecture. The gauntlets (*kote*) are modeled on the so-called Yoshitsune gauntlets in the Nara shrine of Kasuga Taisha. This reproduction is thus a synthesis, containing parts that are historically informed and faithfully reproduced as well as parts that have been reinvented. —AJ

21

紅糸威胴丸具足　細川宣紀所用

DŌMARU GUSOKU-TYPE ARMOR

Red cord lacing

Worn by Hosokawa Nobunori (1676–1732)

Japan, Edo period (1615–1868), 18th century

Iron, gilt bronze, metal, tooled leather, lacquer, silk embroidery, braided silk, fur, feathers

Cuirass front H. 61 cm, sleeve W. 35 cm, total weight 25 kg

Eisei-Bunko Museum, 4098

This magnificent suit of armor, in a revival style, was worn by Hosokawa Nobunori, the sixth-generation lord of the family. The Hosokawa clan has traditionally categorized it as a suit of *dōmaru*-type armor; because it was made in the Edo period and is a full suit (complete with gauntlets, greaves, etc., unlike the more abbreviated earlier examples of dōmaru), it technically it falls into the larger category of *tōsei gusoku* armor.

Suits of Edo-period dōmaru armor such as this (sometimes called *dōmaru yoroi*) are thought to be amalgamations of two distinct earlier types of armor: the dōmaru cuirasses that evolved as lightweight protection for medieval infantry and the formal, archaic *ōyoroi* (see cat. no. 20). During the Edo period, this new type of armor gained the same status as the ōyoroi, becoming known as the "formal armor" (*shikishō no yoroi*)—the most formally correct protective gear—for men of the warrior class. This example faithfully reproduces the characteristics of formal dōmaru suits of armor, with the exception of a few elements such as the construction of the tassets.

The helmet is not only beautiful and dignified but also of exceptionally fine workmanship. Its bowl is an ancient one, made in the Kamakura period (1185–1333), which has been incorporated into this eighteenth-century helmet.

The second son of Hosokawa Toshishige (1646–1687), lord of the Shinden branch of the Kumamoto domain, Hosokawa Nobunori was adopted by the fifth-generation daimyo, Hosokawa Tsunetoshi (1643–1714), and succeeded him to become the head of the clan's main family. He promoted both cultural and martial arts and composed poems in the Chinese style under the pen name Kentankyo, producing such poetry collections as *Kentankyo shishū* and *Kyūjoshū.*
—AJ

22

黒革威肩紅糸威腹巻　細川斉護所用

HARAMAKI-TYPE ARMOR

Black leather lacing, red cord horizontal accent lacing
(*katadori*) on shoulder guards
Worn by Hosokawa Narimori (1804–1860)
Japan, Edo period (1615–1868), 19th century
Iron, leather, lacquer, silk, and gilt metal
Cuirass front H. 56 cm, sleeve W. 29.5 cm.
total weight 21.8 kg
Eisei-Bunko Museum, 4111

This armor in a revival style was worn by
Hosokawa Narimori (1804–1860), the
twelfth-generation lord of the domain, who
saw to the reproduction (cat. no. 20) of the
white-laced *ōyoroi* armor worn by the clan's
first patriarch, Hosokawa Yoriari (1331–1390).

The cuirass (*dō*) is made in the *haramaki*
style dating back to medieval Japan. The
haramaki is an even more simplified form of
armor than the *dōmaru* (see cat. no. 21).
Though similar in many ways, its cuirass is
constructed with an opening at the back
instead of the side to make it easier to put
on and take off.

Except for some incongruities, such as its
replacement of the standard ridged helmet
with a riveted helmet, this haramaki armor
is comparatively true to the style of the
late Muromachi period (1392–1573). The
helmet's hoe-shaped crest (*kuwagata*), with a
lion in gilt bronze, was copied from ancient
armor in the temple Kuramadera, in Kyoto.
The color scheme—black leather, with
horizontal accents of red lacing on the first
two lames on the sleeve protectors—seems
to imitate a suit of ōyoroi armor presented
by the Ōuchi clan to Itsukushima shrine,
in what is now Hiroshima prefecture.

Hosokawa Narimori's administration was
marked by major events and great difficulties as the shogunate approached its demise
at the end of the Edo period. In 1853, after
the arrival of Commodore Matthew Perry's
ships in Uraga, Sagami province (present-
day Kanagawa prefecture), the Hosokawa
was called out to guard Sagami Bay. In 1860,
the family took in eight of the eighteen
rōnin who had assassinated Ii Naosuke in
the famous incident outside the Sakurada
Gate of the shogun's Edo Castle. —AJ

23

栗色革包紺糸威二枚胴具足　細川韶邦所用

TŌSEI GUSOKU-TYPE ARMOR

Clamshell cuirass; chestnut leather-wrapped lames;
dark blue cord lacing (Sansai style)
Worn by Hosokawa Yoshikuni (1835–1876)
Japan, Edo period (1615–1868), 19th century
Iron, leather, braided silk, lacquer, wood, metal, woven silk, gilding
H. 197 cm x D. 120 cm (overall), cuirass front H. 70.0 cm,
cuirass circumference 106 cm, total weight 12.5 kg
Eisei-Bunko Museum, 4116

Suits of *tōsei gusoku*-type armor were developed in the late Muromachi
period (1392–1573) and early Momoyama period (1573–1615),
when mass combat with guns and spears became the main mode of
warfare. It protected the entire body while being light enough to
enable quick and nimble movement.

Hosokawa Sansai (previously known as Tadaoki, 1563–1646), who
won more than fifty battles in his lifetime, made further developments to tōsei gusoku armor based on his own experience. The variant
form of tōsei gusoku he designed came to be known as Sansai style
(Sansai *ryū*). It is characterized by simplicity and practicality, yet
has a refinement that reflects Sansai's aesthetic sensibilities (he was
an expert classicist and tea master). The typical Sansai ryū helmet
is of the Etchū head-shaped (*zunari*) type—so named after Tadaoki's
former office as governor of Etchū—and normally has a crest of
bundled tail feathers from wild birds. The body armor, as a rule,
does not have shoulder guards (*sode*). The cuirass (*dō*) is either black
or chestnut, with plain colors such as black or brown used in the
lacing as well.

The heads of the Hosokawa clan wore Sansai ryū armor for generation after generation; the Sansai style also spread widely among
their vassals. Other daimyo families recognized its advantages and
imitated it, so it became a major influence in the evolution of
Japanese armor.

This suit of armor in the Sansai style was worn by the thirteenth-
generation lord, Hosokawa Yoshikuni (1835–1876). The helmet's
enormous crest—over 120 cm high—is made of lacquered wood.
Its powerful arc evokes an antelope's horns but in fact represents
plants and trees bending in the wind. The cuirass, tassets, gauntlets,
and cuisses are covered with wrinkled leather. With its colorful left
tasset, laced in red (see also cat. no. 72), this is a superb example of
late Sansai-style armor. —AJ

24

紺糸威二枚胴具足　細川斉茲所用

TŌSEI GUSOKU–TYPE ARMOR
Clamshell cuirass, dark blue cord lacing
Worn by Hosokawa Narishige (1759–1836)
Japan, Edo period (1615–1868), 19th century
Iron, leather, braided silk, woven silk, lacquer, silver, metal
Cuirass front: H. 69 cm, circumference 102 cm, weight 17 kg
Eisei-Bunko Museum, 4107

This armor was used by Narishige, the tenth-generation lord of the Hosokawa. At first glance it resembles the medieval *dōmaru*-type armor. However, it has a clamshell cuirass divided into front and back by hinges on the left side; this places it in the category of *tōsei gusoku*.

Tōsei gusoku–type armor was designed to adapt to changes in methods of warfare, such as mass combat and the use of firearms, that had taken place since the Warring States period (late fifteenth and sixteenth centuries). In addition to its helmet and shoulder guards, it included protection for the rest of the body—including jaw guards, gauntlets, and greaves—to shield against spears and other projectiles. Hinges made the cuirass easier to put on and take off. This sort of jumbling of different forms is frequently seen in armor of the mid- and late Edo period (eighteenth and nineteenth centuries), when peace reigned and armor fashions frequently favored appearance over function.

The mail, or *kusari*, of the gauntlets and cuisses (thigh armor) is a variety of what was called *nanban* ("southern barbarian") mail, modeled after the chain mail of European armor. The type seen here, beautifully constructed of finely woven rings, is known as double-link mail (*yaekusari*).

Hosokawa Narishige was a cultured daimyo; himself an accomplished painter, he was also an enthusiastic collector of Chinese paintings. Most of the Chinese paintings currently in the Eisei-Bunko Museum were collected by this individual. —AJ

25

黒革包紺糸威具足　細川護久所用

TŌSEI GUSOKU–TYPE ARMOR
Black leather-wrapped lames; dark blue cord lacing (Sansai style)
Worn by Hosokawa Morihisa (1839–1893)
Japan, Edo period (1615–1868), 19th century
Iron, leather, braided silk, lacquer, wood, metal, silk velvet, silver foil
Cuirass front H. 42 cm, circumference 108 cm
Eisei-Bunko Museum, 4122

The fourteenth-generation family head, Hosokawa Morihisa, wore this suit of *tōsei gusoku* armor. It follows the Sansai style, with an Etchū head-shaped helmet (see cat. no. 23). The curved crest of black-lacquered wood is particularly impressive.

Returning from what had been a highly decorative style to a more solidly practical model, the later Edo period armors in the Hosokawa collection reflect the troubled times at the end of the long feudal era, when the shogunate came to an end. Dark blue was preferred; excess ornamentation was avoided. This tōsei gusoku armor dem-onstrates that trend, with a cuirass covered in wrinkled leather and leather-covered, silver-coated tassets.

Monumental changes took place as the Edo period gave way to the Meiji period. The Hosokawa domain faced crisis during the transition, and Morihisa took an active role in dealing with it. After the Edo shogunate fell and the feudal domains were dissolved, he succeeded his elder brother, Yoshikuni, in the third year of Meiji (1870). As governor of Kumamoto domain, he promoted modernization of the region. —AJ

26 ▶

紺糸素懸威置手拭形兜　細川忠興所用

MILITARY HELMET (KABUTO)

with decoration in the form of a hand towel
Dark blue cord lacing
Worn by Hosokawa Tadaoki
(aka Sansai, 1563–1646)
Japan; Edo period (1615–1868), 17th century
Iron, wood, lacquer, braided silk
H. 23.0 cm x W. 20.2 cm
Eisei-Bunko Museum, 4132

This unconventional style of helmet gets its name from a skull plate that resembles a folded hand towel placed on top of the head. Extant "folded-towel helmets" (*okitenugui kabuto*) bear the signatures of armorers of the Nara Haruta school; it is clear that these were made in Nara or in Uji, Kishū (modern Wakayama prefecture), during the Momo-yama period (1573–1615).

Hosokawa Tadaoki (1563–1645), the second-generation lord, is said to have used this particular helmet. The bowl is made from several thick iron plates, riveted at the sides and top; the nape guard comprises five tiers of narrow, black-lacquered wooden lames (over-lapping plates) laced together with dark blue silk cord. —AJ

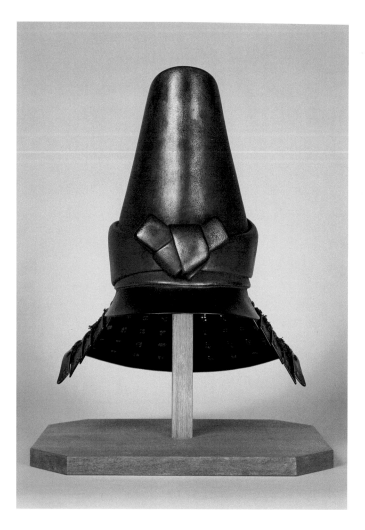

27 ◀

紫糸素懸威鉢巻形兜　細川忠利所用

MILITARY HELMET (KABUTO)

with decoration in the form of a headband
Purple cord lacing
Worn by Hosokawa Tadatoshi (1586–1641)
Japan; Edo period (1615–1868), 17th century
Iron, paper, lacquer, braided silk
H. 34.0 cm x W. 17.5 cm x D. 21.0 cm; weight 2.3 kg
Eisei-Bunko Museum, 4134

For the military leaders of the Warring States era (late fifteenth and sixteenth centuries), the battlefield was a stage. One of their major concerns was how to stand out among tens of thousands of enemies and allies. Distinctive helmets were among the methods developed to awe the enemy and identify oneself to friendly troops. These helmets bore a variety of crests: Buddhist and Shinto deities, animals and plants, fish and shellfish, as well as inanimate objects. Unconventional headgear (*kawari kabuto*) became very popular among military leaders around the Keichō era (1596–1615) at the end of the Momoyama period.

This example, with papier-mâché attachments (*harikake kabuto*), was used by Hosokawa Tadatoshi (1586–1641), the third-generation lord. Only the bowl is made of (thin) iron plate; the headband (*hachimaki*) decoration comprises layers of Japanese paper in the shape of a knotted cloth. The whole helmet was lacquered and coated with silver leaf, which has oxidized to a uniquely beautiful patina. —AJ

28 ▶
菊花文陣笠 細川光尚所用
MILITARY HAT (JINGASA)
with chrysanthemum design
Owned by Hosokawa Mitsunao (1619–1649)
Japan; Edo period (1615–1868), 17th century
Lacquered leather with silver and gold leaf
Diam. 50.7 cm
Eisei-Bunko Museum, 7387

Military hats (*jingasa*) were originally worn in lieu of metal helmets (*kabuto*) by common soldiers and infantry. They were made by soaking rawhide in water and then pounding it into a conical shape. Dried to hardness, the leather was then coated with lacquer and decorated with the company insignia in gold or silver leaf or colored lacquer. The documentary records of Warring States–period daimyo, such as those of the Go-Hōjō and Takeda clans, tell us that infantry were equipped with military hats and cavalry were not.

By the Edo period, the hats were being made in materials such as wrought iron or plaited bamboo as well as in worked leather, and with curving sides or flaring rims instead of simple cone shapes. The hats moved up in status as well, being worn in the retinues of upper-class samurai below the shogun and daimyo.

This military hat is believed to have been owned by Hosokawa Mitsunao (see also cat. no. 70). It is embossed with a two-layered chrysanthemum on a black-lacquered background. Silver leaf is applied to the central flower, and gold leaf to the outer petals; crimson lacquer colors the interior and borders. It is indeed splendid enough for a daimyo's use. —MH

29 ▼
銀桜文付陣笠
MILITARY HAT (JINGASA)
with cherry blossom design
Japan; Edo period (1615–1868), 18th century
Lacquered leather, silver
H. 11.6 cm x Diam. 40.0 cm
Eisei-Bunko Museum, 4435

A cherry blossom, in chased silver on the crown, stands out strikingly against this hat's black lacquered background. Called the Hosokawa cherry blossom, the large-petaled motif is one of the clan's crests: daimyo families were not limited to one family crest but could use multiple emblems.

The standard nine-planet (*kuyō*) device of the Hosokawa was first taken up by Hosokawa Tadaoki (1563–1646), who saw the design on the hilt of a short sword belonging to the warlord Oda Nobunaga, under whom he was serving. Tadaoki took a liking to the motif and had it put on one of his *katabira* (summer kimono). When questioned by Nobunaga about the unusual crest, he explained the circumstances and was then granted permission by the lord to use it as his own. Tadaoki thereafter took the nine-planet motif as his standard crest.

The cherry blossom had been the emblem of the family's main branch since the time of Hosokawa Yoriyuki (1329–1392). After Tadaoki, the Hosokawa family used it as an alternative crest. —MH

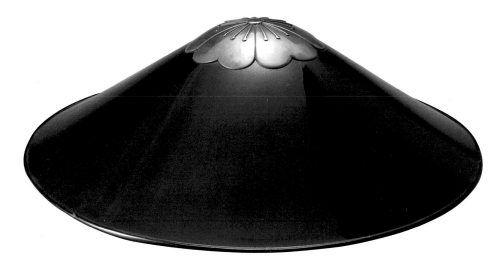

30

「有」字 大馬験 細川宣紀所用

LARGE CAVALRY STANDARD (UMAJIRUSHI)

with the character *ari*

Used by Hosokawa Nobunori (1676–1732)

Japan; Edo period (1615–1868), 18th century

Paste-resist dyed silk

H. 180.0 cm x W. 195.0 cm

Eisei-Bunko Museum, 4223

Cavalry standards (*umajirushi*) were used to indicate the whereabouts of the general on a battle front. They seem to have appeared in the second half of the sixteenth century and were constructed so as to stand out prominently, showing a general's position in battle and distinguishing him from other commanders on the field. Large cavalry standards (*ōumajirushi*), such as this, would be set up in front of a general's headquarters; on the front lines, commanders of lower rank displayed smaller standards (*koumajirushi*)—sometimes small enough to be worn on a pole fitted onto a warrior's back.

Not all generals used flags as cavalry standards; some advertised their locations with other large, distinctive objects on poles. Oda Nobunaga used a paper umbrella, Toyotomi Hideyoshi a gourd, and Tokugawa Ieyasu a golden fan. But the generals of the Hosokawa family used cloth flags such as this one.

This standard, with the character *ari* in white reserve on a black background, belonged to Hosokawa Nobunori (1676–1732). Flags with the character *ari*, like the banner with the nine-planet sign in black on a white background (see cat. nos. 32, 33), came into use after 1600, when Hosokawa Tadaoki (1563–1646) moved the clan to the province of Buzen (present-day eastern Fukuoka and northern Oita prefectures), a domain he had been awarded for his successes at the Battle of Sekigahara. See cat. no. 31 for an explanation of the character *ari* and the Hosokawa family's emblems. —MH

31

「有」字 大馬験 細川治年所用

LARGE CAVALRY STANDARD (UMAJIRUSHI)

with the character *ari*

Used by Hosokawa Harutoshi (1759–1787)

Japan; Edo period (1615–1868), 18th century

Paste-resist dyed silk

H. 168.0 cm x W. 200.0 cm

Eisei-Bunko Museum, 4226

Cavalry standards (*umajirushi*) were set up before or beside a commander's horse to indicate his location on the battlefront. This dark blue banner, with the character *ari* inside a resist-dyed white circle, belonged to Hosokawa Harutoshi (1759–1787).

Ari is one of the characters of Yoriari, in honor of Hosokawa Yoriari (1332–1391), first patriarch of the Hosokawa clan. In this type of standard, the character could be executed in various ways: in white resist against a dyed background or in color against a white background. Before this kind of banner came into use, Hosokawa lords used black cavalry standards with the nine-planet family crest in white. Documentary records confirm that Hosokawa Tadaoki (1563–1646) used just such a black cavalry standard

with a white crest in the Battle of Sekigahara (1600). Cavalry banners with the *ari* character did not come into use until after 1600, when the Hosokawa moved to Buzen province (modern eastern Fukuoka and northern Oita prefectures)—a domain granted to Tadaoki as a reward for military service at Sekigahara.
—MH

32

白地九曜紋幟 細川重賢所用

MILITARY BANNER (NOBORI)
with nine-planet family crest
Used by Hosokawa Shigekata
(1720–1785)
Japan; Edo period (1615–1868)
18th century
Paste-resist dyed silk
H. 387.0 cm x W. 143.0 cm
Eisei-Bunko Museum, 4224

A banner (*nobori*), also called a signal flag
(*noboribata*) or looped flag (*chitsukebata*), is
a type of military standard. It is taller than
it is wide and has loops along one side and
the top for the vertical staff and horizontal
spar to pass through. The nobori derives
from the so-called flowing banner (*nagare-
bata*), which hung from a horizontal arm
attached to the vertical staff by a cord,
allowing the cloth to hang freely (see cat.
no. 54). Nobori were first used to distinguish
allies from opponents in the middle of the
Muromachi period (1392–1573), when
battles were fought between groups of foot
soldiers. Insignia—perhaps a family crest,
the name of a Buddhist or Shinto deity, or
an inspiring slogan—typically appeared in
black, crimson, gold, or silver on a background of white, red, or dark blue.

Combat was originally the job of the
samurai; but the daimyo were battle commanders who were also responsible for
ruling their domains in peace as in wartime.
For that reason, even in the absence of war,
daimyo equipped themselves with weaponry
and military equipment, including banners.

Hosokawa Shigekata's banner bears the
nine-planet family crest in black on a white
background. This design was adopted after
Hosokawa Tadaoki (1563–1646) was rewarded with a new domain for his military
service in the Battle of Sekigahara (1600)
and moved his base from Tango (now northern Kyoto prefecture) to Buzen province
(now eastern Fukuoka and northern Oita
prefectures). —MH

33

白地引両九曜紋幟 細川韶邦所用

MILITARY BANNER (NOBORI)

with bands and nine-planet family crest
Used by Hosokawa Yoshikuni
(1835–1876)
Japan; Edo period (1615–1868)
19th century
Paste-resist dyed silk
H. 382.5 cm x W. 147.5 cm
Eisei-Bunko Museum, 4233

This banner, the property of Hosokawa Yoshi-kuni, has two horizontal bands (*hikiryō*) over the nine-planet (*kuyō*) Hosokawa crest in black on a white background.

Inventories of the military equipment used by Hosokawa Tadaoki (1563–1646) in the Battle of Sekigahara (1600) tell us that between 1582 and Tadaoki's domain transfer in 1600, the Hosokawa used a black banner with a design of diagonal white bands across the top corner. After moving to Buzen province (now eastern Fukuoka and northern Oita prefectures), the family began using a banner with the family crest in black on white, as in this example.

Later, during the Shimabara Rebellion of 1637–1638, Hosokawa banners featured various designs, including the nine-planet crest in dark blue on white; the crest over horizontal bands in white on dark blue; and the crest over horizontal bands in dark blue on white.

According to the official Hosokawa family history *Menkō shūroku,* after the Shimabara Rebellion, Hosokawa Tadatoshi (1586–1641) standardized the clan's banner to have horizontal bands over the nine-planet crest in black on a white background, as in this example. Even then the Hosokawa family banners varied subtly, depending on the presence or absence of the bands.
—MH

34

重要文化財

太刀　銘「守家造」

IMPORTANT CULTURAL PROPERTY

CEREMONIAL LONG SWORD (TACHI) BLADE

By Moriie
Signed "Moriie *tsukuru*" (Made by Moriie)
Japan; Kamakura period (1185–1333)
13th century
Forged and tempered steel
L. (overall) 87.2 cm, blade L. 69.5 cm
curvature 1.3 cm, base W. 3.1 cm
base thickness 0.7 cm
Eisei-Bunko Museum, 1784

A daimyo's possessions fell generally into two categories—articles for official use (*omote dōgu*) and for private use (*oku dōgu*). Official articles included armaments appropriate to the daimyo's rank and clan status among other accoutrements he used on official occasions. The sword was called "the soul of the samurai" and was deemed sacred as the symbol of the warrior. Accorded the highest status among the daimyo's luxurious possessions, swords were the items most frequently given as gifts among the military houses of the shogun, the daimyo, and their retainers. Feudal lords of the Higo domain, the Hosokawa clan collected many fine swords as evidence of their family status. They also acquired sword mountings and decorative sword fittings representing the finest of lacquer craftsmanship.

Osafune, in the province of Bizen (now southeast Okayama prefecture), was the greatest Japanese center of sword manufacture; the town began producing its many fine smiths in the Kamakura period. One of them was Moriie, often called Hatada Moriie because he lived in Hatada, a village

neighboring Osafune. A signature reading "Moriie, resident of Osafune, Bizen" appears on some surviving swords. Moriie seems to have been active around the Kenchō era (1249–1256)—about the same time as Mitsutada, the founder of the Bizen Osafune school of swordsmiths. His style of manufacture emphasizes showiness, boasting bold irregular clove-shaped (*chōji midare*) temper lines alternating with "tadpole" (*kawazugo*) temper lines. This *tachi* sword, an outstanding example of Moriie's work, clearly shows both of these signature characteristics.
—AJ

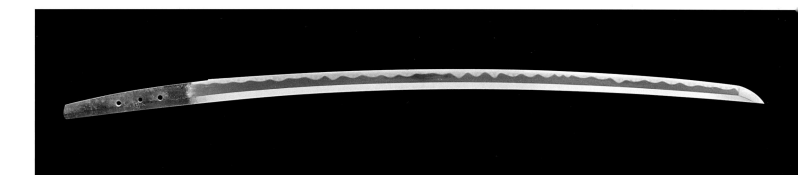

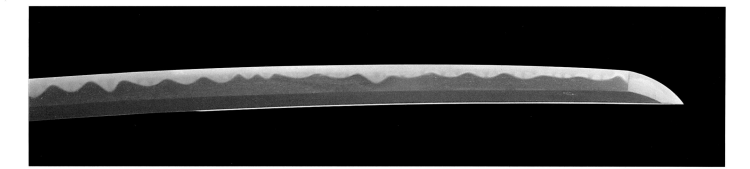

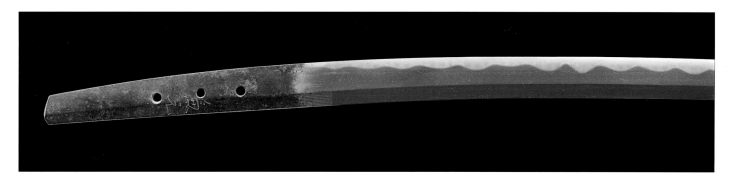

35

刀　銘「兼元」

LONG SWORD (KATANA)
BLADE

By Magoroku Kanemoto II, active c.
1520s–1530s
Signed "Kanemoto"
Japan; Muromachi period
(1392–1573), 16th century
Forged and tempered steel
L. 93.0 cm (overall), L. 73.9 cm
(blade), curvature 1.8 cm
Eisei-Bunko Museum, 6330

During the Muromachi period, the smiths
of Mino (present-day Gifu prefecture) were
second in number only to those of Bizen.
They were scattered around the region, in
such towns as Akasaka, but the greatest
concentration of Mino swordsmiths was in
the town of Seki, and it was the Seki smiths
who became best known for the region's
signature Minomono blades.

Perhaps the leading family of Seki-based
Mino swordsmiths, along with the Kanesada,
was the Kanemoto lineage. The same name
was used by several generations, but the
second-generation Kanemoto—also known
as Seki no Magoroku (Magoroku of Seki)—
was revered as one of the most skilled swordsmith of all time; he was particularly esteemed
for the keenness of his cutting edge.

A classic example of the work of the
second-generation Magoroku Kanemoto,
this sword features a unique temper line
called "three cedar trees" (*sanbon sugi*) that
connects three sharp zigzag (*gunome*) temper lines. —AJ

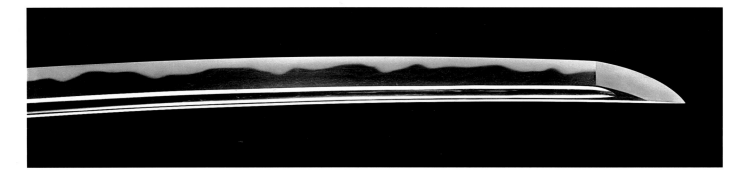

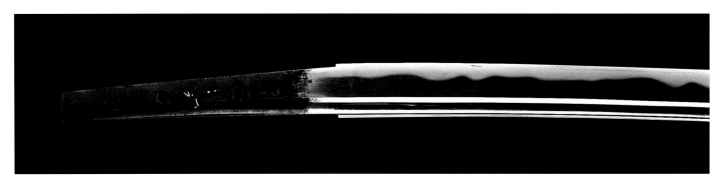

36

刀　無銘志津

LONG SWORD (KATANA)
BLADE

By Shizu Saburō Kaneuji
Unsigned. inscribed "*kaizoku*" (pirate)
Japan; Nanbokuchō period
(1333–1392), 14th century
Forged and tempered steel, gold inlay
L. 85.5 cm (overall), L. 68.3 cm
(blade), curvature 1.2 cm, base W. 3.2
cm, thickness 0.7 cm
Eisei-Bunko Museum, 1788

This blade was founded by a famous Tegai school swordsmith from the province of Yamato, in what is now Nara prefecture. Saburō Kaneuji later lived in Shizu, in Mino province (now Gifu prefecture), from which he got the name Shizu.

Kaneuji was one of the disciples of Masamune, also known as Gorō Nyūdō Masamune, of Kamakura in Sōshū (Sagami province; modern-day Kanagawa prefecture)—perhaps the greatest Japanese swordsmith of all time. Among Masamune's followers, Kaneuji's work is said to have been closest to that of his master. He is famous as the founder of Mino swords (Minomono), which combine the special qualities found in the swords of his native Yamato and the Sōshūmono swords of his master.

This sword has a broad blade with a large point characteristic of the Nanbokuchō period. The "wood" (*itame*) and straight (*masame*) grains of the steel, the wave (*notare*) patterns in the undulating (*gunome*) temper line (*hamon*), and the fine crystallization in the tip illustrate the special characteristics of a Shizu blade. The tang is incised and

inlaid with the inscription *kaizoku* ("pirate") in gold. There is a legend that it was given to one of the vassals of the Hosokawa family by a pirate of the Inland Sea. —AJ

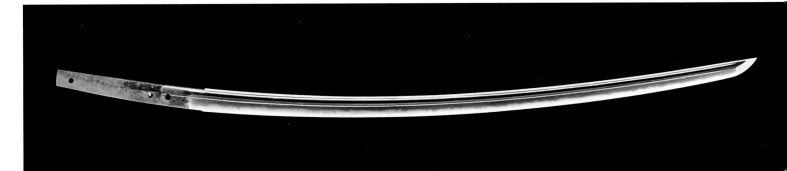

37

太刀　銘「備州長船家助」

CEREMONIAL LONG SWORD (TACHI) BLADE

By Iisuke
Signed "Bishū Osafune Iesuke"
(Iesuke of Osafune, Bishū region)
Japan; Muromachi period
(1392–1573), 15th century
Forged and tempered steel
L. 89.8 cm (overall), L. 71.4 cm
(blade), curvature 2.4 cm,
base W. 3.1 cm.
Eisei-Bunko Museum, 1786

The town of Osafune, in Bizen province (in the southwest of modern Okayama prefecture), produced many famous swordsmiths. The forefather of them all was Mitsutada of the mid-Kamakura period (1185–1333), founder of the Osafune school—the largest school of smiths in Bizen.

Swordsmiths of the Osafune school—such as Morimitsu and Kanemitsu, who flourished during the Ōei era (1394–1428) in the mid-Muromachi period—are referred to as Ōei Bizen; Iisuke, who made this sword, was one of them. The blades of this period don't have the ruggedness of those of the Nanbokuchō period (1333–1392); they are more like swords of the earlier Kamakura period. Some evolution in form is evident, however, in the prominent curvature to the point and in the temper lines, which mostly changed from clove (*chōji*) patterns to irregularly undulating (*gunome midare*) patterns.

Although this *tachi* sword's tang has been shortened, which has in turn has shortened the length of the blade, its form is good. The workmanship on its surface steel and edge well exemplify the characteristics of Ōei Bizen. —AJ

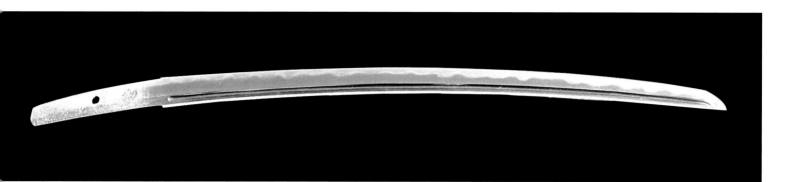

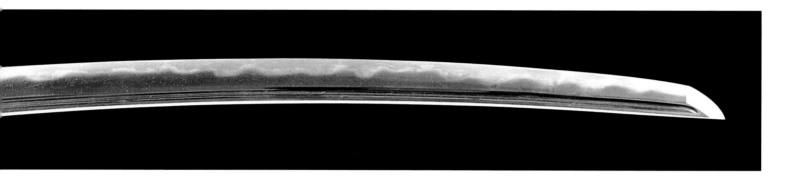

38
脇差　銘「信長」
SHORT SWORD (WAKIZASHI)
BLADE
Signed "Nobunaga"
Japan; Muromachi period
(1392–1573), 15th century
Forged and tempered steel
L. 48.3 cm (blade), curvature 1.2 cm
Eisei-Bunko Museum, 7513

The Nobunaga swordsmiths are said to have originally been from Taima, in Yamato province (now Nara prefecture), and to have moved to Echizen (now Fukui prefecture) at the beginning of the Muromachi period (1392–1573); the Nobunaga name continued for several generations. This sword shows "sand-streaming" (*sunanagashi:* a striation, as if swept with a broom) perpendicular to a large-scale, irregularly undulating (*gunome midare*) temper line. The steel has a "wood" grain (*itame hada*) and is somewhat dark in color, demonstrating the style of manufacture common to the swordsmiths of the northern provinces—Echizen, Echigo, Kaga, etc.

Representative of the Nobunaga type, a mounting (*koshirae*) for this sword was produced in accordance with the tastes of the second-generation lord Hosokawa Sansai (aka Tadaoki 1563–1646). Understated yet intriguing, such mountings included a scabbard of lacquered and burnished ray skin—a very expensive luxury material. This sword's mounting was treasured throughout the Edo period; unfortunately, it is no longer extant. —AJ

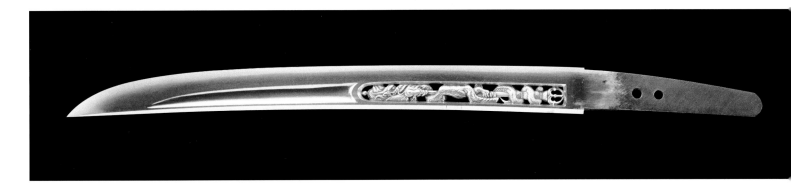

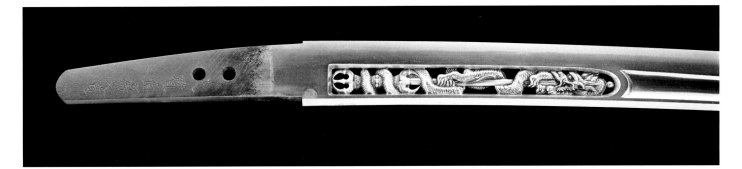

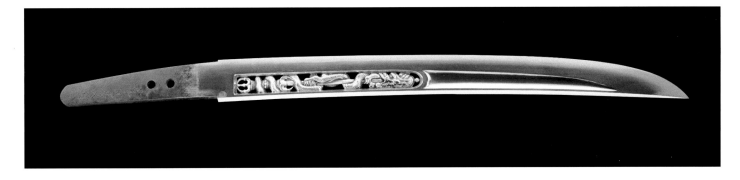

39

脇差　銘「大道直房入道」

SHORT SWORD (WAKIZASHI)
BLADE
Signed "Daidō Naofusa Nyūdō"
Japan; Edo period (1615–1868)
17th century
Forged and tempered steel
L. 47.7 cm (overall); L. 35.7 cm
(blade), curvature 0.4 cm
Eisei-Bunko Museum, 7514

A number of smiths called themselves Daidō;
the earliest was Mutsu-no-kami Daidō. All
came from the province of Mino (now Gifu
prefecture) and are considered to have belonged to the same school. Naofusa Nyūdō
was one of them, but little is known of him.

This short sword (*wakizashi*) blade is
broad and curved, with a layered thickness
characteristic of short swords of the Momoyama
(1573–1615) and early Edo periods. The
openwork near the hilt, of excellent workmanship, depicts the Dragon King Kurikara
(Sanskrit: Kulikala) enveloped in flames. An
incarnation of the Buddhist deity Fudō Myōō
(Sanskrit: Achala Vidyaraja), Kurikara curls
around the sword as if about to swallow it.

This wakizashi was a favorite of Hosokawa
Sansai (aka Tadaoki, 1563–1646). —AJ

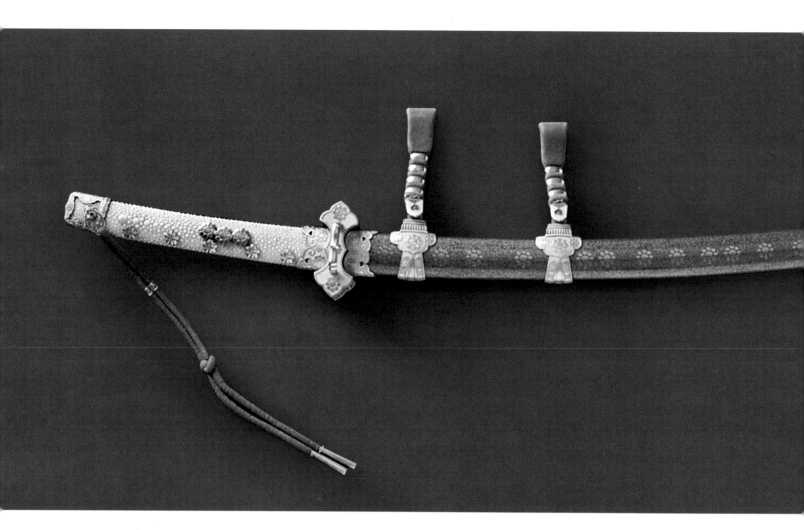

41 ▶

衛府太刀拵　九曜紋銀装

MOUNTING FOR A CEREMONIAL LONG SWORD (TACHI)

with nine-planet family crests and silver fittings
Japan; Edo period (1615–1868), 19th century
Lacquered wood with sprinkled gold (*makie*) decoration, silver, ray skin, leather
L. 98.7 cm, hilt L. 24.5 cm
Eisei-Bunko Museum, 2924-3

Like the gold-decorated *tachi* mounting
shown in cat. no. 40, this imperial guard
sword mounting was made near the end of
the Edo period. Its scabbard is decorated using the *makie* ("sprinkled picture") lacquer
technique, with nine-planet Hosokawa
family crests in gold over a gold pear skin
(*nashiji*) ground—made by sifting fine
metallic powder over wet lacquer to create
an evenly sprinkled effect. The guard, collar,
buttcap, scabbard tip, hilt ornaments, and
other metal fittings are made of silver instead
of gold. This, too, is an elegant, superbly
crafted mounting. —AJ

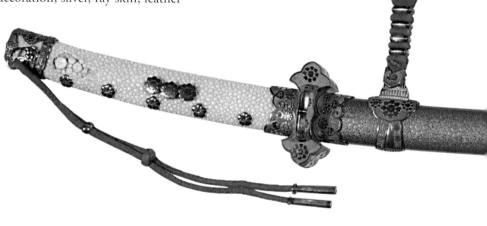

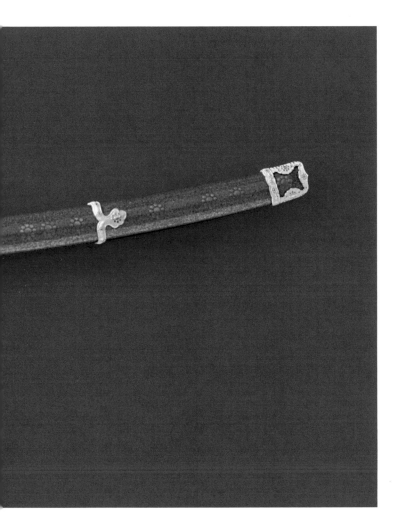

40 ◄

衛府太刀拵　九曜紋金装

MOUNTING FOR A CEREMONIAL LONG SWORD (TACHI)

with nine-planet family crests and gold fittings
Japan; Edo period (1615–1868), 19th century
Lacquered wood with sprinkled gold (*makie*) decoration,
gilt bronze, gold, ray skin, leather
L. 96.0 cm, hilt L. 23.2 cm
Eisei-Bunko Museum, 2924-1

Japanese long swords fall into two categories: the *tachi* (slung long sword), mainly used from the Heian period (794–1185) to the Kamakura period (1185–1333), and the *uchigatana* or *katana* (long sword), which was used from the Muromachi period (1392–1573) through the end of the Edo period. The tachi was designed for cavalry combat; sheathed with the blade edge pointing downward, it was slung from a waist belt, on the warrior's left side. The katana, in contrast, was inserted into a belt with the blade facing up.

The scabbard, hilt, and other accoutrements housing a sword blade are collectively called its mounting (*koshirae*). This particular tachi sword mounting is of a type known as an "imperial guard sword mounting," because it was used by warriors of the imperial palace guard in the Heian period. In later ages it came to be worn ceremonially by men of high-ranking military families on formal occasions. Whether this type of mounting was worn with fittings of gold or silver (see cat. no. 41) seems to have depended on the wearer's rank and on the official garments with which it was worn (either *sokutai* or *ikan* robes); but there are differing explanations of the specific distinctions.

This imperial guard sword mounting was made in the late Edo period. The scabbard is decorated in the *makie* lacquer technique, with nine-planet Hosokawa family crests in gold on a sprinkled gold pear skin (*nashiji*) background; variants of the family's cherry blossom crest adorn the hilt. —AJ

42 ▶

脇差拵　研出鮫蛭巻塗

MOUNTING FOR A SHORT SWORD (WAKIZASHI)

with spiraling bands

Japan; Edo period (1615–1868), 17th–18th century

Lacquered wood, burnished ray skin (*togidashi same*), lacquer with sprinkled gold decoration (*makie*), copper-gold alloy (*shakudō*), gold, gilt bronze

Overall L. 53.0 cm, hilt L. 12.4 cm, scabbard L. 34.5 cm, scabbard W. 4.1 cm, sword guard 7.1 cm x 6.7 cm

Eisei-Bunko Museum, 2906

The scabbard (*saya*) of this mounting is wrapped in a spiraling strip of burnished ray skin edged in gold *makie* (metallic powder set in lacquer); this alternates with a stripe of black lacquer. Burnished ray skin (*togidashi same*) is a variant lacquering effect achieved by applying black lacquer over the bumpy surface of ray skin, letting it dry, then polishing it to create a smooth surface that reveals the skin. High-quality ray skin with an even texture and almost pure white color has been used in this mounting: the circular pattern brought out by the burnishing is beautiful in its delicacy. Imported from the southern regions, ray skin was a very expensive, luxury material.

The mounting also features a sword guard decorated with the Hosokawa nine-planet crest on a background of tool-punched *shakudō* (a copper-gold alloy that oxidizes to blue-black) and a hilt collar (*fuchi*) and buttcap (*kashira*), also of tool-punched shakudō, with incised nine-planet and cherry blossom crests. The hilt ornaments (*menuki*)—nine-planet and cherry blossom crests executed in chased gold—adorn a ray skin hilt. It is not known who owned this mounting, but its components give some sense of his refined taste. —AJ

43 ▼

打刀拵　笛巻変塗

MOUNTING FOR A LONG SWORD (KATANA)
with bands in variant lacquering
Japan; Edo period (1615–1868), 19th century
Lacquered wood, gilt bronze, iron, silver, braided silk
L. 99.6 cm
Eisei-Bunko Museum, 2927

44 ▼

脇差拵　笛巻変塗

MOUNTING FOR SHORT SWORD (WAKIZASHI)
with bands in variant lacquering
Japan; Edo period (1615–1868), 19th century
Lacquered wood, gilt bronze, iron, silver, braided silk
L. 69.3 cm
Eisei-Bunko Museum, 2908

During the Edo period, craftsmen varied the standard lacquer techniques to create a wide range of decorative effects. These variant lacquering (*kawari nuri*) techniques were particularly favored for use on the sheaths of swords, so much so that as a group they are alternatively known as "scabbard lacquering" (*saya nuri*). Hundreds of unconventional lacquering techniques, many very striking, were invented during the period.

For official occasions, Edo period samurai wore their long and short swords in black-lacquered scabbards; but elsewhere they sometimes wore more colorful scabbards. The scabbards in these long and short sword mountings have a striped pattern of rust-colored powder sprinkled on black lacquer, one example of variant lacquering.

The sword accessories, including the sword guards, skewer, and hilt ornaments, are a matching set made by Ishiguro Masaaki (b. 1813) of Edo. They bear decorations that evoke the seasons: butterfly-shaped ornaments (spring) and a silver collar and buttcap with floral scrolls on the large hilt; a scene of geese and reeds (autumn) on the octagonal silver guard; chrysanthemum scrolls on the small silver knife's handle and the skewer. —AJ

45

後藤光孝作　群馬図三所物(小柄・笄・目貫)

SET OF SWORD FITTINGS (MITOKOROMONO)

with design of horses: small knife handle (*kozuka*), skewer (*kōgai*),

hilt ornaments (*menuki*)

By Gotō Mitsutaka (1721–1784)

Japan; Edo period (1615–1868), 18th century

Iron with gold, silver, copper, copper-gold alloy

L. 9.7 cm (*kozuka*), L. 21.3 cm (*kōgai*), L. 4.0 cm (*menuki*)

Eisei-Bunko Museum, 2896

A knife handle (*kozuka*), a skewer (*kōgai*), and a pair of hilt ornaments (*menuki*) make up this matched set of accessories for a *katana* sword mounting. Collectively, they are called *mitokoromono*—"objects of three places." The knife handle would have held a small blade for cutting paper and for other uses. There are various explanations as to how the skewer was used: for scratching the head, and for catching up stray hairs, among others. The small menuki ornaments were bound to the sword's hilt with wrapped leather or braided silk cord, providing for a surer grip. As a rule these accessories were made to the same design, by the same artisan.

Strict standards for sword accoutrements prevailed in the Edo period; only high-ranking members of the warrior class were allowed to attach the knife handle and skewer. The formal mountings used by

daimyo and bannermen were customarily manufactured by the Gotō family.

The first-generation head of the family, Gotō Yūjō (1440–1512), was patronized by the shogun Ashikaga Yoshimasa; thereafter, the family specialized in manufacturing mitokoromono all the way up to its seventeenth generation in the early Meiji period (1868–1912). Catering to the shoguns, the daimyos, and families of high rank, the Gotō family produced work with a distinguished nobility of style. They were regarded as Japan's top makers of decorative sword accessories.

This set of mitokoromono has herds of finely sculpted horses in gold, silver, and copper relief on a blackened *shakudō* (copper-gold alloy) background. It is said to be the masterpiece of the thirteenth-generation Gotō, Mitsutaka (1722–1784). —AJ

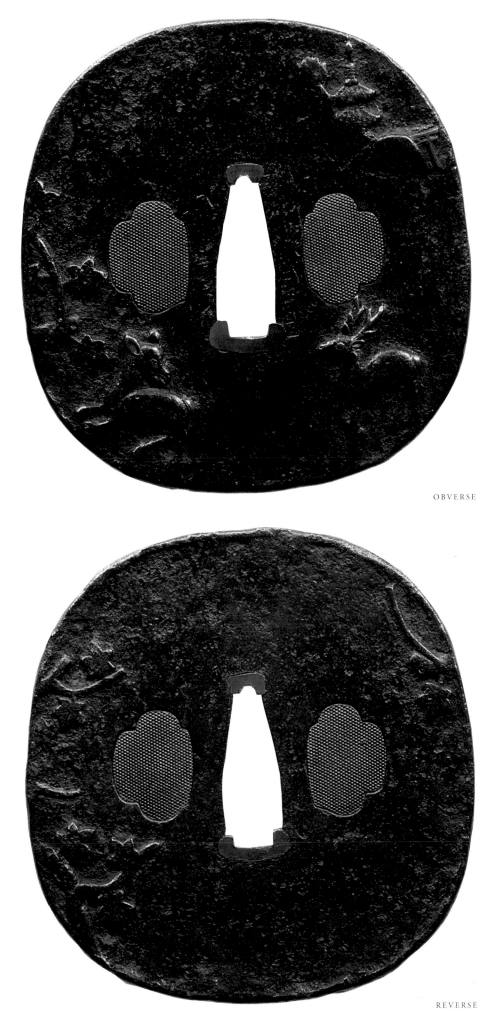

46 ▶

重要文化財

金家作　春日野図鐔　銘「城州伏見住
金家」

IMPORTANT CULTURAL PROPERTY

SWORD GUARD (TSUBA)
with design of Kasuga Plain
Signed "Jōshū Fushimi *jū* Kaneie"
(Kaneie, resident of Fushimi,
Yamashiro province)
Japan; Momoyama period (1573–1615)
16th century
Iron with copper inlay
H. 8.4 cm
Eisei-Bunko Museum, 1504-1

This iron sword guard depicts a scene of
Nara's Kasuga Plain in high relief, executed
in the plow-carving technique (see also cat.
no. 54). In the foreground, a maple branch
extends over a doe looking back at a buck.
In the upper right background, a temple
pagoda and a Shinto torii gate peek out from
distant mountains, evoking autumn on the
plain. The torii is depicted in an inlay of
red copper (*suaka*), which contrasts effectively
against the blackened iron ground. The
signature "Jōshū Fushimi *jū* Kaneie" indicates that the guard was made by an artisan
named Kaneie who resided in Fushimi, in
Yamashiro province (now the southern part
of Kyoto city). Kaneie is known for having
originated the use of pictorial scenery in
sword guard designs. —MH

OBVERSE

REVERSE

47

重要文化財

金家作　毘沙門天図鐔　銘「城州伏見
住　金家」

IMPORTANT CULTURAL PROPERTY

SWORD GUARD (TSUBA)
with design of Bishamonten
By Kaneie
Signed "Jōshū Fushimi *jū* Kaneie"
(Kaneie, resident of Fushimi, Yamashiro
province)
Japan; Momoyama period (1573–1615)
16th century
Iron with gold, silver, and brass inlay
H. 7.8 cm
Eisei-Bunko Museum, 1803

On the obverse of this thinly wrought sword
guard, two slender trees reach skyward at
left; on the right a martial deity stands on
a boulder, his left leg raised, a spear in his
hand, flames at his back. Historically, this
figure has been identified as the guardian
god Bishamonten (Sanskrit: Vaisravana);
however, there is some question as to the
validity of that identification, since the icon
is not carrying the miniature treasure pagoda
that Bishamonten typically holds in his
right hand. In any case, the figure projects
strength and martial dignity.

Rendered in gold and silver inlay, the trees'
foliage; the deity's ears, teeth, and eyes; and
the spear handle, headdress, and flames gleam
against the background of iron. On the
reverse, geese in flight approach two trees.

The signature "Jōshū Fushimi *jū* Kaneie"
indicates that this is a work of Kaneie, of
Fushimi in Yamashiro province (now southern Kyoto city). The pictorial design and the
plow-carved high relief, with touches of gold,
silver, and brass inlay, are hallmarks of Kaneie's
work. —MH

48

鉄舵透鐔　無銘甲冑師

SWORD GUARD (TSUBA)
with rudder design
Unsigned armorer's type
Japan; Muromachi period (1392–1573)
16th century
Iron openwork
H. 9.1 cm x W. 9.1 cm
Eisei-Bunko Museum, 2333

This sword guard of iron has a large design of a rudder represented in openwork. It exemplifies a specific type of Muromachi period *tsuba* classified as an "ancient armorer's" (*ko-katchūshi*) sword guard: such guards were thought to be armorers' products because they use the same openwork techniques seen in armored face masks (*menpō*). In this context, "ancient" (*ko*) distinguishes early, unsigned sword guards from later signed examples. It is now thought that such tsuba were made not exclusively by armorers but also by various other types of artisans with smithy experience. Large, relaxed compositions, like the openwork rudder design of this unsigned piece, characterize armorer's sword guards. —MH

OBVERSE

REVERSE

OBVERSE

REVERSE

49

重要文化財

林又七作　破扇散図鐔

IMPORTANT CULTURAL PROPERTY
SWORD GUARD (TSUBA)
with design of torn fans and cherry
blossoms
By Hayashi Matashichi (1613–1699)
Japan; Edo period (1615–1868)
17th century
Iron with gold inlay
H. 8.4 cm x W. 8.4 cm
Eisei-Bunko Museum, 1796

This unsigned *tsuba* has a design of broken
fans and cherry blossoms executed in inlaid
gold cutouts (*nunome zōgan*) on an iron
ground. Its heavy ground plate gives a sense
of mass and presence, conveying both elegance
and strength. The sophisticated effect in the
places where the broken fans disintegrate—
called "frayed inlay" (*hotsure zōgan*)—is a
technique seen only in the sword guards of
Hayashi Matashichi. With its exquisite inlay
on finely wrought, highest-quality iron,
and a design combining the airy elegance
of cherry blossoms and the boldness of the
broken fans, this guard is viewed as one of
the masterworks of Higo (now Kumamoto
prefecture) metalwork.

This sword guard is unsigned but is considered to be the work of Hayashi Matashichi.
Few of Matashichi's works are signed; that
was common in metalwork made in the
Higo region. The reason for this, we are
told, is that the Higo metal artisans were
considered nobodies until they came of age;
it would have been unthinkably pretentious
to sign a work as a young apprentice. Even
after becoming adults in the social sense,
artists were considered inexpert and in
training until the age of sixty, regardless of
their actual abilities. To sign a work before
then would not have been allowed. —MH

50

林又七作　舞鶴透鐔

SWORD GUARD (TSUBA)

in the shape of a dancing crane

By Hayashi Matashichi (1613–1699)

Japan; Edo period (1615–1868), 17ᵗʰ century

Iron openwork with gold inlay

H. 8.0 cm x W. 8.0 cm

Eisei-Bunko Museum, 1794

This sword guard features an elegant dancing crane with wings outspread. Finely wrought from choice metal, with an excellent patina, it has a subdued finish that exemplifies the highest standard of iron sword guards. The openwork is superb, with each feather depicted in fine lines, well balanced in other areas by thick, stout lines.

It is not signed, but this *tsuba* is judged to be the work of Hayashi Matashichi. Matashichi was a metalworker of seventeenth-century Higo (present-day Kumamoto prefecture) and the first-generation artist of the famous Hayashi lineage. In such family lineages, the first generation generally has superior skills; subsequent generations follow tradition, without innovating and with declining abilities. This was the case with the Hayashi house.

The attribution of unsigned guards to Matashichi has not been done simply because the techniques are in the Hayashi mode and the level of workmanship equals that of the first generation. These works have the same iron color and outstanding openwork technique as sword guards that Matashichi actually signed. —MH

OBVERSE

REVERSE

95

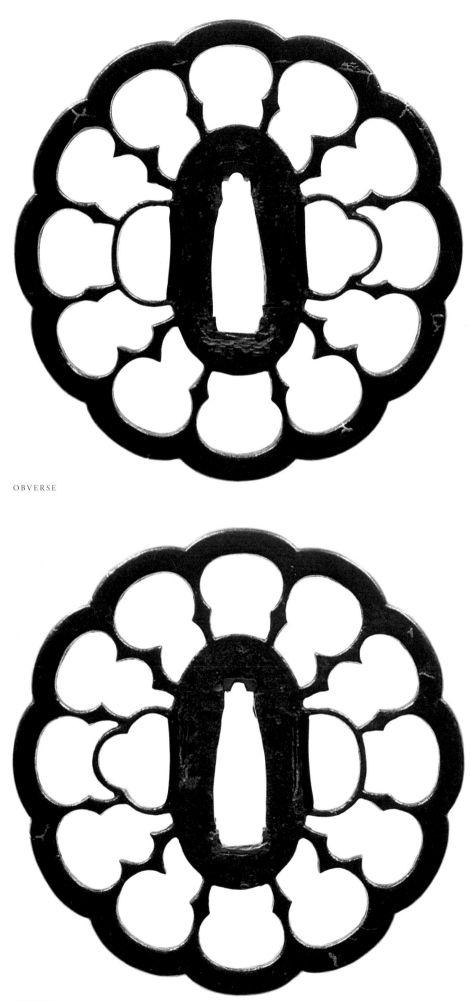

OBVERSE

REVERSE

51

林又七作　十二瓢箪透枯木象嵌鐔

SWORD GUARD (TSUBA)

in the shape of twelve gourds with
withered tree inlay
By Hayashi Matashichi (1613–1699)
Japan; Edo period (1615–1868)
17th century
Iron openwork with gold inlay
H. 7.8 cm x W. 7.8 cm
Eisei-Bunko Museum, 1797

Twelve gourds in openwork encircle this
tsuba's holes for the tang, knife handle, and
skewer. The gourds' outlines are minutely
crafted, crisp and clear, with interesting
variations in shape, and without a hint of
heaviness. Superbly rendered gold "withered
tree" inlay (*kareki zōgan*) resembles the
remains of paper eaten by insects, much like
the "frayed" inlay (see cat. no. 49) thought
to be found only in the sword guards of
Hayashi Matashichi. This unsigned tsuba
has been judged to be the work of Matashichi.

Considered a masterpiece, this guard was
handed down within the Inaba family, lords
of the Yodo domain (now the southern part
of Kyoto city). During the Meiji period it
was acquired by Nishigaki Shirō—a descendant of the artist Nishigaki Eikyū (cat. no. 55)
—who was patronized by the Hosokawa
family. The tsuba later came into the possession of Hosokawa Moritatsu (1883–1970).

Hayashi Matashichi was a metalwork
artist of Higo. His father was a gunsmith
from Owari (modern Aichi prefecture) who
worked for Katō Kiyomasa, lord of Higo,
from the same province. Matashichi, too,
worked for the Katō family as a gunsmith
until the Hosokawa family replaced the
Katō as lords of Higo; thereafter, Matashichi
made sword guards for the Hosokawa.
—MH

52

伝林又七作　水玉透象嵌鐔

SWORD GUARD (TSUBA)
with design of water droplets
Attributed to Hayashi Matashichi
(1613–1699)
Japan; Edo period (1615–1868)
17th century
Iron openwork with gold inlay
H. 8.4 cm x W. 8.1 cm
Eisei-Bunko Museum, 1799

With an openwork design representing large and small water droplets, interspersed with vinelike tendrils of broken droplets in gold inlay, this sword guard has been judged to be an unsigned piece by Hayashi Matashichi. Some scholars have argued that the inlay—while certainly made by the Hayashi family—may not have been the work of Matashichi himself. In any case, the piece is a product of the Hayashi workshop and was executed in techniques associated with Matashichi.

Understatement is typical of sword guards from Higo province, notably those made by the Higo artisans employed by the Hosokawa family. Like the cherry blossom and torn fan design (cat. no. 49) and the dancing crane in openwork (cat. no. 50), this sword guard's restrained but charming droplet motif is both bold and subtle. The combination is said to have appealed to the highly refined tastes of Hosokawa Tadaoki (1563–1646) and it is also seen in his tea utensils and armor. Very probably, then, the Higo metal-work artists who emerged in Tadaoki's life-time and were employed by the Hosokawa house would have had some design direction from the lord himself, presumably their principal patron for such works. —MH

OBVERSE

REVERSE

97

OBVERSE

REVERSE

53

平田彦三作　八ツ木瓜形唐草九曜透鐔

SWORD GUARD (TSUBA)
in the shape of a quince blossom with
floral scrolls and nine planet family crest
By Hirata Hikozō (died 1635)
Japan; Edo period (1615–1868)
17th century
Etched iron
H. 8.5 cm x W. 8.48 cm
Eisei-Bunko Museum, 1798

This guard is shaped like an eight-petal
blossom. The petals, each with a round
opening, surround a ring of floral scrolls
encircling the blade setting (*seppadai*). If
the tang hole or the central floral scroll
roundel is conceived as a large orb, the
design can be seen to depict the nine-planet
Hosokawa crest. The floral scrolls were
first painted in lacquer and then etched
with acid.

There is no signature, but this *tsuba* is
considered to be the work of Hirata Hikozō,
first generation of the Hirata family of
metalwork artists in Higo. A native of Ōmi
province (modern Shiga prefecture), Hikozō
entered the service of Hosokawa Tadaoki
(1563–1645) and moved with his master
to Higo by way of Tango (in the north of
what is now Kyoto prefecture) and Buzen
(eastern Fukuoka prefecture and northern
Oita prefecture) provinces. Though originally
a samurai, Hikozō gave up this profession
while in Buzen.

In Higo, Hikozō lived in the city of
Yatsushiro in central Kumamoto, where
Tadaoki had retired. Documentary evidence
tells us that there he assisted his master in
his hobby of silverwork and frequently sup-
plied the lord with implements for the tea
ceremony and with bronze sword guards.
This tsuba exemplifies the sophisticatedly
simple tastes of Tadaoki. Knowing that
he had a close relationship with Hikozō,
we might assume the lord provided some
aesthetic direction for this work.

Hirata Hikozō might be called a historical forefather of the Higo metalwork artists.
His nephew was Shimizu Jinbei—the first
generation of the Shimizu house, one of
the schools of Higo metalwork artists—
and he was teacher to Kanshirō, father of
Nishigaki Eikyū (1639–1717), who made
the sword guard seen in cat. no. 55. —MH

54

重要文化財

奈良利寿作　牟礼高松図鐔　銘「利寿」

IMPORTANT CULTURAL PROPERTY

SWORD GUARD (TSUBA)

with design of Yoshitsune in battle
at Mure Takamatsu
By Nara Toshinaga (1667–1736)
Signed "Toshinaga"
Japan; Edo period (1615–1868)
18th century
Iron with gold and metal inlay
H. 7.45 cm x W. 7.0 cm
Eisei-Bunko Museum, 7874

This sword guard depicts a large pine tree
and an armored warrior on horseback in
front of a body of water. The iconography
of an armed, mounted warrior facing the sea
under a pine is associated with the historical
battle of Mure Takamatsu (near modern
Takamatsu city, Kagawa prefecture) during
the Genpei War (1180–1185)—a conflict
fought between two warrior clans, the
Minamoto and the Taira.

The warrior on horseback is none other
than the famous general Minamoto Yoshitsune,
who attacked Mure Takamatsu, raided the
military base of the Taira clan at Yashima,
and here faces the Taira's naval fleet on the
sea. The guard's obverse shows a trailing
pine branch with clusters of needles; on the
reverse, a soldier carries a banner (*nagare-
bata*; see cat no. 32) by the pine's trunk. The
branch on the front seems to come from this
trunk, suggesting one continuous scene.

Made from finely wrought iron, the
ground plate is decorated in high relief accomplished with the plow-carving (*sukidashibori*)
technique, in which the chisel is held obliquely.
Gold and other metals add color (*iroe*); the
water is represented in openwork. The skillful modeling of the sloping bank down to
the seaside, the strong relief of the pine, the
raging horse, and the expressions on the warriors' faces all demonstrate superb workmanship.

Nara Toshinaga engraved his signature
between the hole for the tang and the hole for
the small knife handle. Toshinaga was active not
in Higo (Kumamoto prefecture), where the
Hosokawa clan was based, but in Edo (present-
day Tokyo); he is one of the three great artists
of the Nara school (Nara *sansaku*) of metal-
workers, which began in the Momoyama
period (1573–1615) and continued into the
Edo period. Important in its own right, this
sword guard is all the more so because very few
of Toshinaga's works have survived into the
present. —MH

OBVERSE

REVERSE

OBVERSE

REVERSE

55

重要美術品

西垣永久作　田毎の月図鐔　銘「西垣
永久七十歳作之」

IMPORTANT ART OBJECT

SWORD GUARD (TSUBA)
with design of moon reflected in
flooded rice fields
By Nishigaki Eikyū (1639–1717)
Signed "Nishigaki Eikyū *shichijū sai
kore o tsukuru*" (Nishigaki Eikyū made
this at age seventy)
Japan; Edo period (1615–1868), 1708
Brass with gold, silver, copper, copper-
gold alloy (*shakudō*), copper-silver alloy
(*shibuichi*) inlay
H. 7.8 cm x W. 7.35 cm
Eisei-Bunko Museum, 1792

The obverse of this brass guard has an intricate design of rice fields separated by raised
paths. Within each paddy are newly planted
rice seedlings and a reflection of the moon,
in fine single-line gold inlaid into colored
metals such as *shakudō* (copper-gold alloy
with a blackish patina), *shibuichi* (copper-
silver alloy), and pure copper. The diagonal
segmentation of the fields and the openwork in the right bottom section give vitality
to the composition.

The reverse side is decorated with water
lily leaves and horsetails in colored metals;
the leaves' veins and ridges are depicted,
respectively, in gold and silver inlay and
hairline engraving. Its precisely formulated
composition and skillful combination of
materials make this an exemplary work.
To the right and left of the tang hole is the
inscription "Nishigaki Eikyū made this at
the age of seventy."

Nishigaki Eikyū was a metalwork artist
of Higo province (modern Kumamoto
prefecture). His father, Kanshirō worked
for Hosokawa Sansai (aka Tadaoki, 1563–
1646), and his descendants continued to
work for the Hosokawa family all the way
up to the Meiji period. As this piece makes
clear, Eikyū was especially skilled at inlay-
ing in brass. —MH

56

神吉楽寿作　桐紋透唐草象嵌鐔　銘「楽寿」

SWORD GUARD (TSUBA)
with designs of paulownia and floral scrolls
By Kamiyoshi Rakuju (1817–1874)
Signed "Rakuju"
Japan; Edo period (1615–1868)
19th century
Iron openwork with gold inlay
H. 7.85 cm x W. 7.5 cm
Eisei-Bunko Museum, 1800

The sword guard (*tsuba*) often has three openings: a hole for the sword's tang (*nakago ana*; the handle end of the blade) in the center, with an ovoid or semicircular knife handle hole (*kozuka ana*) and a trilobate skewer hole (*kōgai ana*) on either side. The knife and skewer are ancillary implements that attach to the scabbard.

Serving to balance the weight of the blade and the hilt, the guard also protects the hands wielding the sword—but not from an opponent's attack: it would be very dangerous to try to parry a sword's blow with the guard. Rather, the guard prevents the user's hands from slipping up onto the blade while slashing and stabbing at an adversary.

Guards are typically made of iron, bronze, or multilayered leather hardened with lacquer. Various decorative techniques applied to metal guards include line engraving, openwork, relief, and inlay. In the Edo period guards came to be made mainly for aesthetic appreciation rather than for outfitting swords.

This guard, with openwork paulownia crests and double floral scrolls in gold inlay on a quince blossom–shaped base, is the work of Kamiyoshi Rakuju (1817–1874). The signature "Rakuju" appears in gold beside the tang hole. Compared with guards by Rakuju's exemplar Hayashi Matashichi (1613–1699; see cat nos. 49–52), this piece, while finely wrought, conveys an impression of thickness and heaviness, with less artistic depth and elegance. —MH

OBVERSE

REVERSE

OBVERSE

REVERSE

57

神吉楽寿作　武蔵野透唐草象嵌大小鐔　銘「楽寿」

PAIR OF SWORD GUARDS (TSUBA)

with designs of Musashi Plain and floral scrolls
By Kamiyoshi Rakuju (1817–1874)
Signed "Rakuju"
Japan; Edo period (1615–1868), 19th century
Iron openwork with gold inlay
H. 8.4 cm x W. 8.2 cm; H. 7.5 cm x W. 7.2 cm
Eisei-Bunko Museum, 1801

These sword guards (*tsuba*) are formed of iron with an openwork design of eulalia gently swirling around the tang hole. Through the plants we see dewdrops and a barely visible glimpse of the moon. The eulalia grasses are further decorated with floral scrolls in gold inlay. These are guards of considerable elegance and refinement.

The motif of the moon glimpsed through eulalia evokes the scenery of the great plain (*no*) of Musashi, an ancient province that straddled modern-day Tokyo and Saitama prefectures. As the poem goes, "There are no mountains on Musashino for the moon to hide behind; it rises from the grass and sets in the grass": the plain is so vast that the moon rises and sets in its meadows.

The gold-inlaid signature on each guard reveals that the guards were made by Kamiyoshi Rakuju (1817–1874), a metalwork artist of Higo province (modern Kumamoto prefecture). The Kamiyoshi were hereditary artisans from the time of Hosokawa Tadatoshi (1586–1641); they began to specialize in metalwork under Rakuju's grandfather, who was ordered by his lord to learn the traditions and techniques of the Hayashi family of metal artists, also based in Higo. The Kamiyoshi family made sword guards after the fashion of Hayashi Matashichi (1613–1699). In their quality of metal, openwork, and gold inlay, Rakuju's sword guards were unrivaled in his time.

These tsuba came as a set of two, one large and one small, to fit the long (*daitō*) and short (*shōtō*) swords carried by samurai.
—MH

OBVERSE

REVERSE

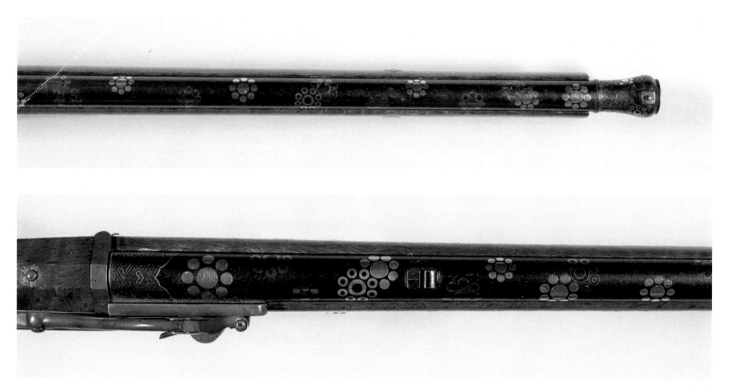

top view details

59 ▶
火薬入
GUNPOWDER CONTAINER
Japan; Momoyama period (1573–1615)
16th–17th century
Bamboo, metal, horn
L. 38.0 cm x W. 9.0 cm
(L. 44 including mouth)
Eisei-Bunko Museum, 7324

58 ▼

九曜紋散紗綾象嵌鉄砲（火縄銃）　銘「肥州住林八助重勝」

MATCHLOCK GUN

with nine-planet family crest
By Hayashi Hachisuke Shigatsu
Signed "Hishū *jū* Hayashi Hachisuke Shigekatsu" (Hayashi Hachisuke Shigekatsu living in Higo)
Japan; Edo period (1615–1868), 17th century
Lacquered iron with gold inlay, wood, metal
L. 101.2 cm
Eisei-Bunko Museum, 7517

This matchlock gun's barrel is decorated with the nine-planet Hosokawa crest in gold. Its inscription tells us that it was made by the metalsmith Hayashi Hachisuke Shigekatsu of Higo province.

Matchlocks were introduced to Japan in 1543 by Portuguese traders who, blown off course, made landfall on the island of Tanegashima, near Kyushu. The Japanese were quick to copy the Portuguese firearms, and many lords employed gunsmiths; the inscription on this piece indicates that it was made for the Hosokawa armory.

Shigekatsu was a metalworker especially known for his inlay technique. His younger brother, Hayashi Matashichi (1613–1699), was also later employed by the rulers of Higo; an outstanding smith, he produced numerous sword guards (*tsuba*) for the Hosokawa clan (see cat. nos. 49–52), some of which have now been designated Important Cultural Properties by the Japanese government.

The brothers' mastery of metal came from their father, a skilled smith in Owari province, where ironworking had a long history. —YW

60

軍配団扇 細川綱利所用

MILITARY LEADER'S SIGNAL FAN (GUNBAI)

with planetary motif
Used by Hosokawa Tsunatoshi (1643–1714)
Japan; Edo period (1615–1868), 17ᵗʰ century
Lacquered leather with gold foil, painted lacquer, sprinkled metallic powder
(*makie*) decoration,
H. 58.2 cm x W. 27.0 cm
Eisei-Bunko Museum, 7389

Military commanders used signal fans (*gunbai uchiwa,* or *gunbai* for short) to direct troop movements. This fan is made of leather coated with black lacquer. Its blade, whose shape suggests a cross section of a gourd, has a riveted border; its handle is decorated in *makie* to resemble a metal fitting; real hardware surrounds the hole for a lanyard.

Circles of gold leaf, bordered in vermilion lacquer, adorn the blade front and back. Within each circle, small orbs in vermilion and black lacquer represent planetary bodies, and numbers in ink indicate the hours of the day.

Wartime decisions were heavily influenced by superstition. Generals commonly used divination to calculate when and where to fight their battles. When going off to battle, they held ceremonies to pray for victory and to celebrate the god of war; if they came home victorious they prayed to him again, in thanks. The planetary symbols and hours on this signal fan could be read to determine auspicious times and locations of combat.

Some warriors acted without regard for such superstitions, but even such famous commanders as Takeda Shingen (1521–1573) and Uesugi Kenshin (1530–1578) practiced soothsaying and magical spells. Augury was still taken seriously in the Tenshō era (1573–1592), despite a dramatic modernization—with innovations in firearms and other weaponry, and in combat methods—of the science of war.—MH

金地日の丸軍配団扇　細川綱利所用

MILITARY LEADER'S SIGNAL FAN (GUNBAI)

with sun motif
Used by Hosokawa Tsunatoshi
(1643–1714)
Japan; Edo period (1615–1868)
17th century
Lacquered iron, gold foil, braided silk,
wood, rayskin
H. 61.7 cm x W. 27.2 cm;
L. 42 cm (tassel)
Eisei-Bunko Museum, 7635

Generals used military signal fans (*gunbai uchi*
or *gunbai*) to command soldiers; but they did
not communicate orders directly to individual
troops. Nor was there an agreed-upon system
for manipulating such a fan to convey specific
instructions. Instead, lieutenants near the general
listened for his verbal orders and watched the
movements of his signal fan, then relayed the
orders to the squadrons. The signal fan's primary
function was to lend form and dignity to the
gestures of the commander.

Originally used to ward off heat, early military
fans were made from plaited bamboo coated
with gold paint or vermilion lacquer. Later fan
blades were made from leather or other material
and embellished with images of the sun, moon,
and stars. Early examples were small, and round
or gourd shaped, but in the Edo period they
evolved into larger, vaguely gourd-shaped implements that might be made of wood or iron as well
as leather. Handles were of lacquered sumac,
bamboo, or sometimes iron.

This signal fan has an iron blade, with the sun
in vermilion on a gilt background. The handle
is covered with ray skin, bound with silk cord
in a diamond pattern to give a firmer grip. The
edge fittings feature floral scrolls and the nine-
planet Hosokawa family crest. —MH

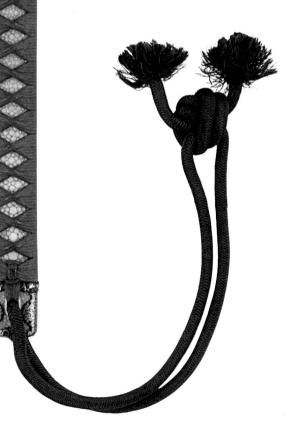

軍扇

FOLDING MILITARY FAN (GUNSEN)

Japan; Edo period (1615–1868), 18th century

Gold foil and color on paper, lacquered wood, braided silk

H. 32.8 cm x W. 50.5 cm

Eisei-Bunko Museum, 4427

Folding military fans (*gunsen*) were used by samurai while in camp during wartime. They usually have eight or sixteen tines, with a broader tine on either end. The sun and moon, in gold or silver and crimson, adorn the fan's faces. While their original function was straightforward—to cool the user in hot weather—folding fans were used for military purposes beginning in ancient times. During the Muromachi period (1392–1573), with the increasing organization of military rituals, folding fans became essential to various ceremonies. The gunsen served as a handheld tray for the presentation of gifts; a samurai might wave his fan to pacify evil spirits on the way to or from the battle-front; and the fan featured in a general's inspection of the decapitated head of an enemy.

Such an inspection might be carried out as follows. First the general would sit on a folding stool (*shōgi*), a gunsen in his right hand. An officer would hand a bow to the general, who would tuck his fan into his belt; take the bow in his left hand; stand it on end; and use it to stand up. He would conduct the actual inspection of the severed head standing at some distance from the stool. After the inspection, he would return to his seat, sit down, return the bow to the officer, and then open the fan completely and fan vigorously three times with his left hand. Finally he would close the fan and return it to his right hand, thus concluding the decapitation inspection ceremony.
—MH

63

采配 細川斉護所用

COMMANDER'S BATON (SAIHAI)

Used by Hosokawa Narimori (1804–1860)
Japan; Edo period (1615–1868), 19th century
Lacquered wood, paper, leather, incised silver
L. 32.7 cm (handle); L. 26.0 cm (tassel)
Eisei-Bunko Museum, 4111-2

Warfare in Japan, formerly conducted through individual combat, changed
during the Warring States period (late fifteenth and sixteenth centuries)
into mass combat. Consequently, various implements were invented to
direct large formations of soldiers. Generals used the baton (*saihai*) to
direct troops in the field.

This baton is associated with the *haramaki*-type armor (cat. no. 22)
also used by the twelfth-generation lord of the Hosokawa, Narimori. Its
tassel, of stout paper cut into long, thin strips, is affixed to a black lacquered
wooden handle, with a cord of dyed leather. Silver caps at the handle's
ends are line-incised with floral scrolls and the nine-planet Hosokawa
family crest on the top. It is a simple yet ingenious design. —JA

64 ◄
梨地束箭蒔絵
SADDLE
with design of arrow fletches on sprinkled ground
Japan; Momoyama period (1573–1615), 16th–17th century
Lacquered wood with sprinkled metallic powder (*makie*)
decoration, silk
Pommel H. 27.4 cm x W. 31.7 cm x cantle H. 38.1 cm
Eisei-Bunko Museum, 4399

65 ▲
梅樹文蒔絵鞍
SADDLE
with design of plum trees
Japan; Edo period (1615–1868), 17th century
Lacquered wood with sprinkled metallic powder (*makie*)
decoration
Pommel H. 27.5 cm x cantle H. 31.8 cm
Eisei-Bunko Museum, 4387

Japanese saddles (*wagura*) have arched pommels and cantles, typically
fashioned from red oak, and seat bars of softer paulownia wood.

   Saddles are generally coated with black lacquer and ornamented
with a variety of designs having auspicious, powerful, or even literary
connotations. The design motifs are executed in the *makie* technique,
in which fine dust of gold, silver, or another metal is sprinkled onto
wet lacquer to form motifs, sometimes over delicately sprinkled
backgrounds. The pommels and cantles are the major areas of decoration. —YW

66 ◄

雷文散蒔絵鞍

SADDLE

with design of stylized
lightning bolts
Japan; Edo period (1615–1868)
17th century
Lacquered wood with sprinkled
metallic powder (*makie*) decoration
Pommel H. 28.5 cm x cantle
H. 32.2 cm
Eisei-Bunko Museum, 4397

67 ►

梨地鶴亀蒔絵鞍

SADDLE

with design of cranes and turtles on
sprinkled ground
Japan; Edo period (1615–1868)
18th century
Lacquered wood with sprinkled metallic
powder (*makie*) decoration
Pommel H. 27 cm x W. 39.0 cm
x D. 38.2 cm x cantle H. 35.5 cm
Eisei-Bunko Museum, 4523

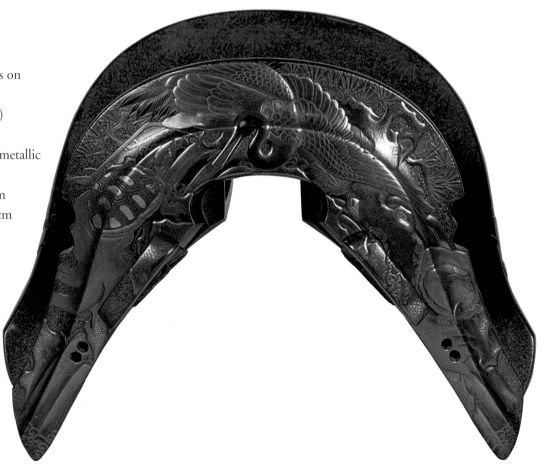

68 ▶

花卉文黄銅鐙 豊臣秀次所持

STIRRUPS
with floral design
Used by Toyotomi Hidetsugu
(1568–1595)
Japan; Edo period (1615–1868)
17th century
Laquered iron with sprinkled metallic
powder (*makie*) decoration
H. 23.5 cm x W. 13 cm x L. 30 cm
Eisei-Bunko Museum, 2194

69 ▼

亀甲に花菱文鐙　銘「江州日野飯島清左
衛門作」

STIRRUPS
with floral hexagonal design
By Iijima Seizemon
Signed "Goshū Hino Iijima Seizaemon *saku*"
(Made by Iijima Seizaemon of Hino,
Ōmi province)
Japan; Edo period (1615–1868)
17th–18th century
Iron with silver inlay and lacquer
H. 27 x W. 121 x L. 27.9 cm
Asian Art Museum of San Francisco,
Transfer from the Fine Arts Museums
of San Francisco, B69M51

70

白ラシャ九曜紋陣羽織 細川光尚所用
SURCOAT (JINBAORI)
with nine-planet family crest
Worn by Hosokawa Mitsunao (1619–1649)
Japan; Edo period (1615–1868), 17th century
Wool (*rasha*) inlaid with wool twill
L. 99.0 cm x W. 54.0 cm (shoulder)
Eisei-Bunko Museum, 4246

A *jinbaori*—military camp (*jin*) jacket (*haori*)—is a surcoat usually worn over a suit of *tōsei gusoku* armor (see cat. no. 23–25). Some surcoats had sleeves but many, like this example, were vests. This rare early jinbaori probably dates to the second quarter of the seventeenth century. It is known to have been worn by Hosokawa Mitsunao, the fourth-generation lord of the Hosokawa, whose military hat is shown in cat. no. 28.

Earlier forms of armor, such as *ōyoroi* and *dōmaru*, were worn over jackets and trouser suits (*yoroi hitatare*) made from opulently patterned silks. The suits of gusoku armor adopted in the sixteenth and seventeenth centuries, however, covered up these decorative undergarments, so high-ranking warriors and daimyo began to wear jinbaori over their battle gear. These were often made of luxurious, sometimes imported materials; conspicuous designs and bold color combinations made strong, clear statements about the rank and identity of their wearers.

This surcoat is made of thick fulled wool (*rasha*), which was an exotic luxury in a country without sheep. It shows European influence in its A-line construction, high standing collar, and long, open back vent with rounded corners (which would have

made it easier to wear over armor). Imported primarily from Europe, wool textiles were available only to the wealthy and powerful.

In the center of the back is a large nine-planet crest that would have distinguished its wearer as leader of the Hosokawa clan. The circles of black wool—partially deteriorated due to the iron mordent used to fix the dye—are inlayed into same-sized cutouts in the white background fabric and stitched decoratively around the joints. The armholes and body are edged in blue.

The black crest on white echoes the design of the clan's banners (see cat. no. 32, 33) used after Mitsunao's grandfather Tadaoki moved the Hosokawa domain from Tango (present-day northern Kyoto prefecture) to Buzen province (now eastern Fukuoka and northern Oita prefectures) in the year 1600. Though few daimyo actually participated in battles during the relatively peaceful Edo period, Mitsunao fought in the Shimabara Rebellion in 1637 together with his father Tadatoshi, before succeeding him as daimyo in 1641. —MR

Reference:
Eisei Bunko, ed., "Bushi no yosooi." *Kikan Eisei Bunko* 29 (January 1989), 12.

71

白緋ラシャ段替わり陣羽織（細川斉茲所用）

SURCOAT (JINBAORI)
with horizontal bands
Worn by Hosokawa Narishige
(1759–1836)
Japan; Edo period (1615–1868)
late 18th century
Wool (*rasha*); silk satin lampas with gilded
paper weft patterning (*kinran*)
L.101 cm x W. 55.8 cm
Eisei-Bunko Museum, 6940

This sleeveless *jinbaori* is made from imported wool in a red-and-white stripe accented with gold-patterned silk. The horizontal bands are not dyed or woven into the cloth; instead, they were made by placing wide strips of red and white felted wool side by side and stitching them together with meticulous, invisible stitches to create the effect of continuous fabric. Such a striped wool textile would have seemed exotic to contemporary Japanese not only for its extravagance (wool was not produced in Japan) but also for the clean lines of its stripes—aesthetically different from the dyed, woven, or ikat-dyed (as in cat. no. 140) horizontal bands of domestically produced luxury textiles.

The body of this surcoat has a standing collar and widely flaring, A-line body—reminiscent of a Portuguese mantle—providing mobility when worn over a suit of armor. The front edges can be fastened with buttons and loops, or opened to reveal a wide, flaring lapel faced with luxurious patterned silk, with cherry blossoms in three sizes over a background of stylized waves (*seigaiha*).

This surcoat was worn by Hosokawa Narishige, whose *tōsei gusoku* armor is shown in cat. no. 24. It probably dates to the second half of the eighteenth century. —MR

Reference:
Eisei Bunko, ed., "Bushi no yosooi." *Kikan Eisei Bunko* 29 (January 1989), 12.

117

72

片袖緋ラシャ陣羽織 細川韶邦所用

SURCOAT (JINBAORI)

with one red sleeve

Worn by Hosokawa Yoshikuni (1835–1876)

Japan; Edo period (1615–1868), 19th century

Wool (*rasha*); silk satin lampas with silk and gilded paper weft patterning (*kinran*)

L. 87.5 cm x W. 145 cm

Eisei-Bunko Museum, 4277-1

This eye-catching surcoat has a white body accented by one red sleeve and a collar faced with opulent patterned silk in designs of Chinese-style dragons and clouds. With its boxy sleeves, four-panel body, and wide collar, it has Japanese-derived tailoring. The collar folds back on itself to create a decorative lapel, resembling warrior coats (*dōfuku*) made from luxury textiles and worn in the sixteenth and early seventeenth centuries by

Japan's military rulers and highest-ranking lords. Made to be worn over armor, this jinbaori has a wide construction with slightly flaring sides.

The single red sleeve on an undecorated white coat reflects the aesthetics of some "Sansai style" (Sansai *ryū*) suits of *tōsei gusoku* armor, such as that shown in cat. no. 23, over which it was worn. There, a single red-laced tasset serves as a striking accent on a sober

suit of brown leather-covered lames laced with dark blue silk cords.

Owned by Yoshikuni, twelfth-generation lord of the Hosokawa domain, and thought to date to the middle of the nineteenth century, this robe reflects the continuity of particular clan-associated aesthetics preserved from generation to generation by the Hosokawa daimyo, even into the end of the Edo period. —MR

73

緋ビロード九曜紋陣羽織 細川護久所用
SURCOAT (JINBAORI)
with nine-planet crest
Worn by Hosokawa Morihisa
(1839–1893)
Japan; Edo period (1615–1868)
19th century
Silk velvet appliquéd with felted wool;
silk satin lampas with silk and gilded
paper weft patterning (*kinran*); braided
silk cord
L. 70.0 cm x W. 45.0 cm
Eisei-Bunko Museum, 4281

Front

This *jinbaori's* European-influenced shape—
with wide, slightly flared sides, large armholes, and standing collar that is detached
from the lapels—had become fairly standard
by the late Edo period. In keeping with the
taste for flamboyant textiles in such garments,
the surcoat is made from luxurious silk cut
velvet in a brilliant shade of deep vermil-
lion, now somewhat faded; its lapels are
faced in Chinese-style multicolored silk with
gilded paper threads and patterned with
five-claw dragons and clouds. Black strips
embellish the shoulders; braided silk cord
loops and knots fasten the lapel. Slim straps
across the chest button to hold the surcoat
in place. In the center of the back, under the
collar, the Hosokawa nine-planet crest is
appliquéd in white felted wool.

Thought to date to the middle of the
nineteenth century, and known to have been
worn by Morihisa, the thirteenth Hosokawa
daimyo, who saw the family into the Meiji
period, this surcoat testifies to the daimyos'
continuing incorporation of luxury textiles
into military wear throughout the Edo period.
—MR

Back

Detail

74

伝矢野三郎兵衛筆　老松牡丹図屏風

OLD PINE TREE AND PEONIES

Attributed to Yano Saburobei Yoshishige (1596–1653)

Japan; Edo period (1615–1868), 17th century

Pair of six-panel folding screens; ink, colors, and gold foil on paper

H. 165.8 cm x W. 350.8 cm (each)

Eisei-Bunko Museum, 4023

Dominated by a gigantic pine and cascading water, this pair of screens presents auspicious symbols. The huge old tree, with its evergreen needles, stands for longevity; the tumbling water, for the restless forces of nature; and the abundant peony blossoms signify wealth. All are abiding elements in Japanese decorative paintings.

Irregular cuts and joins in the paper, hiding apertures for door pulls, indicate that these screens were once mounted as sliding doors (*fusuma*). Their estimated original size and bright and sumptuous golden appear-

ance suggest that the doors might even have been made for a large hall in a castle during the opulent Momoyama period (1573–1615). Their modification, perhaps much later, into free-standing screens is a typical repurposing of old artworks.

The painting has traditionally been attributed to Yano Saburobei Yoshishige, an artist in residence for the Hosokawa Higo domain.[1] —YW

1. Kumamoto Kenritsu Bijutsukan, ed., *Eisei Bunko no byobue* (Kumamoto: Kumamoto Kenritsu Bijutsukan, 1984), 58.

Detail

75

雲谷等顔筆　陶淵明・林和靖図屏風

LANDSCAPE WITH POETS TAO YUANMING AND LIN HEJING

By Unkoku Tōgan (1547–1618)

Japan; Momoyma period (1573–1615), 16th–17th century

Pair of six-panel folding screens; ink and colors on paper

H. 147 cm x W. 358 cm (each)

Asian Art Museum of San Francisco, The Avery Brundage Collection, B60D74+ B60D73+

These screens depict two well-known Chinese poets in landscape settings. In the right screen, Tao Yuanming (365–427), seated in a hut, enjoys a drink while contemplating the chrysanthemums he loved. In the left screen, the Song dynasty poet Lin Hejing and his young servant are looking at a crane— their pet—in full flight. Gentle hills, pine trees, and bamboo surround the poets' modest dwellings.

The representation in art of an ideal life of seclusion became popular in the Muromachi period (1392–1573), when, influenced by the tastes of Zen Buddhist temples, the warrior class began to appreciate the muted expressiveness of delicate ink paintings. While the samurai enjoyed lavish, glittering golden screens in their courts and castles, some of their screens and doors represented literary themes, executed in ink monochrome. This pair bears the seals of the artist Unkoku Tōgan (1547–1618).

Tōgan was born Hara Jihei, into a high-ranking samurai family with connections to the Mōri clan in what is now Yamaguchi prefecture. Impressed by the work of the celebrated painter Sesshū Tōyō, Jihei was allowed to live in Sesshū's former studio. He changed his name to commemorate the honor; the "Tō" in Tōgan relates to Sesshū's religious name, Tōyō, and Unkoku refers to the name Sesshū gave his studio. Further, Tōgan called himself a descendant of Sesshū and worked to perpetuate the master's style of painting. The Unkoku school became influential among elite warriors in nearby domains, including members of the Hosokawa clan.

The Hosokawa family collection includes a pair of late-sixteenth-century screens, *The Seven Sages of the Bamboo Grove,* which are very similar to these in their style and theme. Such examples help to illustrate the extent to which the samurai embraced the gentleman-scholar ideal. In fact, the two official painting schools of the Hosokawa domain derived from Unkoku Tōgan's work. Yano Saburobei Yoshishige (see cat. no. 74),

who had studied the Sesshū-Tōgan style under Unkoku Tōgan, founded the Yano school; Tashiro Tōho (see cat. no. 5), another former student of Tōgan, was employed by the Hosokawa family. —YW

76
一の谷・屋島合戦図屏風
BATTLES OF ICHINOTANI AND YASHIMA
from *The Tale of the Heike*
By an artist of the Kanō school
Japan; Edo period (1615–1868), 17th century
Pair of six-panel folding screens; ink, colors, and gold foil on paper
H. 169.8 cm x W. 372.4 cm (each)
Eisei-Bunko Museum, 4006

The conflict between the two most power-ful warrior clans of the late twelfth century, the Minamoto (Genji) and the Taira (Heike), and the battles they fought, became favorite stories among people of later periods; these tales were told and retold for hundreds of years. Imbued with the Buddhist view that the affairs of this world are transient, that no earthly glory or failure is permanent, they touched people deeply, inspiring them to write poems or to paint imaginary scenes drawn from the stories.

These screens portray the events that took place at Ichinotani (right screen) and the battle conducted at Yashima (left screen). At Ichinotani, Minamoto Yoshitsune (1159–1189), the great Genji general, led his cavalry to the edge of a nearly perpen-dicular cliff. Yoshitsune had intended to attack the Heike camp from the rear, but the escarpment seemed too steep for horses to descend. At that moment, members of

his cavalry saw two stags and a doe running down the cliffside. Yoshitsune sent some riderless horses after the deer. Some fell, but three reached flatter ground and stood there, trembling.

With great care Yoshitsune led his men down the steep slope; they attacked the Heike encampment as planned. Surprised from behind, the bewildered Heike fled into the sea; some soldiers succeeded in swimming to Yashima, located across the inland sea on the island of Shikoku.

In the left-hand screen, boats crowd the bay as the Heike soldiers try to escape from their enemies. The Genji army holds the shore.

The story, as told in *The Tale of the Heike,* has it that battle ceased as night fell. Then a Heike boat appeared, bearing an elegantly attired lady and moving shoreward. Mounted near the prow was a red fan with a golden sun design. The lady gestured, taunting the Genji to shoot at the fan. The Genji general

ordered Nasu Yoichi, a slight young warrior known for "bringing down two birds out of three," to try a shot. Yoichi rode his horse into the sea, but he was still far from the boat when his arrow left the bow. Thudding into the fan an inch from its riveted edge, Yoichi's long shot cut it loose to float on the waves, glittering in the sun's last light. Offshore, the Heike beat the sides of their boats and applauded; the Genji struck their quivers and shouted in exaltation.

Stylistically, this pair of screens is character-ized by crowded presentation with minutely detailed depictions. Saitama Prefectural Museum has a pair of screens very like these;[1] it is thought that both the Eisei-Bunko and Saitama screens were based on a hand-scroll of the same subject. —YW

1. Takeda Tsuneo, ed., *Nihon byōbu-e shūsei,* v. 15 *Fūzokuga.* (Tokyo: Kodansha, 1979), 107–108.

Detail

Detail

77

宇治川・粟津原合戦図屏風

FIRST MAN ACROSS THE UJI RIVER AND BATTLE OF AWAZUGAHARA

from *The Tale of the Heike*

Japan; Edo period (1615–1868), late 17th century

Pair of six-panel folding screens; ink, colors, and gold foil on paper

H. 152.0 cm x W. 352.2 cm

Asian Art Museum of San Francisco; Avery Brundage Collection, B60D60+, B60D61+

Many tales of war were written during the thirteenth century, and *The Tale of the Heike* (*Heike monogatari*), which told of the conflict between the powerful Genji (Minamoto) and Heike (Taira) warrior families, was among the most popular. Consequently, episodes from *Heike* appear in many paintings.

These screens depict two episodes, "The First Man Across the Uji River" and "Battle of Awazugahara." The Uji River scene (right) recounts an 1184 contest of military tactics and horsemanship between two Minamoto warriors. On a military campaign, Sasaki Shirō Takatsuna and Kajiwara Genta Kagesue approached the Uji. The river was in flood, and its bridge was out of commission; they had no choice but to swim their horses

across, each man competing to be first. They dashed toward the river, with Kajiwara in the lead. Close behind him, Sasaki shouted, "The Uji is the biggest river in the west. Your saddle looks loose, make it tight!" With Kajiwara's attention diverted, Sasaki seized the lead, crossed the river, and ascended the opposite bank. Kajiwara's horse was caught in the current and made land far downstream.

The screen shows four mounted samurai dashing toward the Uji. Kajiwara leads on his black horse, and Sasaki follows on his chestnut. The painting depicts the moment when Sasaki shouted.

The left screen illustrates an episode from the chapter detailing the death of Kiso Yoshinaka. Lady Tomoe, a heroic warrior,

has donned armor and entered into battle to protect her beloved husband, Kiso Yoshinaka (1154–1184), a cousin of Minamoto Yoritomo. Tomoe has just pulled her enemy Onda Hachiro Moroshige from his horse; holding him across her saddle, she now prepares to slit his throat.

In this superb example of the warrior-painting genre, lively figures are set against a grand gold background whose simplicity helps focus the viewer's attention on the action. —YW

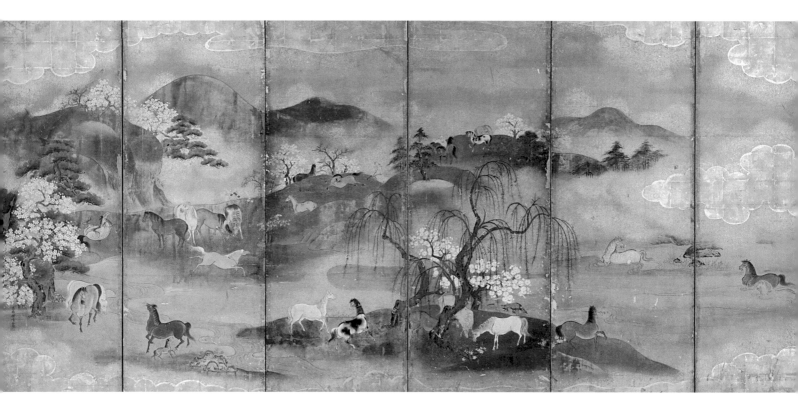

Detail

78

狩野探信筆　牧馬図屏風

GRAZING HORSES

By Kanō Tanshin (1653–1718)

Japan; Edo period (1615–1868), 1715–1718

Pair of six-panel folding screens; ink, colors, and gold on paper

H. 158.9 cm x W. 356.8 cm (each)

Eisei-Bunko Museum, 4016

These screens depict a glorious spring day in a peaceful riverside pastureland. The hills are covered with fresh greenery and densely dotted with flowering cherry trees. A distant waterfall cascades into the river, which flows placidly in the foreground. Horses of various colors and markings are enjoying the warm day, some grazing or playing, some lying at the water's edge, some swimming.

In the fifteenth and sixteenth centuries, during the Warring States (Sengoku) period, horses were indispensable parts of a warrior's armaments; as tools of combat they were valued in terms of their energy, strength, and stamina. In the newly peaceful Edo period (1615–1868), warriors saw their horses

differently. Certainly the horse was still the symbol of a courageous warrior, but the tendency now was to cherish the animal for its beauty and nobility. The breeding farms of the samurai sought to produce horses of perfect proportion, with colorful coats and beautiful markings, spots, or patterns.

These screens were not made to portray a living herd or the pasture of any particular warrior family. Rather, in their idealization of animals and setting, they reveal the affection and respect of the warrior for the horse.

Kanō Tanshin signed his work with the honorific title Hōgen, which he received in 1715. These screens, then, date from between 1715 and his death in 1718. —YW

Detail

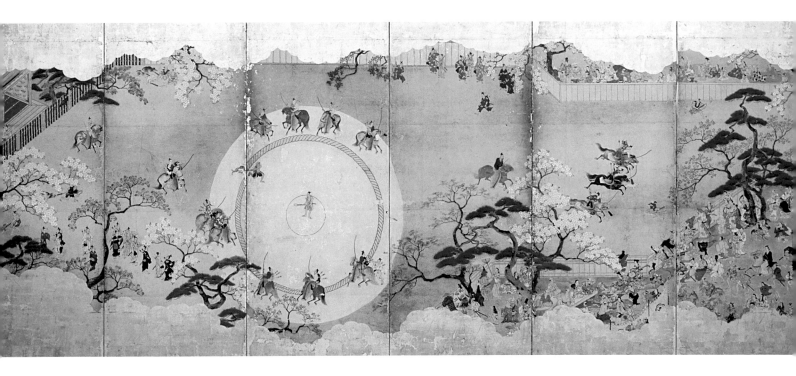

79

犬追物図屏風

DOG CHASING

Japan; Edo period (1615–1868), late 17th century

Pair of six-panel folding screens; ink, colors, and gold foil on paper

H. 139.9 cm x W. 351.8 cm (each)

Eisei-Bunko Museum, 4005

These screens depict the "dog-chasing event" (*inuoumono*), a popular archery drill for mounted warriors of the Edo period. (The other principal drills were *yabusame*—performed in shrine precincts by archers who shot at three stationary targets while riding at a gallop—and *kasagake*, where archers shot at a straw hat, again from a galloping horse.) *Inuoumono* was the most difficult drill: the target was a running dog.

Mounted samurai sought to hit the dog, which understandably was moving as fast as it could, with thickly padded arrows. The competition made formidable demands on the warrior's skill as equestrian and archer. Dating from the Muromachi period (1392–1573), the dog-chasing event became a spectator sport popular among common men, women, and children as well as with the aristocrats who practiced it. Closely codified rules stipulated the size of the field and the number of dogs and participating archers for each round. Only when the dog passed over a rope could the archers try to hit it, and then only in the torso: shots that struck its head or limbs drew penalty points.

In the right screen, the recorder's booth at the end of the field holds officials. Spectators fill the viewers' stands along the field's sides. —YW

Detail

80

阿蘇下野狩図屏風

HUNTING ON THE SHIMONO PLAIN BENEATH MOUNT ASO

Japan; Edo period (1615–1868), 18th–19th century

Pair of six-panel folding screens; ink, colors, and gold foil on paper

H. 178.8 cm x W. 379.8 cm (each screen)

Eisei-Bunko Museum, 4058

This pair of screens depicts an annual hunt conducted on the Shimono plain at the foot of Mount Aso, Japan's largest active volcano. Directed by the grand priest of Aso shrine, the hunt was meant both to protect the harvest from animals and to give participants an opportunity to practice their fighting skills while furthering their warrior spirit. The grand priest was also the head of the Aso clan; this hereditary dual position continued for six hundred years, as did the hunt. Toward the end of the sixteenth century, the clan went into decline and the Shimono hunt beneath Mount Aso, with its blend of strenuous activity and dignified ceremony, ceased. This pair of screens, created two hundred years later, recalls the lost warrior family.

In the right screen, mounted hunters pursue animals on an open plain. Fires have been set to turn the fleeing animals from possible routes to safety. In the leftmost panel, a group of warriors surround their lord.

In the left screen, the hunt is finished and the participants, scattered in groups, enjoy picnics. Most wear white robes and black headgear—an indication of the hunt's dual purpose as a religious activity. At far left, people gather, perhaps for post-hunting games. —YW

81

細川幽斎筆　秋草図和歌扇面

AUTUMN PLANTS AND WAKA POETRY
ON FAN PAPER

By Hosokawa Yūsai (aka Fujitaka, 1534–1610)

Japan; Momoyama period (1573–1615), 16th–17th century

Hanging scroll; ink and colors on paper

H. 121.5 cm x W. 66.0 cm (image)

H. 121.5 cm x W. 71 (overall)

Eisei-Bunko Museum, 3391

On a fan-shaped paper decorated with autumn flowers flourishing
around a stream, Fujitaka wrote a famous poem by Sosei Hōshi.
Extracted from the early tenth-century imperial poetry anthology
Kokin wakashū (Collection of Poems Ancient and Modern), it reads:

ぬれてほす山路の菊の露のまに
いつか千とせを我はへにけむ

Nurete hosu	Did an age slip by
yamaji no kiku no	during those fleeting moments
tsuyu no ma ni	when I dried my sleeves
itsu ka chitose o	drenched by chrysanthemum dew
ware wa henikemu	on the path through the mountains?[1]

Fujitaka was a cultured man who excelled in composing and
teaching *waka* poems—the classical Japanese form. He was also well
trained in the tea ceremony, music, and fine cuisine; yet he was a
fierce warrior as well. His life's work was central to the only occasion in Japanese history in which literary scholarship proved more
materially powerful than military force. (Details appear in the text
accompanying cat. no. 5.) —YW

1. Helen Craig Mc Cullough trans., *Kokin Wakashu: The First Imperial Anthology
of Japanese Poetry.* (Stanford: Stanford University Press, 1985), no. 273, 68.

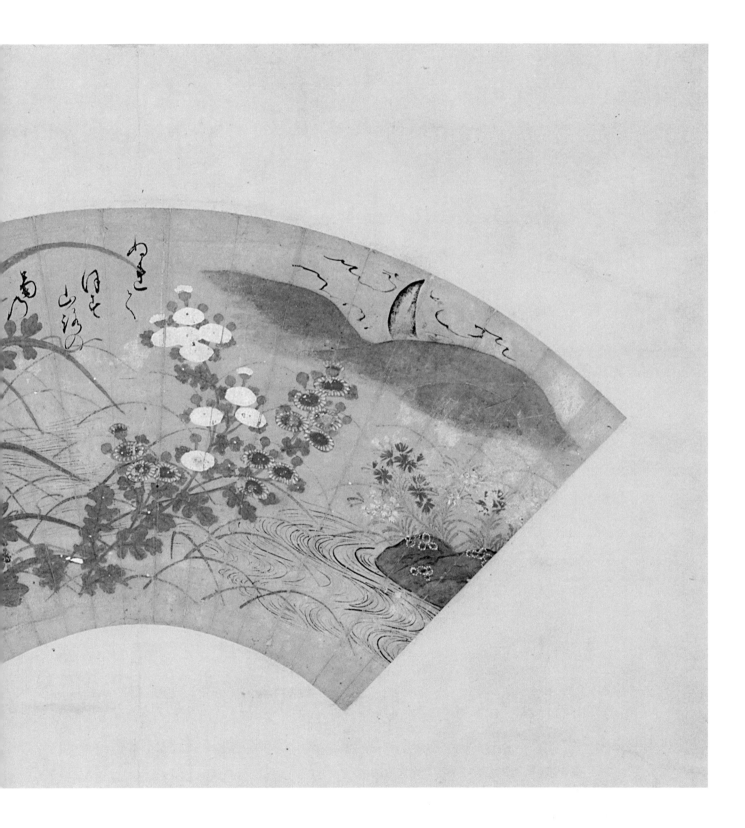

清見潟
庚
四寸
九歩

82

狩野養長筆　牡丹芍薬生写

SKETCHES OF TREE PEONIES AND CHINESE PEONIES

By Kanō Osanaga (1815–1875)

Japan; Edo period (1615–1868), 1856

Album (60 leaves)

ink and colors on paper

H. 24.3 cm x W. 27.2 cm

Eisei-Bunko Museum, 3755

In 1756 Hosokawa Shigekata (1720–1785), the tenth-generation Hosokawa lord, founded a garden, called Banjien, for the propagation and study of medicinal plants. Botany and horticulture became particular interests of the people of Higo: the domain produced Higo peonies, Higo chrysanthemums, Higo camellias, Higo irises, Higo morning glories, and other flowers.

This album of paintings presents the result of the Higo cultivation projects. It names and illustrates thirty-one types of tree peony and twenty-nine types of Chinese peony.

The album's box is inscribed "By the painter in service." Kanō Osanaga was "painter in service," or artist in residence, to the Hosokawa house in the spring of 1856.

Hosokawa Narimori (1804–1860), the twelfth-generation lord, was another Higo daimyo with a strong interest in botany. He supported an organization called the Flower League, and his ship *Naminashi Maru* (used for state visits to Edo; see also cat. nos. 16 and 17) was decorated with paintings of 170 flower species. —YW

雲井霍 辰
五寸五歩

Ceiling of interior of ship *Naminashi Maru*

琉球牡丹

83

赤星閑意、松山敬誠、松岡敬廉筆　群芳帖
SKETCHES OF FLOWERS
By Akahoshi Kan'i (1835–1888), Matsuyama Takamasa
(1807–1865), and Matsuoka Takakiyo (d. 1859)
Japan; Edo period (1615–1868), 19th century
Album (89 leaves); ink and colors on paper
H. 36.8 cm x W. 28.7 cm
Eisei-Bunko Museum, 3705

Flowering irises were widely cultivated in the early years of the Edo
period; but in the Genroku era (1688–1707), when several decades
of peace allowed horticulture and botany, like many other branches
of the arts, to flourish, many new varieties of iris began to appear.

This album contains illustrations of Japanese water irises (*Iris
ensata*), variants of wild iris species propagated in Higo. In the album's eighty-
nine pages, each flower is limned in seven hues, including purple,
pink, indigo, and lapis lazuli. The painters were professional artists
in the employ of the Hosokawa family. —YW

連

新歓

初露

難波津

右二于禮松山巌敬誠画

139

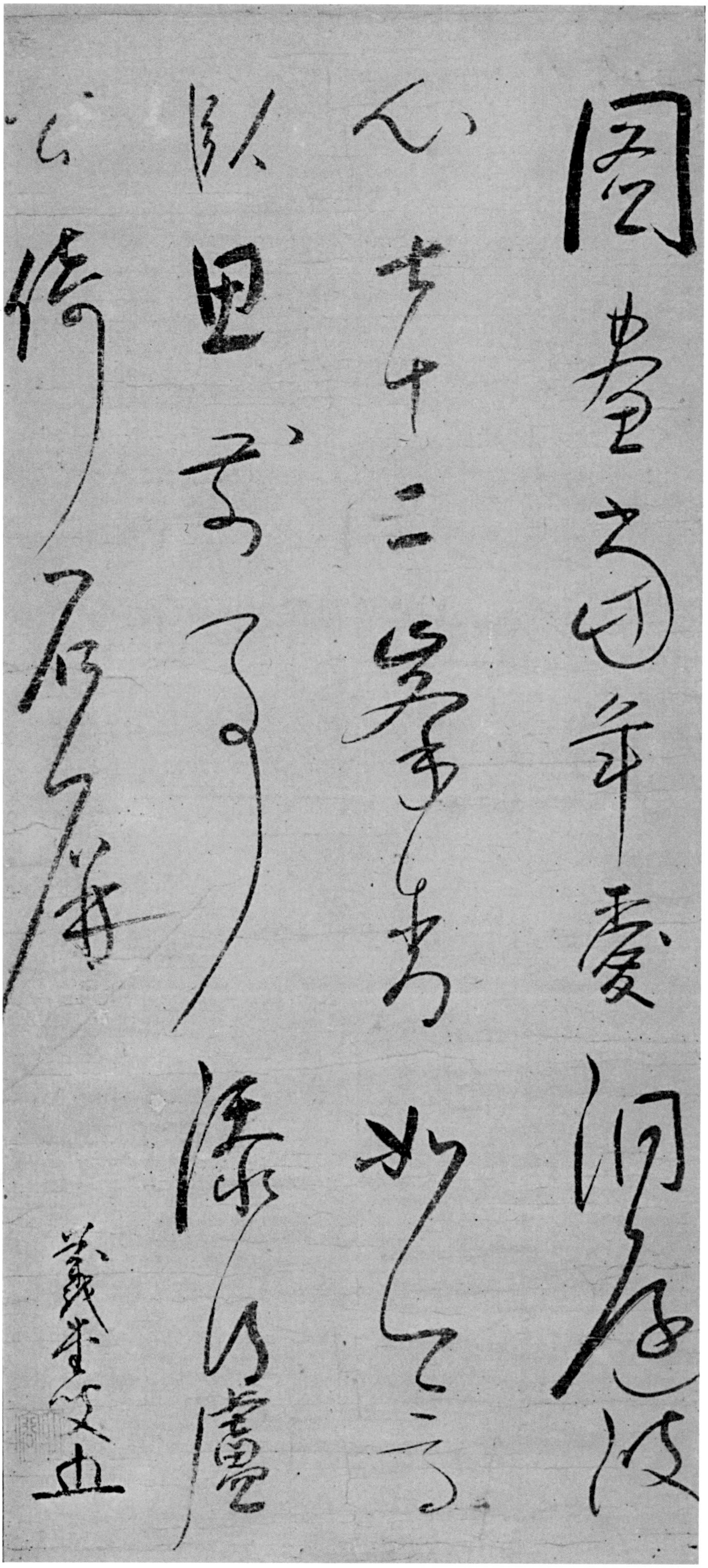

84

義堂周信筆　七言絶句

CALLIGRAPHY

Chinese poem of seven–character phrases
By Gidō Shūshin (1325–1388)
Japan; Nanbokuchō period
(1333–1392), 14th century
Hanging scroll; ink on paper
H. 65.1 cm x W. 31.0 cm (image)
W. 36.8 cm (overall)
Eisei-Bunko Museum, 305

圓畫當年愛洞庭波
心七十二峯青　如今高
臥思前事　添得盧
公倚石屏　義堂叟　（花押）

*While sketching that year, I came to love
　"Lake Dongting."
In the bosom of its waves were seventy-two
　peaks of blue.
Now in a moment of leisure I recall these
　past events.
To that sketch I have added Master Lu
　leaning against a stone wall.*[1]

This powerful calligraphic work was done
by Gidō Shūshin, a famous Zen priest in
Kamakura and, later, in Kyoto.

The passage, by the Song dynasty poet
Xuedou Zhongxian (980–1052), concerns
the Curweifen peak, located in the Jiuyi
Mountains surrounding China's Lake Dongting. The poem is included in *Biyanlu*
(Blue Cliff Record), a Chinese collection
of koans compiled in 1125, which is used
in Japanese Rinzai Zen training. It is not
known when the Hosokawa family came into
possession of this strong work of calligraphy,
but the acquisition indicates the family's
interest in Zen Buddhism.

Gidō Shūshin was born in Tosa, now Kōchi
prefecture, on the island of Shikoku. After
studying Rinzai Zen under the eminent Zen
master Musō Sōseki (1275–1351), he founded
the Hōonji temple in Kamakura—the central temple of Japanese Zen Buddhism in
his time. The shogun Ashikaga Yoshimitsu
later asked him to become the head priest
of Kenninji temple, and later of Nanzenji
temple, both in Kyoto. Shūshin was the
Ashikaga shoguns' private teacher of Zen
Buddhism. —YW

1. Translation adapted from Victor Sōgen Hori, *Zen
Sand: The Book of Capping Phrases for Kōan Practice.*
(Honolulu: University of Hawai'i Press, 2003),
559–560.

85

一休宗純筆 「諸悪莫作衆善奉行」

CALLIGRAPHY

Verses of precepts of the seven Buddhas
By Ikkyū Sōjun (1394–1481)
Japan; Muromachi period (1392–1573)
15th century
Hanging scroll; ink on paper
H. 125.0 cm x W. 32.0 cm (image)
H. 188 x W. 38.4 cm (overall)
Eisei-Bunko Museum, 1076

Assertively calligraphed by the famous Zen
monk Ikkyū Sōjun, this scroll is a kind of
devotional icon. It reads:

> *Do not commit evil deeds;*
> *Strive to do good deeds.*

These are the first two of four verses known
as *Shichibutsu tsukai no ge* (Verses of precepts
of the seven Buddhas), extracted from the
early Buddhist sutra *Sōichi agon kyō* (Sanskrit:
Ekottara-āgama-sūtra), which was translated
into Chinese during the Eastern Jin dynasty
(317–419). The subsequent two verses, not
included in this calligraphy, would have read:

> *Purify your thoughts—*
> *This is what the Buddha teaches.*

The calligraphy style falls between the cleri-
cal (*kaisho*) and semicursive (*gyōsho*) modes.
Executed in bold, rough strokes, the brushwork evokes the monk's powerful nature.
He worked so quickly that he accidentally
omitted the character for "good" from the
second verse. Ikkyū later added the character, in small precise calligraphy, to the right
of the line. A square relief seal, "Ikkyū," is
impressed at lower left.
   Hosokawa Sansai (1564–1646) is said to
have purchased this scroll in Kyoto.—YW

86

澤庵宗彭筆　「放下着」

CALLIGRAPHY

"Free yourself from all attachments"

By Takuan Sōhō (1573–1646)

Japan; Edo period (1615–1868)

17th century

Hanging scroll; ink on paper

H. 28.0 cm x W. 64.0 cm (image)

H. 108.5 cm x W. 70.5 cm (overall)

Eisei-Bunko Museum, 434

Takuan Sōho was the abbot of Daitokuji, a leading Zen temple of the Rinzai school in Kyoto. A calligrapher, poet, and tea master, Takuan acted as a mentor to the Hosokawa family. Here his message, *hōge-jaku*—"Free yourself from all attachments," or "Put it down, let it go"—is the Zen advice to let material and even spiritual attachments fall away.

His calligraphy style is bold and free; his brush movement conveys the subtlety of Zen thought. —YW

87

細川韶邦筆 「豁如」

CALLIGRAPHY

"Magnanimity"

By Hosokawa Yoshikuni (1835–1876)

Japan; Edo period (1615–1868)

19th century

Hanging scroll; ink on paper

H. 127.5 cm x W. 55.5 cm (image)

H. 187 x W. 75.5 cm (overall)

Eisei-Bunko Museum, 3591

Lord Hosokawa Yoshikuni wrote these two characters reading *katsujo* (Chinese: *huoru*) in semicursive style. The word refers to the capacity to be generous and open, to embrace everything and everyone; it appears in canonical Chinese histories describing the personalities of the Chinese dynasts Han Gaozu (reigned 206–194 BCE) and Tang Gaozu (reigned 618–627 CE) as loving and benevolent rulers.

Yoshikuni was the last daimyo of the Hosokawa family. In 1868, the emperor Meiji was restored to power; Tokugawa Japan became imperial Japan, and the 250-year rule of shogun and daimyo came to an end.

—YW

143

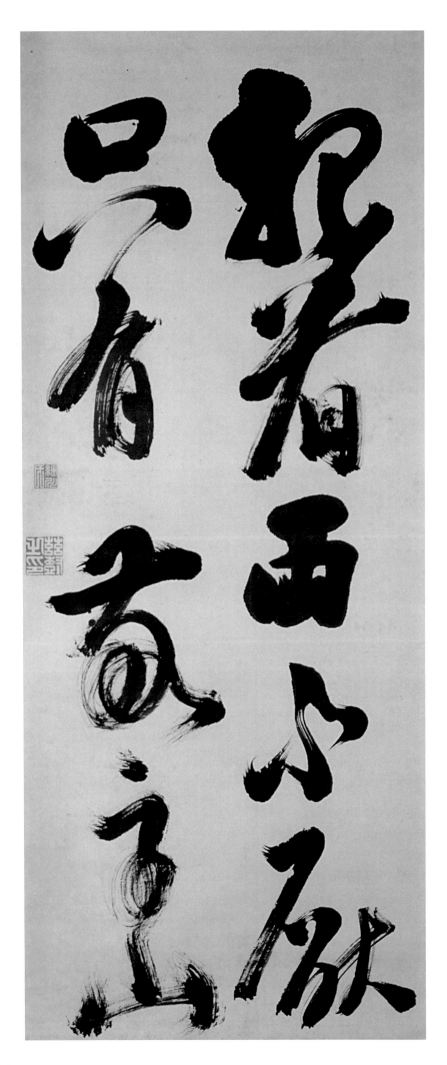

88

細川斉樹筆　五言絶句

CALLIGRAPHY

Chinese poem of five-character phrases
By Hosokawa Naritatsu (1789–1826)
Japan; Edo period (1615–1868)
18th–19th century
Pair of hanging scrolls; ink on paper
Each: H. 137.0 cm x W. 58.0 cm (image)
H. 231.5 cm x W. 77.5 cm (overall)
Eisei-Bunko Museum, 3569

The Japanese adopted the Chinese writing system
in antiquity; they appreciated Chinese literature and
particularly loved Chinese poetry.

Lord Hosokawa Naritatsu (1789–1826) inscribed
these scrolls with a poem entitled "Sitting Alone
on Jingting Mountain" in two pairs of five-character
phrases. It was written more than a thousand years
before him by the renowned Tang dynasty poet Li
Bai (Li Bo, 701–762).

Flocks of birds fly high and vanish;	衆鳥高飛尽
A single cloud, alone, calmly drifts	弧雲独去間
Never tired of looking at each other—	相看両不厭
Only Jingting Mountain and me.[1]	只有敬亭山

Lord Naritatsu expressed Li Bai's work in bold, powerful curvilinear characters. —YW

1. Adapted from translation by Irving Y. Lo in Wu-chi Liu and
Irving Yuchen Lo, eds., *Sunflower Splendor: Three Thousand Years
of Chinese Poetry* (Bloomington: Indiana University Press, 1974).

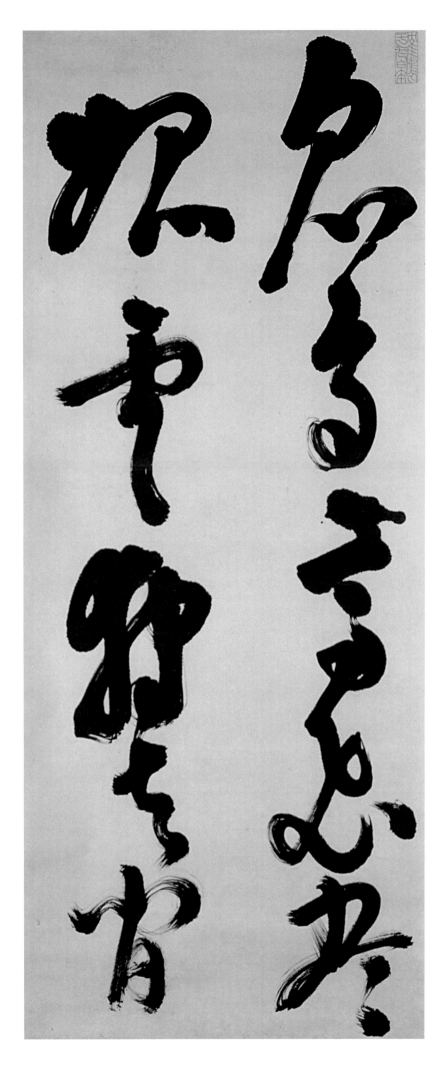

89 ▲

宮本武蔵作　木刀

WOODEN TRAINING SWORDS

By Miyamoto Musashi (1584–1645)
Japan; Edo period (1615–1868), 17th century
Oak
L. 101.8 cm; L. 61.0 cm
Matsui Bunko, M2

The martial artist Miyamoto Musashi founded and perfected the Niten Ichi school of swordsmanship, in which a long and a short sword are used together. These wooden swords are a Niten Ichi practice set attributed to Musashi himself. Carved from oak, both swords have oval-section handles and hexagonal "blades." They are a little thicker than the practice swords used for training by the Niten Ichi school today.

These wooden swords have been handed down in the Matsui family, secretariat elders to the Hosokawa lords of Higo for many generations. Miyamoto Musashi was invited to Kumamoto in 1690 by the lord Hosokawa Tadatoshi; this invitation took place through the offices of Matsui Okinaga, house elder of the Higo domain. Okinaga's adopted son Matsui Yoriyuki (1617–1666; sixth son of Hosokawa Tadaoki, adopted by Okinaga at the age of five) was a pupil of Musashi in the martial arts and supported Musashi in his last years.

After Musashi's death, Yoriyuki hired two of the old warrior's disciples to work for the Matsui family. Subsequently many members of the family studied in the Niten Ichi school, whose practice flourished in the military training grounds of the Matsui clan's castle at Yatsushiro, Higo province (now in Kumamoto prefecture). This is how wooden swords, saddles, and paintings made by Miyamoto Musashi came to be heirlooms of the Matsui family. —AJ

Reference:
Shin Kumamoto Shishi Hensan Iinkai, ed., *Shin Kumamoto shishi tsūshi hen*, 3 (Kumamoto: Kumamoto shi, 2001).

90 ▶

寺尾勝延書写　宮本武蔵　五輪書

THE BOOK OF FIVE RINGS (GORIN NO SHO)

By Miyamoto Musashi (1584–1645); transcribed by Terao Katsunobu
Japan; Edo period (1615–1868), 17th century
Set of five handscrolls; ink on paper
(Vol. 1) H. 17.5 cm x W. 1190.2 cm; (vol. 2) H. 17.7 cm x W. 932.8 cm; (vol. 3) H. 17.7 cm x W. 1203.5 cm; (vol. 4) H. 17.8 cm x W. 936.4 cm; (vol. 5) H. 17.7 cm x W. 367.8 cm
Eisei-Bunko Museum, 774

Miyamoto Musashi, also known as Niten, was the most famous swordsman and painter of his day. He won renown by developing a style of fencing using two swords. He was considered a personification of the samurai spirit and the embodiment of the ideal military man.

Many facts of Musashi's life are obscure, but he is thought to have been born in either Mimasaka (now a part of Okayama prefecture) or Harima (now Hyogo prefecture). Like many other samurai whose lords had fought and died on the losing side in the Battle of Sekigahara in 1600, Musashi became a masterless samurai (*rōnin*). While he lived as a wandering samurai he engaged in duels when he was challenged and is said to have fought sixty-eight times without ever being vanquished. His last duel was fought against Sasaki Kojirō in 1612 on Ganryū Island.

In 1640, Musashi was offered the position of sword instructor by Hosokawa Tadatoshi (1586–1641), the lord of the Higo (Kumamoto) domain, and he traveled to Higo to accept the position. There Musashi was provided a salary in the form of rice, and he spent his last years in relative peace.

The Book of Five Rings (*Gorin no sho*) synthesizes Musashi's swordsmanship teachings. He is said to have written it in a mountain cave (Reigendō) in 1643. On his deathbed, Musashi gave the book to his trusted disciple Terao Katsunobu. The original of the book was lost, but Katsunobu's copy has survived in the Hosokawa family. —YW

Contents:

Volume one: "Scroll of Earth" (*Chi no maki*), the basics of Niten-style swordsmanship.

Volume two: "Scroll of Water" (*Mizu no maki*), a detailed discussion of swords.

Volume three: "Scroll of Fire" (*Hi no maki*), swordsmanship in general and war fittings.

Volume four: "Scroll of Wind" (*Kae no maki*), more on swordsmanship in general and war fittings.

Volume five: "Scroll of Sky" (*Sora no maki*), conclusion on the goals of swordsmanship.

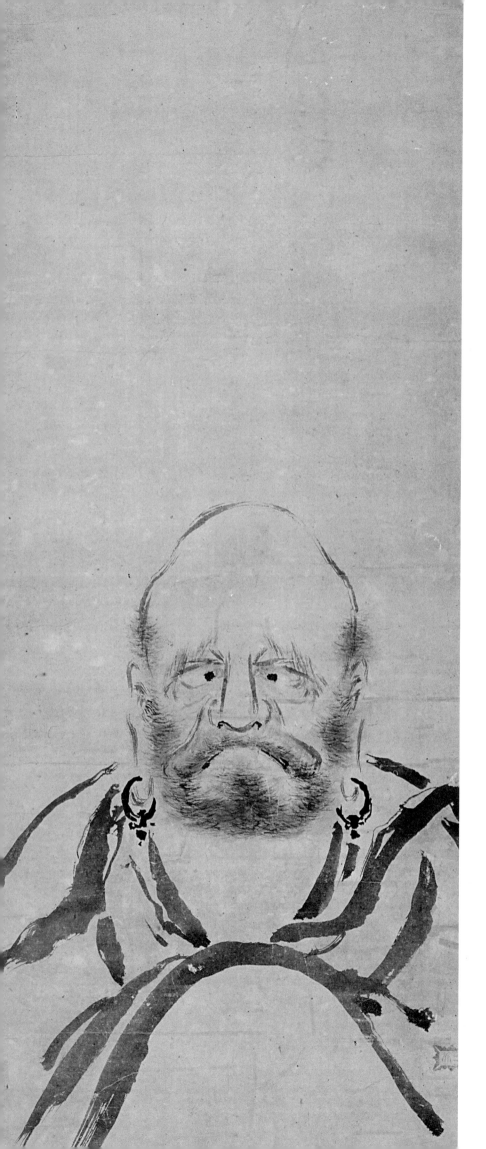

91

宮本武蔵筆　正面達磨図

BODHIDHARMA

By Miyamoto Musashi (1584–1645)
Japan; Edo period (1615–1868)
17th century
Hanging scroll; ink on paper
H. 91.4 cm x W. 38.6 cm (image)
H. 180 cm x W. 56.2 cm (overall)
Eisei-Bunko Museum, 775

Miyamoto Musashi painted Bodhidharma—
the first patriarch of Zen Buddhism—with
his eyes crossed, signifying intense meditation. His hair and beard are rendered in
repeated strokes of dark gray; his robe, in
rough, thick lines of black ink. His down-
turned mouth is another coded indication
of the profundity of his meditation. —YW

92

宮本武蔵筆　面壁達磨図

BODHIDHARMA
MEDITATING IN FRONT
OF A WALL

By Miyamoto Musashi (1584–1645)
Japan; Edo period (1615–1868)
Early 17th century
Hanging scroll; ink on paper
H. 56.7 cm x W. 26.7 cm (image)
H. 173.9 cm x W. 49.5 cm (overall)
Eisei-Bunko Museum, 776

The legendary swordsman Miyamoto Musashi
painted this image of Bodhidharma, the
first patriarch of Zen Buddhism. According
to legend, Bodhidharma sought enlightenment through meditation while seated
facing a wall.

This painting portrays Bodhidharma at
a moment when he has turned away from
the wall to meet the viewer's eye. With
an overgrown moustache and drooping
eyebrows, his exhausted face expresses the
severity of his exercise.

Zen (Chinese: Chan) Buddhism was
transmitted to Japan through China. Unlike
other schools—Pure Land Buddhism, for
example, which taught trust in the Buddha
Amida (Sanskrit: Amitābha), a supernatural
being who could alleviate human suffering—
Zen taught self-reliance as the essential
means by which to attain enlightenment.
This aspect of Zen appealed particularly to
the warrior class: as professional fighters,
they could rely on no one but themselves.
—YW

'93

宮本武蔵筆　野馬図

WILD HORSE

By Miyamoto Musashi (1584–1645)

Japan; Edo period (1615–1868), 17th century

Hanging scroll; ink on paper

H. 46.4 cm x W. 25 cm (image)

H. 146.3 cm x W. 45.5 cm (overall)

Matsui Bunko, M1

Miyamoto Musashi's painting of a wild horse—seen from the left and rear, as if the animal were about to run away—is remarkable for its economy of brushwork. Quickly captured in ink, the eye, hooves, and tail reveal the painter's superb ability to convey, with no more than a suggestion, both the horse's physical essence and its untamed spirit.

The horse was an important part of samurai armament; well-formed, energetic, and high-spirited horses were much sought after among members of the warrior class. —YW

Detail

94

重要文化財

伝宮本武蔵筆　芦雁図屏風

IMPORTANT CULTURAL PROPERTY

WILD GEESE AND REEDS

Attributed to Miyamoto Musashi (1584–1645)

Japan; Edo period (1615–1868), 1640–1645

Pair of six-panel folding screens; ink on paper

H. 155.5. W. 361.5 cm (each)

Eisei-Bunko Museum, 1738

Miyamoto Musashi, the greatest swordsman of his day, served as sword instructor to the Hosokawa family. He was a renowned painter as well as a famous samurai. This pair of screens—said to have been commissioned by Hosokawa Tadatoshi (1586–1641), the third-generation lord of the Hosokawa daimyo family—suggest that Musashi's art was influenced by Kaihō Yūshō's late-sixteenth-century sliding-door panels at Reitōin

and Zenkyoan, subtemples of Kenninji in Kyoto. Kaihō Yūshō (1533–1615) was an earlier warrior-turned-painter.

The screen at right depicts a group of dark-feathered geese gathering to rest or to feed; in the left-hand screen white geese are already at rest on the ground. Executed decisively, the scenes are filled with energy and movement, evoking Musashi's adroit swordmanship. —YW

95

白隠慧鶴筆　達磨図

BODHIDHARMA
By Hakuin Ekaku (1686–1769)
Japan; Edo period (1615–1868), 1767
Hanging scroll; ink on paper
H. 46.8 cm x W. 55.6 cm (image)
H. 227.9 cm x W. 78.7 cm (overall)
Eisei-Bunko Museum, 98

直指人心
見性成仏

Pointing directly at the human heart,
See your own self to attain Buddhahood.[1]

The great Zen monk Hakuin presents here a powerful image of Bodhidharma, first patriarch of the Zen school of Buddhism. According to legend, the Indian Bodhidharma was seriously committed to attaining enlightenment and brought the foundations of Zen from India into China. His teachings were then transmitted through China to Japan, where they profoundly influenced Buddhist thought. With their emphasis on self-reliance, Bodhidharma's teachings appealed especially to members of the warrior class.

The artist is the influential Zen teacher Hakuin Ekaku (1685–1769), a native of Hara, Suruga province (now eastern Shizuoka prefecture). At the age of fifteen he entered the Zen temple Shōinji, which remained his base throughout his long life of traveling and teaching. He moved on to a series of temples before returning to Shōinji, and then founded the temple Ryūtakuji in Mishima in 1761. Hakuin is considered one of the most important Zen masters of the Edo period.

In this painting, Hakuin depicts the Bodhidharma as a fiercely spiritual man with penetrating eyes that see everything before him and beyond. The representation speaks to the monk's precept that the true understanding of Buddhism, and the way to attain enlightenment, come not through words but through "pointing directly at the human heart and mind."

Bodhidharma's exotic facial features reflect the Japanese conception of people from India. Hakuin established a formula in his Bodhidharma portraits—large face; roughly drawn hair, eyebrows, and beard—and followed it with little variation; thus the group came to be known as "Hakuin's Hundred Bodhidharma Portraits." Most striking are the teacher's eyes, which tell the viewer: "See yourself to attain Buddhahood."

Besides the Bodhidharma portraits, Hakuin created an enormous number of paintings and works of calligraphy in a variety of subjects; he used them in his teaching.

The inscription to the left of the figure's forehead reads: "Under a *sal* tree, a man of eighty-three years, Hakuin, brushed this painting." —YW

1. Hakuin extracted this passage from *Chuanxin fayao* (J: *Denshin hōyō*), by Huangbo Xiyun (d. 850).

96

白隠慧鶴筆　円相図

ENSŌ, BUDDHIST CIRCLE OF ENLIGHTENMENT

By Hakuin Ekaku (1686–1769)

Japan; Edo period (1615–1868), 18th century

Hanging scroll; ink on paper

H. 46.8 cm x W. 55.6 cm (image); H. 151.8 cm x W. 59.5 cm (overall)

Eisei-Bunko Museum, 105

遠州浜松よひ茶の出所
むすめやりたやいよ茶をつミに

*Hamamatsu in Tōtōmi province produces
good tea,
[Parents] would wish to send their daughters
there to harvest tea leaves.*

This single-stroke circle (*ensō*) symbolizes
enlightenment; in a way, it is a picture of
Zen thought; but the ensō can be interpreted
in many ways. Suggesting that each person
embodies the universe, it can also represent
a state of mind or express absolute truth.
It signifies everything and/or nothing; it
includes and/or excludes. To suddenly comprehend these concepts may trigger a sudden
moment of enlightenment.

The ensō may look easy, but it is difficult
to execute. Not all Zen painters or callig-
raphers produced good ensō. In this work,
Hakuin produced an excellent one. He
began at the lower left, gradually pressing
the brush harder, then moved it quickly up
and back and down while pressing still harder—
and lifted it to close the circle where it began.
The varying speed of the hand and pressure
of the brush create an expressive circle. Among
Hakuin's numerous Zen artworks, this is
the only ensō he is known to have made.

The inscription does not refer to any Zen
teaching; its words come from a popular
folk song. —YW

97

白隠慧鶴筆　隻手布袋

BUDAI'S ONE HAND CLAPPING

By Hakuin Ekaku (1686–1769)

Japan; Edo period (1615–1868)

Hanging scroll; ink on paper

H. 92.7 cm x W. 29.2 cm (image); H. 186.3 cm x W. 46.6 cm (overall)

Eisei-Bunko Museum, 51

若いものともや何を云うてもな
隻手の音を聞かねば
皆たわ事の皮だぞよ
さる所の八十二才　のおやぢ

All you young people
No matter what you say, everything is superficial
Unless you hear the sound of one hand clapping.
—A man of eighty-two years who lives in a certain place

Borrowing the figure of the humorous deity Budai (Japanese: Hotei), Hakuin presents a powerful reference to his famous Zen koan, "What is the sound of one hand clapping?" Below the rapidly written inscription, the plump, dome-headed Budai squats—right hand raised, palm outward—on a big bag. Common sense tells us that Hakuin's chosen koan is nonsensical: one hand by itself cannot make a clapping sound. Nor, of course, can anyone hear soundless sound; that is the key to the paradox.

Enigmatic and illogical, koans were used in Zen teachings as instruments for training monks to despair of placing an ultimate dependence upon reason, and thus forcing them into sudden, intuitive moments of enlightenment.

In the Zen perspective, it is the most humbling experience for a man to try to listen to the soundless sound, which eventually leads him from the realm of common sense to a transcendental state of complete freedom.

The historical Budai was an eccentric but genial monk who lived during the Latter Liang Dynasty (907–922) and who was said to have wandered in the region of Ningbo, living on alms. Stories of Budai spread to Japan, where he came to be considered something of a holy fool; a popular folk deity and one of the Seven Gods of Good Luck, he is associated with earthly abundance. —YW

98

仙厓義梵筆　達磨図

BODHIDHARMA

By Sengai Gibon (1750–1837)

Japan; Edo period (1615–1868)

Hanging scroll; ink on paper

H. 97.1 cm x W. 27.8 cm (image); H. 165.5 cm x W. 41.2 cm (overall)

Eisei-Bunko Museum, 521

学者の学者くさきハ
猶可忍
仏の仏くさきハ
不可忍

One can endure a scholar who looks and behaves like a scholar,
But one cannot endure a Buddha who looks and behaves like a Buddha.

As if to illustrate his antipathy—expressed in this painting's inscription—to a Buddha who resembles the Buddha, Sengai painted a remarkably odd and comically ugly image of Bodhidharma, who transmitted Zen (Chinese: Chan) Buddhism from India to China. He portrays this legendary monk with a pointed head, a squared nose, and mischievous eyes. His month is hidden under an overgrown moustache.

Like Hakuin before him (see cat. nos. 95–97), Sengai was a prominent Zen monk who traveled far beyond the prestigious temples of Kyoto and Kamakura. Born in the mountainous Mino province (present-day Gifu prefecture), he received Zen training in Yokohama. He then moved to Hakata, on the southwestern island of Kyushu, where he became the 123rd abbot of Shōfukuji temple. It was during his last twenty years, while he was living as a layman near that temple, that Sengai produced most of his paintings. His works are characterized by quick, often wild strokes, and robust humor.
—YW

99

仙厓義梵筆　虎図

TIGER

By Sengai Gibon (1750–1837)

Japan; Edo period (1615–1868)

Hanging scroll; ink on paper

H. 39.7 cm x W. 52.2 cm (image)

H. 131.4 cm x W. 69 cm (overall)

Eisei-Bunko Museum, 606

猫か虎か当てて見ろ
Guess if this is a cat or a tiger.

Sengai used a limber, wobbly line to draw this catlike animal. Its stance is ambiguously threatening, its eyes are wide, and its long tail curves back over its head.

This painting needs no explanation. Whether cat or tiger, the creature seems to be trying to look fierce; but the effort is insufficient. Despite its tigerish posturing, it still looks like a pussycat. —YW

100

仙厓義梵筆　武渓老師安居図

THE ZEN PRIEST BUKEI
IN RETREAT

By Sengai Gibon (1750–1837)
Japan; Edo period (1615–1868), 1822
Hanging scroll; ink on paper
H. 130.4 cm x W. 51.0 cm (image)
H. 228.3 cm x W. 72.3 cm (overall)
Eisei-Bunko Museum, 511

子育龍象
絶無慈心
正傍喪身失命
噫武渓多毒淫

When Master Bukei taught his Zen students,
Who had determination and excellent potential,
He did not have compassion for them at all.
Many of them nearly lost their minds and ruined their lives.
Oh, Master Bukei, you had a lot of poison.

In this relatively complex composition, Sengai presents a scene of his Zen master in retirement. The artist refers to this phase of the master's life as *angyo* or *ango* (lit., "to dwell in peace"), a term that can refer to peaceful living or to an extended Buddhist training session in a rural location—essentially a retreat from the secular world.

Sengai took up training in Zen when he was nineteen years old under the master Gessen Zenne (1702–1781), who was later renamed Bukei. A priest of the Rinzai school, Bukei was known for his austere, uncompromising approach to training—Sengai's inscription may not be too much exaggerated in its woeful description of his teacher's methods. But in painting his teacher's portrait, when he himself was seventy-three years old, Sengai depicts his mentor with great affection.

A narrow path runs from the bottom left of this painting, turning aside at a small hut with a figure inside, and then ascending through paddy fields to another hut. A black-robed figure sits within the hut; this must be Bukei. To the left of the inscription quoted above, Sengai added: "I made this painting in response to a request for a scene of Bukei in ango retreat" and dated the piece the sixteenth day of the seventh month, 1822. In the Rinzai Zen school, ango began on the sixteenth day of the fourth month and ended on the fifteenth day of the seventh month. Sengai's date of execution was not chosen randomly. —YW

101

伝細川忠興作　茄子形提重

SAKE BOTTLE AND FOOD BOX SET (SAGEJŪ)

in the shape of an eggplant

Attributed to Hosokawa Sansai (aka Tadaoki, 1563–1646)

Japan; Edo period (1615–1868), 17th century

Lacquered wood

H. 25.5 cm x W. 17.5 cm x D. 13.8 cm

Eisei-Bunko Museum, 6535

This ingeniously conceived picnic set combines an eggplant-shaped sake flask, a food container, and a sake cup in the shape of an eggplant leaf, attached to the bottle stopper.

Warriors were expected to be highly cultured men, but the ability to create such a complex and charmingly proportioned piece as this was very unusual. It would have required great patience and talent—which appear to have come naturally to the brilliant warrior Hosokawa Sansai. —YW

103 ◄

黒塗九曜紋入壺椀

DEEP BOWL

with nine-planet family crest

Japan; Edo period (1615–1868)

18th century

Lacquered wood with painted lacquer decoration

H. 7.0 cm x Diam. 10.0 cm

Eisei-Bunko Museum, 6536

104 ▼

黒塗九曜紋入平椀

SHALLOW BOWL

with nine-planet family crest

Japan; Edo period (1615–1868)

18th century

Lacquered wood with painted lacquer decoration

H. 5.4 cm x D. 12.3 cm

Eisei-Bunko Museum, 6536

The set includes deep and shallow bowls suitable for a variety of foods. The bowls are decorated with the nine-planet Hosokawa family crest in red. —YW

102 ◄

黒塗九曜紋入椀　二対

伝細川忠興所用

COVERED BOWLS

with nine-planet family crest, two pairs

Said to have been owned by

Hosokawa Tadaoki

(aka Sansai, 1563–1646)

Japan; Edo period (1615–1868)

16th century

Lacquered wood with painted lacquer decoration

H. 12.0 cm x Diam. 14.0

H. 6.8 cm x Diam. 13.5 cm

Eisei-Bunko Museum, 6536

These two pairs of covered bowls were rediscovered in the twentieth century together with five small dishes (cat no. 105) in another family's collection. They are rare objects associated with Lady Hosokawa Gracia (1563–1600), the wife of Hosokawa Tadaoki, who died prematurely in order to avoid being taken hostage at Osaka Castle in 1600.

These bowls were given by Gracia to her lady-in-waiting upon her marriage to a samurai named Hirata, from what is now Tottori prefecture. They are decorated with the Hosokawa family crest, which means that they were made after Gracia married Hosokawa Tadaoki in 1578.

The two pairs of bowls would have been used to hold individual portions of food at a meal. —YW

105 ▲

唐花漆絵皿　五客　伝細川忠興所用

DISHES WITH FLORAL ROUNDELS

Set of five

Said to have been owned by Hosokawa Tadaoki (aka Sansai, 1563–1646)

Japan; Edo period (1615–1868), 16th century

Lacquered wood with painted lacquer decoration

H. 3.8 cm x Diam. 19.4 cm

Eisei-Bunko Museum, 6539

106 ▲

木箸　二膳　伝細川忠興所用

CHOPSTICKS

Two pairs

Said to have been owned by Hosokawa Tadaoki (aka Sansai, 1563–1646)

Japan; Edo period (1615–1868)

17th century

Wood

L. 35.7 cm, L. 35.1 cm

Eisei-Bunko Museum, 6544

There are few extant objects associated with Gracia (1563–1600), wife of Tadaoki, who died young when captured at Osaka Castle. These small dishes are among them.

The dishes were discovered in the twentieth century, when the Hosokawa household contacted descendents of the Hirata family, into which one of Hosokawa Gracia's ladies-in-waiting had married centuries before. The wooden box containing this set tells that it was given by Gracia to her lady-in-waiting when she married Hirata.

Executed in wood painted with lacquer, the dishes' small size suggests that they were used for sweets to be served with tea. Two pairs of covered bowls from Gracia (cat no. 102) were also found in the same family collection. —YW

Detail of leaf-shaped dish

107 ▼
木の葉形錫皿　五客
LEAF-SHAPED DISHES
Set of five
Japan; Edo period (1868–1912), 18th century
Pewter
L. 23.6 cm x W. 10.5 cm (each)
Eisei-Bunko Museum, 6542

These pewter dishes are shaped like curled oak leaves. In Japanese custom, serving pieces and tableware come in pairs or in sets of five, ten, twenty, or more. —YW

108
花鳥図沈金菱形重箱
LOZENGE-SHAPED TIERED FOOD BOX (JŪBAKO)
with design of birds and flowers
Japan; Edo period (1615–1868), early 17th century
Lacquered wood with incised and gold inlaid decoration
H. 17.2 cm x W. 26.2 cm x D. 14.5 cm
Eisei-Bunko Museum, 6406

This four-layered box of red lacquer is unusually ornate. Every surface, including the top, is decorated with a window-like cartouche filled in with black lacquer and embellished with the technique of *chinkin*, in which the lacquered surface is incised and then filled in with gold.

The images shown in the windows have mostly naturalistic or scenic themes and include birds, flowers, animals, insects, clouds, fish, and pavilion-dotted landscapes and seascapes. —YW

109
桜折枝柴蒔絵行厨
PICNIC SET (KŌCHŪ)
with design of cherry blossoms and bundled branches
Japan; Edo period (1615–1868)
19th century
Lacquered wood with sprinkled metallic powder (*makie*) decoration; incised silver
H. 18.0 cm x W. 36.0 cm x D. 36.0 cm
Eisei-Bunko Museum, 2149

This style of picnic set became popular in the Momoyama period (1573–1615). Its compact form neatly holds tiered boxes for food and sake cups on one side and plates and a sake flask on the other. The gourd-shaped silver sake bottle is incised with cherry sprays and bundled branches. Identical motifs are repeated on the sides of the lacquered wood food boxes and on the carrying case, this time using the technique of *makie*— in which metallic dust is sprinkled onto wet lacquer. The case's top is affixed with a bronze handle for portability. —YW

110

竹椿蒔絵重箱

TIERED FOOD BOX (JŪBAKO)

with design of bamboo and camellia

Japan; Edo period (1615–1868), end of 18th century–beginning of 19th century

Lacquered wood with sprinkled metallic powder (*makie*) decoration

H. 47.3 cm x W. 27.2 cm x D. 28.9 cm

Eisei-Bunko Museum, 6498

This tiered food box is decorated with images of bamboo and camellia, executed in the combined techniques of *makie* (powders of gold and other metals sprinkled into wet lacquer to create motifs) and *takamakie* (relief *makie*).

The powerful vertical bamboo design draws the eyes upward, while the other decorative elements disperse the vertical focus, making a delicate, diffuse secondary pattern. —YW

111

叢梨地違鷹羽紋散食籠

FOOD CONTAINER (JIKIRŌ)
with scattered falcon feather crests
Japan; Edo period (1615–1868), 19th century
Lacquered wood with sprinkled metallic powder (*makie*) decoration
H. 22.5 cm x Diam. 33.0 cm
Eisei-Bunko Museum, 7367

Scattered falcon feather crests over a mottled pearskin (*muranashigi*)
background adorn this lidded container. The pearskin (*nashiji*) effect
was made by sprinkling metallic dust or flakes, usually gold, onto
wet lacquer, which then dries to create a smooth and elegantly
embellished surface.

This container was used to hold cooked rice. —YW

113 ◄

芒菊桐蒔絵碁筒、碁盤
GO GAME BOARD AND GO STONE CONTAINERS
with design of eulalia, chrysanthemums, and paulownia
Japan; Momoyama period
(1573–1615), 16th century
Wood (board); lacquered wood with sprinkled metallic powder (*makie*) decoration (containers); stone (playing pieces)
H. 21.5 cm x W. 44.1 cm x D. 44.6 cm
Eisei-Bunko Museum, 1581 or 1253?

112 ◄

桐九曜紋散蒔絵香道具
INCENSE GAME BOX AND IMPLEMENTS
with design of scattered nine-planet family crests
Japan; Edo period (1615–1868)
18th century
Lacquered wood with sprinkled metallic powder (*makie*) decoration, silver, bronze, mica
H. 13.2 cm x W. 24.0 cm x D. 16.0 cm
Eisei-Bunko Museum, 2161

Participants in *kōdō* ("Way of Incense"), the incense game, enjoy the perfume of a burning chip of scented wood or a combination of wood and other materials. The appreciation of fragrance originated in Buddhist ceremonies; transmitted to Japan in the sixth century and thereafter, this aesthetic pursuit became popular in aristocratic social occasions, outside of any religious context.

Simply burning a single aromatic wood could be enjoyed in a solitary or social setting. But in a popular pastime, guests would bring their own incense (mixtures of pulverized aromatic woods and animal scents, kneaded with honey and other substances)

and the group decided which it liked best. Eventually people created rules and procedures, as with the tea ceremony and flower arrangement. Special precautions were required: participants were not to use scents in their hair or clothes, and they refrained from eating any strongly flavored or aromatic food for a day before the gathering.

In the Edo period, an incense game set was included in a bridal dowry. This exquisite set, made for a Hokosawa family member and decorated with the family's nine-planet crest, includes metal "fire incense tools," an incense box, braziers, and a tray of mica plates called *ginban* ("silver plates"). —YW

Sen Rikyū (1522–1591), the great tea master, is said to have owned this Go set.[1] The board is made of wood and is about 9 cm thick. The set includes 159 white stones and 158 black stones of natural shape, instead of being formed artificially. These playing pieces are kept in two lacquered containers decorated with paulownia, chrysanthemums, and eulalia in the technique of *makie*—in which fine gold and metallic dust are carefully sprinkled into wet lacquer. This particular type of work, with its gold motifs on a black background, is known as Kōdaiji *makie* (named for a temple in Kyoto for which many examples were commissioned) and is typical of highest-quality Momoyama period lacquerware.

Thought to have originated in ancient China or India, the game of Go arrived in Japan during the Asuka period (552–645). It was popular in both court and temple circles, and eventually was embraced by the warrior class. The stone containers were often lacquered and exquisitely decorated with makie designs. —YW

1. Kumamoto Kenritsu Bijutsukan, ed., *Eisei Bunko no shitsu kōgei.* (Kumamoto: Kumamoto Kenritsu Bijutsukan, 1983), cat. no. 49.

114

交趾獅子香炉

INCENSE BURNER WITH LION

Cochin type

China; Ming dynasty (1368–1664), 17th century

Earthenware with green glaze, appliqué, and impressed decoration

H. 14.2 cm x Diam. 9.8 cm

Eisei-Bunko Museum, 2042

Bears' heads appear in high relief above this stout cylindrical incense burner's three short legs. Two opposed S-shaped lugs serve as handles. Three registers of impressed decoration circle the surface. The broad central register is of a geometric pattern, with a narrow band of square spirals at the top and another of flower heads at the bottom. The eye-catching sculptural lid sits tightly inside the burner's mouth; two tiers of round daises decorate its flat surface. An open-mouthed Chinese lion squats at the top and serves as the knob for the lid, which is perforated to emit incense. A shiny green glaze coats the burner all over, pooling in dark tones at indented areas, such as the three decorative registers' demarcation lines. The pooling enhances the sharp profile of the vessel, whose design is inspired by similar metalware forms such as the *lian* containers of the Han dynasty (206 BCE–220 CE).

The Chinese had purified clothes and rooms with incense since the Han period, considering the action a necessary aspect of good manners among the elite class. Incense burning, in both secular and religious uses, induced a calm mind and a pleasurable ambience. Consequently, burners of various materials and in numerous forms found a regular place throughout the history of Chinese decorative art. Auspicious symbols are often incorporated into their designs; among the most common are those related to Taoism or Buddhism, such as Penglai Island (legendarily inhabited by the Taoist immortals) and the Chinese lion seen on this fine example.

When Buddhism was introduced to Han China, the Buddhist lion, protector of dharma, came along. Over the time it became as well the regal guardian of Chinese imperial palaces, temples, and government offices. Incorporating characteristics of both lion and dog, the Chinese lion is a staple motif in Chinese decorative art and daily life. The Chinese believed that the ferocity of the lion—as well as of other beasts, such as the bears on this burner—would help expel evil spirits. To burn incense in this vessel, then, was to evoke such protection against evil with symbolic potency.

In Japan this incense burner was also used to cleanse rooms; the permeating aroma of the burning incense would help create a tranquil environment.

The Japanese used two attributive terms for this type of green-glazed low-fired earthenware. One is "Dutch ware," because those wares were brought into Japan by Dutch traders, the only Western merchants permitted to trade with Japan during the seventeenth century. Another is "Cochin (Japanese: Kōchi) ware," as it was thought to be made in that region. The term Cochin is derived from the Chinese *Jiaozhi,* an ancient name for a broad area including part of southwestern China and northern Vietnam. A recent study has shown, however, that this ware was probably made in China's Fujian province, on the east coast.[1] —JC

1. The study concluded by examining an incense box of the same style unearthed from the Tuanhang kiln in Fujian province. See Fukuyama Bijutsukan, ed., *Daimyō cha no meihō* (Hiroshima: Fukuyama Bijutsukan, 2005), 111.

115

油滴天目茶碗

TEABOWL

Yūteki Tenmoku type

Cizhou ware

China; Southern Song dynasty (1127–1279), 12th–13th century

Stoneware with black glaze and iridescent oil spot markings

H. 6.9 cm x Diam. 18.8 cm (mouth); Diam. 5.7 cm (foot)

Eisei-Bunko Museum, 1471

Shaped like a trumpet's mouth, this teabowl has slanting walls that rest on a small, shallow ring-foot and flare dramatically up to an everted lip. It is covered inside and out in black glaze with tiny, silvery oil spots; the glaze stops short above the foot. Halfway down from the rim, on the interior, five circular clusters of oil spots in pale russet are placed at even intervals. The unglazed foot area reveals that beneath the black glaze is a white body of fine clay, with an iron-rich slip coating fired to a deep purplish brown.

Chinese black-glazed teabowls are known in Japan as *tenmoku,* after the Japanese pronunciation for the mountain Tianmu in China's Zhejiang province, where Japanese monks went to study Zen Buddhism in and after the twelfth century. Black teabowls were part of the paraphernalia of Zen practice in China; monks also brought them back to Japan. Most of those teabowls were produced at the Jian kilns in Fujian province of southeast China, which reached their production zenith by specializing in dark-

glazed wares. Their trademark product is the teabowl in two typical forms; one is seen here and the other in cat. no. 116. These teabowls became synonymous with the Jian ware and were widely copied elsewhere.

While crafted in the Jian ware style, this large teabowl was made in a northern kiln: its clay and glaze character are different. Two striking features attest to the potter's consummate skill. One is the rare large size with a bold, flaring mouth that creates a sense of expansion in the bowl form. Another is the oil spot (Japanese: yūteki) glaze, deep black with tiny silvery flecks, so called because those silver speckles sparkle like drops of oil on water. A layer of high-iron slip is applied beneath the glaze to achieve this effect. During the high firing (1300°C), the bubbling glaze carries concentrated iron to the surface, where it crystallizes into varied markings and colors. Often two or more crystalline-iron colors can be found on the same piece—as in this example, with russet, silver, and blue oil spot markings.

The success of an oil spot glaze depends on both the potter's deliberate calculation and the kiln's capricious transformation.

The Chinese began drinking tea as a beverage (rather than for medicinal effects) in the first century BCE. Various ways of ingesting tea have been practiced through out its history; consequently, many types of tea utensils have been devised. By the eleventh century CE, the drinking of powdered tea had attained its highest sophistication in China (see details in the entry for cat. no. 116), and the tradition still continues in the Japanese Way of Tea (*chanoyu*). Not only was the drink to be meticulously prepared, but also particular teabowls were to be used. To meet the standards of the time, the finest tea must produce a consistent white froth, and the black teabowl was the best for creating visual contrast. The teabowl shown here would be an ideal choice for this highly developed tradition. —JC

116

黄天目茶碗

TEABOWL

Ki Tenmoku type

Jian ware

China; Southern Song dynasty (1127–1279) or Yuan dynasty (1279–1368), 13th–14th century

Stoneware with black glaze and yellow banded decoration

H. 6.7 cm x Diam. 12.2 cm (mouth); Diam. 4.4 cm (foot)

Eisei-Bunko Museum, 2003

This teabowl has a funnel shape atop a small, shallow ring-foot; its walls rise gradually about halfway through the form, then turn in steeply toward the mouth to form a nearly vertical rim. A silver band caps the mouth lip. Slightly coarse in texture and fired a purplish brown, the body clay is covered with a dark brown glaze over a yellow slip coating, which is revealed in bands on the bowl's unglazed lower portion and around its mouth.

The form and the potting are typical of ware from the Jian kilns, which achieved its greatest fame during the Song dynasty. This teabowl and the one seen in cat. no. 115 are the two classic forms of Jian ware made in Fujian province; these designs were much copied by major kiln centers in both southern and northern China. Their broad success

had deep roots in the tea culture of the period. The Song people enjoyed a particular white-foamed tea, which is prepared by vigorously pouring boiled water into finely ground tea powder, then whipping it to a fine consistency. The deep, rather straight-walled form of this teabowl was considered more agreeable for whipping, and the black glaze showed the white froth to the best visual effect.

Refined appreciation of tea in China was taken further in the game *dou cha* (tea contest). Fashionable in Chinese high society, the game considered many qualities of a good tea. Finely textured white foam was best, while the worst tea was characterized by an early appearance of the water ring mark inside the bowl. This ring was caused by the separa-tion of tea powder from water as the

mixture cooled. The Jian teabowl's thick wall held the heat longer—much longer when the bowl was heated before use.

Highly revered in Japan, Jian teabowls have been known by perhaps a dozen specific Japanese terms, based on their kaleidoscopic variations of crystalline markings in the black glaze, since the fourteenth century. This example is traditionally categorized as the *ki tenmoku* (yellow tenmoku) type because of the yellow tone in the lower part of the bowl and around its mouth.[1] The additional embellishment of a silver metal band on the rim highlighted the status of both the tea-bowl and its owner. —JC

1. This bowl is stored inside two boxes. The characters *ki tenmoku* are written in ink on each of the box covers.

117

堆黒屈輪天目台

TEABOWL STAND

with pommel scrolls

China; Ming dynasty (1368–1644), 15th–16th century

Carved black lacquer with red lacquer layers

H. 9.2 cm x Diam. 15.7; Diam. 9.3 cm (mouth)

Eisei-Bunko Museum, 2140

Designed to hold a teabowl such as cat. no. 115 or 116, this lacquer stand carries a carved decoration of pommel scrolls all over the external surface; the interior is lacquered in plain black. Through beveled cutting, the thick black exterior lacquer reveals evenly spaced thin layers of red lacquer beneath. The surface is polished to a smooth sheen.

The style of carving seen on this stand appeared first in the twelfth century. Known as *tixi* in China (*guri* in Japan), it usually incorporates marbled lacquer, beveled cutting, and a design involving a single motif of pommel scrolls. The marbled lacquer is formed by applying layer upon layer of lacquer in thin films, alternating the desired colors—black and red, in this case. To build up the thickness of lacquer coating on this teabowl stand required dozens of applications, and each layer took several days to harden before the next application. The beveled cutting technique is both deep and of a characteristic angle, resulting in rather broad grooves that outline the motifs in bold strokes and add a relief-like depth to the design; further, this cutting angle reveals the colored bands of marbled lacquer to the best effect. The pommel scroll motif, a trefoil pattern with pleasing enclosed curves, is named after the shape of the ring-pommel of early Chinese swords. It is a classic motif in Chinese carved artworks; over the time many subtle variations in lines and sculptural forms of this deceptively simple pattern announced the carver's ability and adroitness. This teabowl stand exemplifies the enormous effort and artistic ingenuity lavished on Chinese carved lacquer wares.

The teabowl stand was introduced in China in the fourth century or earlier. This fifteenth-or sixteenth-century example is in the Song dynasty (960–1279) style, which featured a small, bowl-like holder on a wide flange supported by a high stem. When a teabowl sits on this type of stand, its lower part cannot be seen. The stand's design may thus explain why many teabowls, especially those made in the Song period, have a precariously tiny foot (see cat. no. 115). Lacquer teabowl stands appear to have been preferred to ceramic stands in Chinese tea-drinking culture, to judge from historical literature and paintings—probably, to at least some extent, because of the lacquer wares' light weight and insulating quality. Artistic carving and the lacquer's buttery texture surely offered aesthetic reasons for the stands to be paired, as they often were, with thickly glazed ceramic bowls of similar surfaces. —JC

118 ▲
朱塗天目台
TEABOWL STAND
Negoro type
Japan; Muromachi period (1392–1573), 16th century
Lacquered wood
H. 6.7 cm x Diam. 15.3 cm; Diam. 8.3 cm (mouth)
Eisei-Bunko Museum, 2103

119 ▼
粉引｜茶碗　銘「大高麗」
TEABOWL
entitled "Ōgōrai" (Great Goryeo)
Kohiki type
Korea; Joseon dynasty (1392–1910),
15th–16th century
Stoneware with white slip
H. 9.5 cm x Diam. 17.8 cm (mouth);
Diam. 6.7 cm (foot)
Eisei-Bunko Museum, 1350

This stand was made to support a narrow-footed black-glazed Chinese teabowl—the type known as *tenmoku* in Japan (see cat. nos. 115, 116)—when presenting tea to an honored guest. Such stands were often valued as artistic works in themselves. Unlike the exquisitely carved lacquer teabowl stands of China, this simple example was made in Japan, perhaps in the area of present-day Wakayama city, a Buddhist center and home to the famous temple of Negoroji. Until

Regent Toyotomi Hideyoshi (1537–1598), wary of the priesthood's temporal power, suppressed Buddhism in Japan, Negoro was famous for specialty lacquer wares typified by a black undercoating finished with red lacquer, which would gradually wear off over time creating a pleasing two-tone effect. This piece may not be from Negoro proper, but it reflects the characteristics of Negoro ware. —YW

Japanese tea lovers had eclectic taste in their selection of tea utensils. Good collections might have included a variety of pieces from China, Southeast Asia, and Korea. This bowl, named Ōgōrai ("Great Goryeo"—named after the Korean dynasty, 918–1392), is one of the most famous tea pieces in the Hosokawa family's collection. It was originally made as a ewer with a spout. The spout was removed and the ewer repurposed as a teabowl. Many years of use have given the patched area an interesting surface pattern.

While the tea practitioners of Japan admired formal, symmetrical ceramics, they also found joy in imperfection, as exemplified in this piece. —YW

120 ▼

三島暦手茶碗

TEABOWL

Mishima koyomide type
Korea; Joseon dynasty (1392–1910),
15th–16th century
Tool-stamped and incised stoneware
with slip inlay
H. 4.5 cm x Diam. 16.1 cm (mouth);
Diam. 5.5 cm (foot)
Eisei-Bunko Museum, 1248

Japanese connoisseurs consider slip-inlaid
Punchong ware—known as Mishima in
Japan—to be one of the representative forms
of Korean ceramics from the early Joseon
dynasty. Mishima teabowls were much
admired by Japanese tea practitioners of
the time.

Applied by brush, the white slip decoration shows vividly against the iron-rich, dark
brown body clay. An ash glaze was applied
to the entire bowl before it was fired, creating a complex surface effect.

The wooden box in which this bowl is
stored is inscribed by renowned tea master
and architect Kobori Enshū (1579–1647).
—YW

121 ▶

雲鶴茶碗

TEABOWL

with design of clouds and cranes
Korea; Joseon dynasty (1392–1910), 16th–17th century
Stoneware with slip inlay
H. 7.0 cm x Diam. 12.2 cm (rim); Diam. 5.7 cm (foot)
Eisei-Bunko Museum, 1196

Japanese tea practitioners fell in love with
all sorts of Korean ceramics—even everyday rice bowls, which they repurposed as teabowls. The design of clouds and cranes
on this bowl was made by carving into the
body of the bowl and laying a white clay
slip into the design.

The crane symbolizes longevity through
its association with Taoist immortals. This
piece is one of several types of imported
bowls called *gohon* (honorable book), which
were ordered from Korea using a design
book. The name came to be applied to any
teabowl with the pink-and-gray spotted
effect visible here.

The ceramic arts of Japan and Korea are
intimately intertwined: major innovations
in ceramic technology often accompanied
Korean potters who came to Japan—volun-
tarily, or as hostages brought back by Japanese
warrior tea masters.

This particular bowl had another famous
owner besides the Hosokawa family—the

Edo period Zen priest and painter Sengai
Gibon (1750–1837). Gibon was the 123rd
head of Shōfukuji, a Zen temple in Fukuoka
city. A tea scoop by Gibon came into the
Hosokawa collection with this tea bowl.

Sengai Gibon is known as a painter of
witty, humorous Zen subjects; three of his
paintings (cat. nos. 98–100) are included
in this publication. Each of these works
might have been used as the scroll in a tea
room alcove and would be likely to stimulate
animated discussion during the gathering.
How interesting to imagine a tea gathering, hosted by a member of the Hosokawa
family, in which this teabowl and one of
Gibon's scrolls helped guests to remember
and honor that engaging Zen artist. —DC

122 ▶

蕎麦茶碗

TEABOWL

Sobade type

Korea; Joseon dynasty (1392–1910)

16th century

Glazed stoneware

H. 6.8 cm x Diam. 16.1 cm (mouth);

Diam. 5.7 cm (foot)

Eisei-Bunko Museum, 2008

A blue-gray ash glaze lightly coats this thin-walled bowl. Korean bowls in this style were highly valued by Japanese tea practitioners, who called them *sobade* (soba type); perhaps the speckled grayish glaze reminded the users of soba noodles. The production date is estimated to be around the middle of the Joseon dynasty of Korea. Bowls like this were imported into Japan toward the end of the Muromachi period (1336–1573). —YW

123 ▲

安南染付寿字茶碗

TEABOWL

with character for "longevity"
Annan type
Vietnam; 17th century
Stoneware with underglaze blue
H. 6.8 cm x Diam. 13.1 cm (mouth); Diam. 6.2 cm (foot)
Eisei-Bunko Museum, 1250

An illustrated album belonging to the Hosokawa family indicates that this blue-and-white Vietnamese tea bowl had become part of the family collection by the eighteenth century.[1] Although this type of stoneware, with cobalt designs under a clear glaze, had been produced in northern Vietnam since the fourteenth century, it is not noted in Japanese inventories of heirloom ceramics before the 1590s,[2] when burgeoning international trade led to the importation of a wider variety of objects from Southeast Asia. At the same time, tea practice was gaining popularity with the merchant classes and a new mode of tea gathering developed. In this type of tea practice, called "grass hut tea" after the simple setting where it was practiced, "imperfect" utensils were appreciated for their rusticity. Antique Chinese ceramics (*karamono*) were intentionally grouped with less refined but subtly striking newer pieces, of either East Asian or Southeast Asian origin, to play up intentional contrasts.[3]

Much of our knowledge of early imported Southeast Asian ceramics in Japanese collections comes from connoisseurs' guides, diaries of tea gatherings, and inventories of important collections. Contemporary Japanese records describe this type of glazed ceramics as "Annan ware," after the Chinese name for what is now northern Vietnam. Most glazed Vietnamese tea bowls in Japanese collections are patterned like this one, with a double lotus petal band above the foot and a floral scroll on the body. The character for "long life" (Japanese: *kotobuki*), is painted on the center of the bowl's interior. Another characteristic of ceramics of this type is a wash of brown that colors the underside of the bowl. The use of gold to repair the rim emphasizes that this object was treasured and deemed worthy of repair. —NR

1. Fukuyama Bijutsukan, ed., *Cha no geijutsu: Daimyō cha no meihō* (Fukuyama; Fukuyama Bijutsukan, 2005), 53.
2. Louise Allison Cort, "Vietnamese Ceramics in Japanese Contexts," in *Vietnamese Ceramics: A Separate Tradition* (Chicago: Art Media Resources, 1997), 66.
3. Ibid.

124 ▶

南蛮芋頭水指

FRESH WATER JAR
(MIZUSASHI)
in the shape of a large taro
Vietnam; 16th century
Stoneware with ash glaze, lacquer repairs
H. 22.7 cm x Diam. 20.0 cm (mouth)
Diam. 9.4 cm (foot)
Eisei-Bunko Museum, 1352

Covered vessels such as this one were used to hold fresh water used in a tea gathering. The jar's small mouth suggests that it was originally made as some other kind of storage vessel but was adapted for a new use (with an added lid) when it reached Japan. Jars of this shape were called *imogashira,* often playfully translated as "potato head" after a type of taro (a bulbous tuber). A simple brown ash glaze covers the vessel; cracks have been repaired with red lacquer.

This jar has a long provenance that has undoubtedly added to its prestige. It is thought to have been owned by the tea master Sen Rikyū (1522–1591), famous for transforming the Way of Tea with his use of rustic pottery and simple utensils.[1] One of Rikyū's students, Sumioshiya Sōmu (1534–1603), owned the jar in 1587: records show that the vessel was used then in the grand tea gathering at the Kitano Shrine in Kyoto.[2]

Hosokawa Sansai, a senior disciple of Sen Rikyū, acquired the jar in the late sixteenth or early seventeenth century. One of the boxes that held the vessel is inscribed by Sansai and notes that the jar came from Cochin—the Mekong delta of northern Vietnam. Noting its similarity to a dated vessel of similar appearance, Louise Cort suggests that this jar might date from the sixteenth century.[3] —NR

1. An inscription on the base of the jar is identified as the mark of Sen Rikyū in two sources: the records of the great Kitano tea gathering and the Hosokawa family records, *Odōgu yuraizu.* Miho Museum, ed., *Eisei Bunko, Hosokawa-ke no meihō* (Shigaraki: Miho Museum, 2002), 261.
2. Louise Allison Cort, "Buried and Treasured in Japan: Another Source for Thai Ceramic History," in *Thai Ceramics: The James and Elaine Connell Collection* (Oxford: Oxford University Press, 1993), 29.
3. Ibid., 29–30.

126 ▶

楽宗入作　赤楽茶碗

TEABOWL

Red Raku ware

By Raku Sōnyū (1664–1716)

Japan; Edo period (1615–1868), 18th century

Glazed earthenware

H. 8.2 cm x Diam. 12.1 cm (mouth); Diam. 5.7 cm (foot)

Eisei-Bunko Museum, 2001

This bowl is thought to have been made by Raku Sōnyū, the fifth-generation artist in the Raku family. Its box is signed with the character "Raku" (楽). Few ceramicist families have continued in a lineage stretching more than four hundred years, as the Raku family has done in Japan; however, Sōnyū was adopted into the family by the fourth-generation artist, Ichinyū. In 1708 he became a Buddhist monk, taking the name Sōnyū for this retirement from the world. He was cousin to two other great Japanese artists, Ōgata Kōrin and Ōgata Kenzan, who formed the decorative art style called "Rinpa" (literally "school of the Rin," with Rin referring to the last part of Kōrin's name).

The Chinese character for raku (楽)—meaning pleasure, comfort, or ease—is said to derive from the middle character of the name of a sixteenth-century palace called the Jurakudai (聚楽第), built in Kyoto by the powerful warlord and patron of the arts Toyotomi Hideyoshi (1536–1598). The story goes that the Raku potters dug clay from Hideyoshi's palace grounds, and that the warlord presented a golden seal bearing this character to the second head of the Raku family. From that time forward, many Raku wares have borne an impression of this seal, usually near the foot of the bowl. The Raku family were among the first ceramic artisans in Japan to "sign" their work with such a mark and thus became the first individually known ceramic artists, whereas previously only the kiln might be indicated by a mark.

In tea practice, the teabowl creates a physical connection between host and guest. The host prepares the beverage by measuring pow-

125 ◀

瀬戸茶碗　銘「念八」

TEABOWL

entitled "Nenpachi"

Seto ware

Japan; Momoyama period (1573–1615), 16th century

Glazed stoneware mended with lacquer and gold powder

H. 8.0 cm x Diam. 14.8 cm (mouth); Diam. 6.4 cm (foot)

Eisei-Bunko Museum, 2007

The overall design of this bowl was achieved by glazing in two colors over a surface featuring a cross-hatched design carved into the side of the bowl, perhaps representing an abstract fence. The surface has been further enlivened by having been mended in several places with lacquer dusted in gold. The practice of mending tea ceramics is an art form in its own right in Japan, where often the mended work is thought to be more aesthetically appealing than before the breakage.

According to the Hosokawa collection inventory (*Gohōmotsu chō*), compiled during the Meiji and Taisho periods, "The name 'Nenpachi' was given in reference to the fact that the bowl was acquired on the twenty-eighth of the eighth month." The character for *pachi* (or *hachi*) in "Nenpachi" is the number eight. —YW

dered tea into the bowl, using a scoop like those included in this catalogue (cat. nos. 132–135), then adding hot water and blending tea and water together with a bamboo whisk. Host and guest in turn cradle the teabowl in their hands; the guest's lips touch the bowl's rim when drinking. Raku teabowls are known for their pleasing tactile qualities.

Compared to ceramics fired at a higher temperature, and despite their visual bulk, Raku bowls feel soft and light in the hands. Their thick walls conduct heat slowly, containing the heat of the tea while gently warming the hands. Traditionally Raku bowls are without decoration, but the host may find a particular aspect of the bowl most pleasing to the eye and choose to present that side to the guest. —DC

127

重要美術品

楽長次郎作　黒楽茶碗　銘「乙御前」

IMPORTANT ART OBJECT

TEABOWL ENTITLED "OTOGOZE"

Black Raku ware

By Raku Chōjirō (d. 1589)

Japan; Momoyama period (1573–1615), 16th century

Glazed earthenware

H. 8.2 cm x Diam. 10.8 cm (mouth), Diam. 5.0 cm (foot)

Eisei-Bunko Museum, 1297

Raku first, Hagi second, Karatsu third.

Japanese saying from the Edo period (1615–1868), expressing the order of preference for Japanese teabowls used in the thick tea portion of a full tea gathering; still quoted by tea people today.

As much of a celebrity among tea practitioners as any movie star in the wider world, this piece is attributed to Japan's most famous potter, Raku Chōjirō, whose tea bowls most fully embody a revolution in Japanese taste.

Tea drinking originally centered around the appreciation of refined Chinese masterworks. Beginning in the late fifteenth century, a succession of merchant-class tea masters developed a more rustic style of tea, called *wabicha.* They admired the artless beauty of handcrafted, Japanese objects and incorporated such utensils—some of which were found objects, repurposed from other uses—into their teas.

This bowl takes its poetic name from the jolly, rotund female deity Otafuku, also known as Otogoze. It is thought that the bowl's voluptuous shape inspired the name. In the Hosokawa family history, *Menkō shūroku,* there is a record of the art objects and tea utensils owned by Hosokawa Sansai (1563–1646) entitled the "Oiemeibutsu

no taigai," which mentions it by name and states that it was loved by Sansai, who had Chōjirō fire this bowl for him.[1] Sansai carved two of the tea scoops in this catalogue (cat. nos. 132 and 133).

Not much is known about Raku Chōjirō, but it is believed that he began his career as a roof tile maker, and his legendary biography associates him with Japan's famous tea master Sen Rikyū.[2] Raku bowls are hand built, then sculpted and trimmed with a knife or spatula, resulting in a distinctly individual form. In early Raku wares such as this, the raw clay was coated with a lead glaze and fired in a small-scale kiln. The current head of the family, Raku Kichizaemon XV, is innovating on his family's storied tradition by creating abstract scenes in multiple colors on his teabowls.

"Raku" carries multiple meanings. It is the name of one of Japan's most prestigious artistic families, founded by the artist who made this teabowl; and it describes tea-

bowls fired in small kilns by generations of the Raku family. Born in 1949, Raku Kichizaemon is the fifteenth-generation head of this artistic lineage. Potters around the world today use "raku" to describe a type of low-temperature firing that was inspired by Japanese Raku but which has morphed into something completely different, untethered to Japanese tradition. —DC

1. Miho Museum, ed., *Eisei Bunko: Hosokawa-ke no meihō* (Shigaraki: Miho Museum, 2002), 227, 258.
2. The traditional history is recounted on the Raku family website: "Chojiro is thought to have been a son of Ameya of Chinese origin. He founded Raku ware under the guidance of Sen no Rikyu who established chanoyu, the tea ceremony, exclusively making red and black tea bowls for the tea ceremony." (http://www.raku-yaki.or.jp/rekidai/r1-e.html) However, some scholars, such as Morgan Pitelka shed doubt as to whether there is any evidence that Chōjirō and Rikyū ever met. Morgan Pitelka, *Handmade Culture: Raku Potters, Patrons, and Tea Practitioners in Japan* (Honolulu: University of Hawai'i Press, 2005), 17–30.

128

古瀬戸茶入　銘「白鼠」

TEA CONTAINER (CHAIRE)

entitled "Shironezumi" (White Mouse)

Ko-Seto ware

Japan; Muromachi period (1392–1573), 15th century

Glazed stoneware; ivory

H. 4.5 cm x Diam. 8.0 cm; Diam. 5.1 cm (mouth); Diam. 3.5 cm (foot)

Japan; *Eisei-Bunko Museum,* 1265

Ceramic containers with ivory lids (*chaire*) such as this (see also cat. no 129) held the powdered tea used in preparing thick tea (*koicha*) in a tea gathering. Thick tea is made with a larger proportion of tea to water, giving the beverage the consistency of heavy cream. Because more tea is used, thick tea is usually prepared with a higher quality of green tea.

The source of the poetic name White Mouse is not certain. Some have speculated that the mouse is a reference to the Japanese god of wealth, Daitoku. A legend tells of a rat or mouse (it is the same word in Japanese) that protected Daitoku from a demon.

Since the mid-fourteenth century, famous persons, Zen monks, samurai lords, and venerated tea masters have bestowed poetic names on tea utensils that made an impression on them. Such a name for a tea object might derive from the name of the owner or creator, or the place where it was made, or from a Japanese poem, legend, or story. The name adds to the artwork's personality and value, and the owner of such a piece will consider its name as well as its function and appearance when selecting appropriate utensils for a particular tea gathering. Looking closely at paraphernalia like this piece, and discussing their poetic names, are among the pleasures of participating in the gathering. The guest is greatly honored to be served tea from an object with an interesting name given by a famous person.

This tea container is comparatively large and open, taking a shape inspired by Chinese models known as "open sea" (*taikai*). It was made at the Seto kilns near Nagoya.

Traditionally, ceramic tea containers had lids of carved ivory. Today lids are made either from ivory that people owned before 1989, when the international ivory trade was banned, or from other materials, such as plastic or bone. —DC

仕覆　笹蔓縞緞子、唐花宝尽緞子
Tea container pouch (shifuku) with bamboo and ivy;
tea container pouch (shifuku) with myriad treasures
and scrolling vines
Japan; Edo Period (1615–1868), 17th–18th century
Silk damask and braided silk
H. 10 cm x W. 8 cm (each)

129 ▶

瀬戸茶入　銘「山桜」

TEA CONTAINER (CHAIRE)

entitled "Yamazakura" (Mountain Cherry)
Seto ware
Japan; Muromachi (1392–1573)
or Momoyama period (1573–1615)
16th century
Glazed stoneware; ivory
H. 8.4 cm x Diam. 7.6; Diam. 4.0 cm (foot)
Eisei-Bunko Museum, 2027

This Seto ware jar was used to hold powdered green tea for making "thick tea" (see also cat. no.128). It was given the poetic name Yamazakura, "mountain cherry," referring to the wild cherry trees (*Prunus serrulata spontanea*) that grow all over Japan and whose blossoming is celebrated each springtime. The name is painted on the tea container's special storage box. Hundreds of Japanese poems mention *yamazakura;* it is possible that this container was named with a particular poem in mind, but the name may also have been inspired by the impression of "scenery" in the glaze—a golden brown with two trailing lines of black. A similarly named tea container in the collection of the British Museum is thought to have been so called because the "glaze is reminiscent of the bark, faded by time, of the *yamazakura* (mountain cherry)."[1]

Two silk pouches accompany this container; both are modern replacements of traditional fabrics. One has the design of bamboo and ivy (*sasatsurushima donsu*), and the other has "myriad treasures" and scrolling vines (*karabanatakarazukushi donsu*). Only one pouch was used at a time; the host of a tea gathering would select the fabric based on seasonal and thematic as well as visual considerations. The bamboo-and-ivy design could be used year round as both plants are evergreen. "Myriad treasures," also suitable for any season, may lend itself particularly well to a celebratory tea gathering at New Year's, for example.

The cloth pouches are considered inseparable parts of the artwork. Before a tea gathering, the host prepares by filling the tea container, then encloses it in one of its pouches. The guests first see the container when it is still clothed in its pouch. In the course of making tea, the host removes the container from the pouch; after the tea has been consumed, the tea container, tea scoop (cat. nos. 132–135), and pouch circulate for closer examination by the guests as the host shares interesting details about the artworks with them. —DC

1. http://www.britishmuseum.org/explore/highlights/highlight_objects/asia/t/tea-caddy,_with_its_set_of_bag.aspx

130

梅牡丹堆朱茶器

TEA CONTAINER (CHAKI)

with peony and plum design

China; Ming dynasty (1368–1644),16th–17th century

Carved red lacquer

H. 8.9 cm x Diam. 6.0; Diam. 3.1 cm (foot)

Eisei-Bunko Museum, 1252

This tea container (*chaki*) takes its unusual shape from two elongated, neatly joined hemispheres. Its organic form, resembling a red jujube date, is enhanced by pleasing curves that outline the whole without interruption. While the inside and the slightly indented top and bottom are lacquered in plain black, a carved decoration covers the surface, with thick red lacquer of plum blossoms (top half) and peonies (bottom half) bordered by two narrow bands of geometric patterns and lotus petals. The design also has incised details of leaf veins and flower filaments. Plum and peony are two staple motifs in Chinese decorative art; in carved lacquer decoration they often symbolize the seasons of winter and spring.

This tea container was imported from China to Japan for its formidable craftsman-ship. The making of even a small carved-lacquer piece was not only labor intensive and time consuming, it also demanded errorless carving skill. A thick layer of solid red was painstakingly prepared through many applications of liquid lacquer. The carving technique required an overall vision in decorative design as well as consummate precision in cutting into the thick lacquer. Such carving skills were never surpassed outside China. The cutting style shown on this tea container, with slightly rough edges around the motifs, compares favorably with late Ming dynasty lacquer wares often attributed to southwestern China's Yunnan and Sichuan provinces, the commercial center of lacquer production. It is not unlikely that this piece was made to order for the Japanese market, for similar design practice was flourishing in ceramics traded to Japan during the first half of the seventeenth century.

During a Japanese tea gathering, the host takes the powdered tea from the container with a specially crafted bamboo tea scoop, the *chashaku* (see cat. nos. 132–135). Tea containers traditionally served as a visual focus for aesthetic appreciation; thus, a Chinese carved-lacquer tea container like this one was a luxury item treasured by the Japanese elite. The Japanese shared with the Chinese a sophisticated taste for the elegant, often understated visual appeal of carved lacquers. Moreover, to possess such a Chinese item was itself a symbol of political and cultural power in the Japan of the time. —JC

131

青貝中次

CYLINDRICAL TEA CONTAINER (NAKATSUGI)

Japan; Edo period (1615–1868), 16th–17th century

Lacquered wood with inlaid mother of pearl and sprinkled gold powder (*makie*)
decoration

H. 7.5 cm x Diam. 6.0 cm

Eisei-Bunko Museum, 1253

This container held powdered tea for the preparation of *usucha*, or thin tea. Although it is impossible to know the exact details of the tea procedure practiced four hundred years ago, we may obtain a basic sense of how this piece might have been used by looking at contemporary practice, which has been handed down in an oral tradition stretching back to the days of Hosokawa Sansai and Sen Rikyū.

During a traditional tea gathering, which lasts about four hours, a simple but elegant meal is served in small dishes and lacquer bowls (see cat. no. 102), with a little sake. After sweets and a short break, the guests reenter the tea room and are served thick tea; everyone drinks from a bowl passed hand to hand. Usually a Raku tea bowl (see cat. nos. 126 and 127) is used for thick tea. Again, various sweets are served, followed by thin tea, which might be scooped into the bowl from a container such as this one.

The shape of this container is known as "middle joint" (*nakatsugi*), indicating a work with a cylindrical shape and a relatively deep lid that meets the base nearly at the center of the body. It is thought to have been created for use as a medicine container, but repurposed as a tea container.

This piece is said to be in the *nanban* style. *Nanban*—literally, "southern barbarian"—originally described works of art, including ceramics and lacquers, that were made for export—primarily to Europe—in the late sixteenth or early seventeenth centuries. Although the term certainly has a derogatory tone, in this case *nanban* does not imply that the piece is of any lesser value; in fact, it was and is treasured for it uniqueness.
—DC

細川三斎作　茶杓

TEA SCOOP (CHASHAKU)

By Hosokawa Sansai (aka Tadaoki, 1563–1646)

Japan; Momoyama period (1573–1615) or Edo period
(1615–1868), 16th–17th century

Bamboo (scoop); bamboo and wood (tube)

L. 17.7 cm x W. 0.9 cm (scoop tip)

Eisei-Bunko Museum, 3211

133

細川三斎作　茶杓

TEA SCOOP (CHASHAKU)

By Hosokawa Sansai (aka Tadaoki, 1563–1646)

Japan; Momoyama period (1573–1615) or Edo period
(1615–1868), 16th–17th century

Bamboo (scoop); bamboo and wood (tube)

L. 18.1 cm x W. 0.95 cm (scoop tip)

Eisei-Bunko Museum, 3212

A bamboo scoop is used to measure powdered green tea into the bowl during a tea gathering. These two were carved by Hosokawa Sansai, one of the Hosokawa family's most important tea masters and one of Sen Rikyū's seven disciples. (A portrait of Sansai is included in this publication; see cat. no. 7.) Sansai, with his father Yūsai, founded the Hosokawa family's impressive collection of tea utensils, now at the Eisei-Bunko Museum.

Tea scoops often have a protective container created from a tube of bamboo, and may also have a wooden box to encase the scoop within its bamboo tube. Sometimes these containers have inscriptions written in ink or lacquer that might include the artist's signature, the tea scoop's poetic name, or a full verse associated with the piece. As far as we know, neither of these scoops has a name, and both were made before the practice of attaching poetic names to scoops was typical. The bamboo tube for cat. no. 133 is signed "Made by Hosokawa Sansai." It also has a silk bag to enwrap the scoop in its box.

Bamboo scoops began to be made in the late fifteenth century and were based on Chinese ivory models.[1] Initially, they were intened as disposable functional utensils made new for each gathering and given away as a memento. Gradually, scoops came to be among the most highly prized utensils because of their strong personal connection to the maker.

This shift in material, from expensive ivory carved in China to bamboo, a material that grows plentifully in Japan, relates to the shift in tea aesthetics to favor rusticity and locally made utensils. Tea scoops are regularly made by amateurs, and yet today they are among the utensils presented to guests after drinking tea, for close examination. Earlier tea gatherings featured the ostentatious display of finest-quality imported Chinese ceramics, metalware, and painting; that an unassuming object such as this, carved by an amateur artist from a material growing everywhere in Japan, would warrant such attention is truly remarkable. It speaks to the philosophy behind rustic tea (*wabicha*).

The tea master Takeno Jōō (1502–1555) was the first tea master to use the term *wabi* to describe this new attitude toward sharing a bowl of tea. Jōō's letter to Rikyū defines wabi as follows: "The word ... has come to mean straightforward, considerate, and not arrogant. Of the months of the year, the tenth most represents wabi. Lord Teika's poem expressed it well:

> The Month without God tells no lies.
> What more sincere than the first drops of an autumn shower?
> Whose are the honest tears that fall?"[1]

The tenth month of the lunar calendar corresponds roughly to November, and was poetically known as "the Month without God"—a time when it was thought that all the gods in Japan gathered at Izumo, leaving the rest of the country without gods. It was also a time when the trees are bare and cold rains fall. Jōō also quoted the following poem by Fujiwara Teika as evocative of wabicha:

Miwataseba	*As I gaze far about—*
Hana mo momiji mo	*There's neither blossom*
Nararikeri	*Nor crimson leaf.*
Ura no tomaya no	*At sea's edge: a rush hut*
Aki no yūgure	*In autumn dusk.*[2]

Jōō's student, Rikyū, quoted this poem by Fujiwara Ietaka to define wabi:

Hana o nomi	*To those who wait*
Matsuran hito ni	*Only for flowers*
Yamazato no	*Show them a spring*
Yukima no kusa mo	*Of grass amid the snow*
Haru o misebaya.	*In a mountain village.*[3]

Hosokawa Sansai was not only at the center of major events of tea history. He, as a warrior, and his family made history at the founding of the early-modern Japanese state. At fifteen he fought in the service of Oda Nobunaga (1534–1582), the first of Japan's three unifying warlords. He married Akechi Tama (best known by her Christian name, Hosokawa Gracia), the daughter of a warrior who eventually rebelled against Nobunaga, leading to Nobunaga's ritual suicide (*seppuku*) and forcing Hosokawa Gracia into seclusion. Sansai also led troops in battles for the second of Japan's unifiers, Toyotomi Hideyoshi (1537–1598), who ended Japan's hundred years of civil war. Sansai was close to Tokugawa Ieyasu (1543–1616), first shogun of the Tokugawa period (1615–1868). In 1600 Hosokawa Gracia was taken hostage in Osaka Castle by an enemy of Ieyasu; preferring death to captivity, she ordered a servant to kill her. This horrifying event is thought to have solidified Sansai's loyalty to Ieyasu, founder of the shogunate which would rule Japan for 250 years. —DC

1. Takeno Jōō, "Wabi no fumi," in *Shinshū Chadō Zenshū*, ed. Kuwata Tadachika, vol. 8, 17, cited in Sen Sōshitsu XV, *The Japanese Way of Tea: From Its Origins in China to Sen Rikyū*, translated by V. Dixon Morris (Honolulu: University of Hawaii Press, 1998), p. 152.
2. Takeno Jōō, cited in Dennis Hirota, trans., *Wind in the Pines: Classic Writings of the Way of Tea as a Buddhist Path* (Fremont, CA: Asian Humanities Press, 1995), 233.
3. William Theodore De Bary, Donald Keene, Yoshiko Kurata Dykstra, George Tanabe, and Paul Varley, *Sources of Japanese Tradition: From Earliest Times to 1600* (New York: Columbia University Press, 2001), 390–391.

132   133

134

千宗旦作　茶杓　銘「小木刀」

TEA SCOOP (CHASHAKU)
entitled "Kobokutō" (Small Wooden Sword)
By Sen Sōtan (1578–1658)
Japan; Edo period (1615–1868), 17th century
Bamboo
L. 17.5 cm x W. 0.9
Eisei-Bunko Museum, 1262

Surely a treasured item in the Hosokawa collection because of its maker's importance to early tea history, this scoop was carved by Sen Genpaku Sōtan.

A grandson of Sen Rikyū, and father to the progenitors of the three Sen traditions of tea—Ichiō Sōshu (1593–1675; Mushakōjisenke), Kōshin Sōsa (1613–1672; Omotesenke), and Sen Sōshitsu (1622–1697; Urasenke)—Sōtan is celebrated in an annual memorial ceremony called Sōtanki. The scoop shown here might have been used during one such occasion.

This work is carved from *gomadake,* a type of bamboo with a pattern resembling sesame seeds (*goma*), which is also known as *sabidake* or "rusted bamboo." *Sabi* is an aesthetic concept meaning "to have patina or rust," from the verb *sabiru,* "to get rusty." Originally a literary term, *sabi* in tea meant appreciation of utensils that had a natural patina and an atmosphere of tranquility. Rikyū is quoted in an eighteenth-century book: "Becoming patinated is good. Causing to be patinated is bad."[1] In other words, using naturally "imperfect" bamboo such as this is preferable to altering an unblemished piece of bamboo to make it look old or weathered.

The poetic name Small Wooden Sword (Kobokutō) is written in black ink on the scoop's tubular box. The curve of the scoop is quite sharp, and the handle is relatively narrow and straight; perhaps this inspired the name. The startling image of this small piece of bamboo as a sword contradicts common sense, and may be likened to a Zen riddle in which ideas challenge rational thought. It is not known who gave the name or why, but one could speculate that the image intended has to do with martial discipline: several Japanese sword traditions practice using wooden weapons. Another interpretation may suggest a Buddhist image of the sword as a conceptual weapon that cuts through ignorance. Any guest might ponder such intriguing questions during and long after a tea gathering in which this scoop was used. —DC

1. *Genryū chawa,* cited in *A Chanoyu Vocabulary: Practical Terms for the Way of Tea.* Translated by the Urasenke International Association, edited by the Tankosha Editorial Department (Kyoto: Tankosha Publishing Co. Ltd., 2007), 176.

135

千宗左作　茶杓　銘「西王母」

TEA SCOOP (CHASHAKU)

entitled "Seiōbo" (Xiwangmu, Queen Mother of the West)

By Sen Sōsa (probably Sen Sōsa VIII, aka Sottakusai 1744–1808)

Japan; Edo period (1615–1868), 18th–19th century

Bamboo

L. 19.2 cm x W. 0.9 cm

Eisei-Bunko Museum, 1258

This tea scoop is thought to have been carved by Sen Sōsa, the eighth-generation head of the Omotesenke tradition of tea, one of three lineages tracing their history to Sen Rikyū both in blood heredity and in teaching. Rikyū's grandson Sen Genpaku Sōtan (1578–1658), who carved the tea scoop shown in cat. no 134, had four sons; three of them established tea schools that still thrive today. The names of these traditions—Omotesenke, Urasenke, and Mushakōjisenke—stem from the location on the family property where each tea master lived and gave instruction. *Omote* means "front," *ura* means "back," and Mushanokōji is the name of a street bordering that plot. *Senke* means "school of the Sen family." The name Sen Sōsa is handed down to each new head (*iemoto*) of the Omotesenke lineage. The current head of the family, Jimyōsai (born 1938), is the fourteenth-generation master of this tradition.

The name given this scoop refers to a female Taoist immortal, the Queen Mother of the West, known in China as Xiwangmu. She had a palace in the Kunlun Mountains, where she cultivated a magical peach tree that bore fruit every three thousand years; anyone who ate its fruit became immortal. Thus the peach is an auspicious symbol of immortality or longevity in much East Asian art.

The reasons for naming this particular scoop after the Queen Mother of the West probably have little to do with its appearance: tea scoops' names can be more impressionistic than descriptive. Like the calligraphy scroll that hangs in the alcove during a tea gathering, tea scoops are often made by famous tea masters or respected Zen monks, and it is the artist's intellect that generates interest, more than the skill with which the piece is crafted. And yet many of these scoops are exquisitely carved. Although some masters certainly were skilled amateur bamboo carvers, it is said that others only applied the final touches to a scoop chiefly crafted by a professional.

Near the end of a tea gathering, the tea scoop, tea container, and sometimes other utensils such as a cloth pouch are presented to the guests for a close look. Each guest examines these artworks, passing them one by one to the next guest. The opportunity to handle the utensils, which may have an interesting history, is one of the great delights of the tea gathering. The feeling might be compared to the experience of being allowed to handle Shakespeare's quill during a quiet, intimate gathering at a friend's house.

This scoop has more heft than the other tea scoops in this catalog (cat. nos. 132–134). It has a relatively thick stem and does not taper as much as the others. —DC

136

松竹梅文芦屋釜

HOT WATER KETTLE (KAMA)
with design of pine, bamboo, and plum
Ashiya type
Japan; Momoyama period (1573–1615), 16th century
Cast iron, bronze
H. 17.5 cm x Diam. 25.0 cm
Eisei-Bunko Museum, 2126

Used to heat water for tea in a tea gathering, this kettle was made in the Ashiya area of what is now Fukuoka prefecture, Kyushu. The place was famous for its tea kettles produced in the fifteenth and sixteenth centuries; production has begun again in recent years, with artisans replicating the style and techniques of this important early kettle-making center.

The design of pine, bamboo, and plum is a popular motif in many Japanese mediums. Known as the "three friends of winter," these plants symbolize long life and happiness; each contributes certain positive qualities to the collective symbolic power. Pine trees, evergreen and tough, live long. Bamboo,

a grass, is also evergreen and is strong yet flexible. Plum trees represent bravery, being the first trees to bloom in late winter, often when snow still covers the ground. An old pine tree and flowering plums are depicted on one side of the kettle; the other side is decorated with bamboo and pine needles. The host may present the side that guests might find most meaningful, and that which best complements the theme of their gathering.

Works like this are made by casting the design into the iron using clay molds. Rough edges are filed smooth after the molds are removed. The mask of a mythological demon (*kimen*) is cast into the lugs on either side of the kettle. This design, unique to Ashiya

kettles, is thought to derive from the *taotie* mask found on many ancient Chinese bronzes. The demons' manes continue onto the body of the kettle, and the lugs have holes to which open carrying rings are attached.

Iron must be handled carefully to avoid oxidation and the corrosion caused by oil deposits from human fingers: even a cool kettle is never touched directly by the hands. After use, these kettles must be dried completely, usually by heating, to keep rust to a minimum. On this kettle, the area below the waist is a later replacement.

Many tea people consider water boiled in an iron kettle a delicious drink in its own right. —DC

137
大西浄清作　四方釜
SQUARE HOT WATER
KETTLE (KAMA)
By Ōnishi Josei (1603–1682)
Japan; Edo period (1615–1868)
17th century
Cast iron, copper alloy, partially gilded
H. 22.4 cm x D. 16.0 cm
Eisei-Bunko Museum, 1280

Iron kettles have been made in Japan since at least the eighth century, when they were first documented in temple lists. They are the only category of tea utensil in which Japanese-manufactured works have always been more valued than imported objects.

Used to heat water for a tea gathering, the kettle was placed over a carefully prepared charcoal fire built in front of the guests; it also provided warmth to the tea room in winter. This kettle was commissioned from the artist by the warrior tea aficionado Hosokawa Sansai (1564–1646). A family record of important objects (御家名物之大概, *Oiemeibutsu no taigai*) lists it as one of Sansai's favored tea utensils. This record also states that Sansai chose the poem that trails on the kettle's four walls in an elegant, flowing script:

Miwataseba	*As I gaze far about—*
Hana mo momiji mo	*There's neither blossom*
Nakarikeri	*Nor crimson leaf.*
Ura no tomaya no	*At sea's edge: a rush hut*
Aki no yūgure	*In autumn dusk.*

By Fujiwara Teika (1162–1241). From the *New Anthology of Ancient and Modern Verse* (an anthology of approximately two thousand Japanese poems compiled and edited between 1200 and 1220.[1]

The kettle became known as Tomaya—"rush hut," a reference that tea people would associate with this poem, which was cited by tea master Takeno Jōō as embodying the spirit of rustic tea (*wabicha*). Cherry blossoms and autumn foliage are gloriously beautiful, like the finest tea wares from China, but it is within the solitude of a humble hut at dusk along the shore that one can explore rich internal landscapes: "People in the world of society spend their time wondering when blossoms will open on this hillside or that grove, day and night turning all their attention outside themselves and never realizing that those blossoms and leaves lie within their own hearts and minds."[2]

Jōsei was the second-generation artist of the Ōnishi kettle-making family. He was kettle maker for the Tokugawa shogunate, which ruled Japan from 1615 to 1868. —DC

1. Translated by Dennis Hirota in *Wind in the Pines: Classic Writings of the Way of Tea as a Buddhist Path* (Fremont, CA: Asian Humanities Press, 1995), 233.
2. From book one of the *Nanpōroku*, a compendium of Rikyū's Way of Tea recorded by his disciple, the Zen monk Nanbō Sōkei. Hirota, 234.

鬱金地金花菱鳳凰文唐織
NOH COSTUME, KARAORI ROBE
with design of phoenixes and flowers on floral lozenges
Japan; Edo period (1615–1868), 18th–19th century
Silk twill weave with silk and gilded paper supplementary weft patterning
L. 147.0 cm x W. 142.0 cm
Eisei-Bunko Museum, 2405

The *karaori* is named for the material from which it is made. *Karaori* ("Chinese weave") textiles used for the Noh theater are by rule a 1:2 twill ground weave with supplementary pattern wefts in floating silk floss of various colors. Often, supplementary wefts of finely cut strips of paper coated with gold leaf are inserted to create an additional layer of decoration.

Karaori are by nature colorful and luxurious, but this robe conveys a distinctly noble sensibility. The yellow background is covered with an underpattern of floral lozenges—a motif similar to those found in Japanese aristocratic garments—over which sprays of chrysanthemum, cherry blossom, and peony, and colorful phoenixes are scattered at unusually wide intervals. The phoenix is an imaginary bird that originated in China and became closely associated with the emperor in Japan. The combination of phoenix and Chinese peony gives the robe an exotic feeling, making it an appropriate costume for a Noh play such as *Yōkihi,* which relates the tragic story of Tang dynasty imperial concubine Yang Guifei (719–756).[1] —MR

1. A contemporary reproduction of this robe has been made by Noh costume maker Yamaguchi Akira of the Asai Gallery of Noh Arts. See Kirihata Ken and Yamaguchi Akira, eds., *Karei naru nō shōzoku no bi* (Tokyo: Asahi Shimbunsha, 1998), 54, 182.

139

金地撫子蝶文唐織

NOH COSTUME, KARAORI
ROBE

with design of butterflies and pinks
Japan; Edo period (1615–1868)
18th century
Silk twill weave with silk and gilded
paper supplementary weft patterning
L. 152.0 cm x W. 146.0 cm
Eisei-Bunko Museum, 2408

This lavish *karaori* Noh robe combines three varieties of butterfly in flight over an underpattern of pinks. The brilliant gold background was executed with supplementary wefts of gilded paper strips. Pinks (*nadeshiko*)—*Dianthus plumarius* and related species—bloom from late spring through early fall and suggest maidenly charm; butterflies had associations with magic and immortality, but could also be considered spirits of the dead. The swallowtail (*ageha*) butterfly with

both wings uplifted was the medieval crest of the Taira clan, whose battles with the Minamoto clan in *The Tale of the Heike* (*Heike monogatari*) are alluded to in many Noh plays. This robe contains red, and so it would have been suitable for roles of young women.

As is standard in karaori textiles, a single pattern block is repeated up and down the textile. Here, each block covers the full width of the cloth (the back between the sleeves is made from two widths, with a central

seam, and each of the sleeves is one width) and the length of three butterflies. The weaver has mitigated the sense of repetition by inserting different colors into each repeat; he has also used mirror images of the same pattern for alternate sides of the garment. Using such techniques, Noh costume makers created opulent and highly individual garments using a limited variety of patterns and a limited color palette. —MR

140

段替松菊桐萩文唐織

NOH COSTUME, KARAORI ROBE
with alternating color blocks and design of pine,
chrysanthemum, paulownia, and bush clover
Japan; Edo period (1615–1868)
approx. 1800–1839
Silk twill weave with silk and gilded paper
supplementary weft patterning
L. 149.0 cm x W. 150.0 cm
Eisei-Bunko Museum, 2417

Noh costumes fall into a range of categories. The *karaori, atsuita, nuihaku,* and *surihaku* are four costume types that are shaped after the kimono-like *kosode* robe. Originally worn as an underlayer, the *kosode* had become a standard outer garment for elite Japanese society by the late Muromachi (1392–1573) and Momoyama (1573–1615) periods. Among the costumes, the karaori is the only one normally worn as the outermost garment (*uwagi*). The incorporation of such full-length robes into the Noh theater probably stemmed from wealthy patrons' practice of giving luxury kosode to favorite actors as rewards for outstanding performances.

Karaori robes—used primarily for women's roles—can be further categorized as "colored" (*iroiri*) or "colorless" (*ironashi*) depending on whether or not they display the safflower-

dyed color red (*beni*), which is associated with young, unmarried women. With its designs of pine trees, chrysanthemum, lattices covered with winding grape vines (traditionally identified as paulownia within the Hosokawa collection, due to an inscription on its original paper wrapper), and bush clover over an underpattern of mist-like horizontal gold lines, this robe is a "colorless" karaori, suitable for the role of an older woman or, possibly, an aristocratic man.

The striking ochre and pale blue checkered background was created by tie-dyeing the warp (vertical threads) to create alternating ochre and blue blocks; wefts of the same color were then inserted into the respective sections. Ikat tie-dyeing in the vertical threads creates a delicate feathered effect at the upper and lower edges of each

section. Careful alignment of contrasting colors when tailoring created the checkered effect. As is standard in karaori, all the motifs are woven: silk or gilded paper supplementary wefts were inserted by hand into each row.

The daimyo collection of the Ii family, now housed in the Hikone Castle Museum, contains a karaori that is identical except for having been woven with different colors.[1] Noh costume makers often used the same weaving pattern for more than one garment; by changing the colors, and sometimes the orientation, of each pattern block, they could create robes that were individually unique and visually distinctive. —MR

1. Hikonejō Hakubutsukan, ed., *Tokubetsuten Ii ke denrai no nōmen nōshōzoku.* (Hikone: Hikonejō Hakubutsukan, 1987), 128.

141

霰鱗地桐鳳凰丸文厚板

NOH COSTUME, ATSUITA ROBE

with paulownia and phoenix roundels on checkered triangles

Japan; Edo period (1615–1868), 18th century

Silk twill weave with silk supplementary weft patterning

L. 156.0 cm x W. 143.2 cm

Eisei-Bunko Museum, 2420–2

An *atsuita* is a full-length Noh costume in the form of a *kosode* (kimono). It is generally worn as an inner robe (*kitsuke*) under a jacket and, usually, wide trousers for the roles of male characters, deities, or mythical animals; accordingly, atsuita designs are frequently bold and geometric. The use of the color red (*iroiri*) can express youth.

The word *atsuita*—"thick board"—refers to the hefty supports around which luxury patterned textiles were wrapped before being exported from China.[1] Domestic atuita textiles used in the Noh theater have a range of weave structures: some are twills, and some have richly brocading supplementary weft patterns. This example is of a type sometimes characterized as *atuita karaori,* combining brocading *karaori* motifs with the more geometric designs typical of atsuita. Such a robe has a broader use than a twill atsuita and might sometimes be chosen for female roles.

The designs are in two layers: a geometric underpattern combines triangles, or "scales," which can signify demonhood, with the miniature checks found in aristocratic textiles. The upper pattern layer has the more representational motifs of phoenix medallions and paulownia sprays. Phoenix iconography came to Japan from China. Purported to live in a paulownia tree and to feed on bamboo seeds, the mythical bird was considered a highly auspicious symbol of wise rule. To the viewer, such evocative motifs would meld with the poetry, music, and dance of the Noh play to create a richly nuanced performance.
—MR

1. Iwao Nagasaki and Monica Bethe, *Patterns and Poetry: Nō Robes from the Lucy Truman Aldrich Collection at the Museum of Art, Rhode Island School of Design.* (Providence, RI: Museum of Art, Rhode Island School of Design, 1992), 157.

142

紅地青海波州浜に松帆文縫箔

NOH COSTUME, NUIHAKU ROBE
with design of seashore, pines, and sails over
stylized waves
Japan; Edo period (1615–1868)
18th century
Silk with silk embroidery and stencil-pasted
gold foil
L. 145.5 cm x W. 144 cm
Eisei-Bunko Museum, 2441

Shaped like a *kosode* (kimono), the *nuihaku* is usually made of silk satin with designs in embroidered silk floss and stencil-pasted metallic leaf. This example features scattered stencil-pasted gold leaf sandbars amid a sea of stylized, auspicious waves (*segaiha*). The one, two, or sometimes three square, wind-filled sails—each embroidered differently—suggest distant ships passing behind the pine-lined islands and create an evocative scenery over the brilliant vermilion background.

In the Noh theater, the nuihaku is most commonly used as an underrobe (*kitsuke*) for the roles of female characters, high-ranking men, or deities. For women's roles, it is often worn wrapped only around the lower part of the body and folded at the waist in the *koshimaki* style. Beneath it would be worn a *surihaku* underrobe decorated with gold or silver leaf; above, depending on the role and the play, might be a *karaori* (pulled up at the waist in the *tsuboori* style) or a gossamer outer robe such as a *chōken* or *mizugoromo*.

A nuihaku has a softer and more pliable hand than the stiff woven karaori and *atsuita* robes (see cat. nos. 138–141). Because the motifs are applied to the surface, the patterns can be arranged more freely than in woven garments. In this example, the clumped arrangements of similar motifs on a repeated background pattern seem to have been inspired by *karaori*, but their subtle variations would not have been possible in a woven textile. —MR

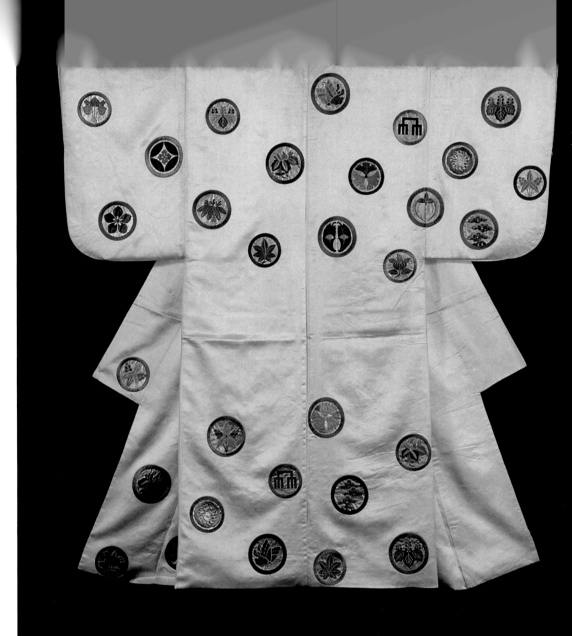

143

白地丸紋尽縫箔

NOH COSTUME, NUIHAKU ROBE

with design of myriad crests

Japan; Edo period (1615–1868), 18th century

Silk satin with silk embroidery and pasted gold foil

L. 141.5 cm x sleeve width 138.0 cm

Eisei-Bunko Museum, 2444

Nuihaku robes combine two techniques—embroidery (*nui*) and pasted gold or silver foil (*haku*)—that were popular among high-ranking members of society in the Momoyama period (1573–1615). Often given by daimyo or other wealthy samurai patrons to favorite actors, such robes eventually found their way into the standard Noh costume repertoire. Nuihaku are usually worn for the roles of women, boys, or aristocratic young men.

Robes like this one, with scattered roundels of stylized family crests (*mon*) on a blue, black, red, or white satin ground, are most closely associated with the roles of

female demons in plays such as *Dōjoji, Aoi no Ue,* or *Kanawa.* For such a role, a nuihaku would be worn not over the shoulders but wrapped around the lower body in the *koshimaki* (waist wrap) style. A silk *surihaku* underrobe, bearing geometric designs in gold leaf, would cover the upper half of the body.

Although straightforward geometric motifs on a plain background are can create a severe impression—appropriate for demon roles—this kind of robe might also be selected by an actor in the role of a young boy in a play such as *Kokaji* or *Tamura.* —MR

References:

Kanze Yoshimasa, Shōda Natsuko, *Enmokubetsu ni miru nō shōzoku.* (Tokyo: Kōdansha, 2004), 49.

Tokugawa Yoshinobu, Ōkochi Sadao, trans. By Monica Bethe and Louise Cort, *The Tokugawa Collection Nō Robes and Masks.* (New York: Japan Society, 1977), 122–123.

Tokugawa Bijutsukan, ed., *Tokugawa Bijutsukan no meihō.* (Nagoya: Tokugawa Bijutsukan, 1995), 116.

144

紺地麻葉沢瀉丸文狩衣

NOH COSTUME, KARIGINU ROBE

with design of arrowhead roundels on stylized hemp leaf pattern

Japan; Edo period (1615–1868), 18th century

Silk satin lampas with gilded paper supplementary weft patterning (*kinran*)

L. 148.0 cm x W. 201 cm

Eisei-Bunko Museum, 2496

The *kariginu* (literally, "hunting robe") used in the Noh theater is modeled after a type of informal robe worn by aristocratic or warrior-class men. In Noh, it is used as a formal costume for the highest-ranking male roles. There are two styles, lined and unlined. The lined type, such as this, usually has clean, bold patterns in gold on a plain ground, giving it a strong, masculine feel. Lined

kariginu are worn for the roles of deities, demons, or other supernatural beings. Here, round crests of triple arrowheads punctuate the hexagonal background diaper of starlike concentric triangles, known in Japanese as a hemp leaf (*asa no ha*) pattern. The arrowhead is an aquatic plant that grows in streams and rice paddies, for which reason it symbolizes plentiful water. —MR

145

紫地桜花筏文狩衣

NOH COSTUME, KARIGINU ROBE

with design of cherry blossoms and rafts

Japan; Edo period (1615–1868), 18th century

Silk complex gauze (*ro*) with silk supplementary weft patterning

L. 164.5 cm x W. 207 cm

Eisei-Bunko Museum, 4911

While its round neckline, partially unattached double-width sleeves, and long narrow body form a distinctly masculine silhouette, the complex gauze (*ro*) with which this unlined *kariginu* is constructed gives it a different translucence and lightness than its lined counterpart in cat. no. 144. The design of cherry blossoms, cherry sprays, and rafts, executed in brocading supplementary wefts of white silk, contribute to the gentler impression; the background, now somewhat faded to brown, was purple when the piece was new.

Fallen cherry petals drift together as they float downstream; the "flowers and rafts" (*hana ikada*) motif, often found in visual art and literature, is thought to derive from the "rafts" formed by clustering petals as they float down a stream. The design conveys both the glory of spring and the transience of life.

Unlined (*hitoe*) kariginu robes are generally chosen for the roles of aged gods, fallen warriors, and young male courtiers of high stature. This costume might convey the poetic sensibility of a youthful aristocrat.

When skillfully selected, the costumes' colors and motifs complement the masks' expressions and the poetic language of the Noh script to give the viewer a richly layered, evocative, theatrical experience.

—MR

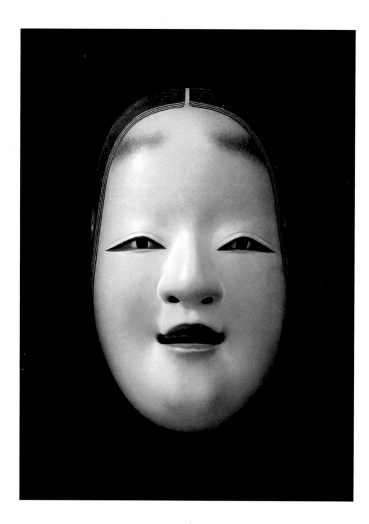

146 ◄

能面　小面

NOH MASK, KOOMOTE

Japan; Edo period (1615–1868), 18th century

Ink and colors on wood

H. 21.2 cm x W. 13.3 cm

Eisei-Bunko Museum, 6513

Koomote means "little mask"; this diminutive name reflects the young, maidenly figures this category of mask is used to portray in Noh plays. A Koomote mask is distinguished by pleasingly fleshy cheeks and chin, which contribute to its youthful quality, and by the three smooth, uncrossing strands of hair on either side of the face—it is the only mask with this hairstyle.

As is typical for its type, this mask is carved to be smaller than the actor's face, giving it not only sweetness but also an elegance and purity associated with the aristocratic maiden. Blackened teeth and high painted eyebrows convey the character's high rank; both are practices associated with the courtier classes.

In the Edo period, certain types of masks became associated with specific schools of Noh. While all five main schools of Noh use Koomote, it is especially favored by the Konparu and Kita schools for *shite* (protagonist) roles of young women. —MR

147 ►

能面　中将

NOH MASK, CHŪJŌ

Japan; Edo period (1615–1868), 18th century

Ink and colors on wood

H. 20.2 cm x W. 14.1 cm

Eisei-Bunko Museum, 6517

Noh theater employs a variety of different mask categories. Each type has specific characteristics; some are associated with roles in specific plays.

The type of mask called Chūjō is said to have been modeled after the famous ninth-century courtier and poet Ariwara no Narihira. Its gentle mouth and eyes, blackened teeth, and raised eyebrows convey the sensitivity of the aristocratic young gentleman, while the wrinkles of concern between the brows suggest melancholy or pathos.

This mask would be used for such roles as Kiyotsuna, Atsumori, or Tsunamasa, all aristocratic youths who were the losers in historic battles chronicled in the medieval epic *The Tale of the Heike (Heike monogatari)*. The pale, delicate face is carved in such a way that the expression subtly changes when viewed from different angles, expressing a range of emotions as the actor moves around the stage. —MR

能面　小面

back view

148

黒地揚羽蝶文素袍・袴

KYŌGEN COSTUME, SUŌ JACKET AND HAKAMA TROUSERS

with design of butterflies

Japan; Edo period (1615–1868), approx. 1800–1840

Ramie or hemp tabby with stenciled paste-resist dyeing (*katazome*)

L. 85.5 cm x W. 202.0 cm (jacket); L. 179.0 cm (trouser)

Eisei-Bunko Museum, 7565-1, 7565-2

Kyōgen is an often comedic theater in the colloquial language of the Edo period. Its plays are performed during interludes between the more formal, sometimes austere plays of Noh. Unlike the heavily brocaded or gold-patterned Noh robes, the costumes used for Kyōgen tend to be informal, constructed from crisp, slightly translucent textiles of hemp or ramie decorated with freehand or stencil-dyed patterns.

The *suō* outfit worn in Kyōgen, a V-neck jacket with extra-long pleated trousers (*nagabakama*), is derived from a garment similar to the *hitatare* (see cat. no. 19), which was originally worn ceremonially by lower-level members of the warrior class. Its use as Kyōgen costume may have begun when samurai patrons gave garments to the actors as laudatory gifts.[1] In the theater context, *suō* are normally unlined; this example is unusual for its ramie lining. As is typical, it has leather ties at the neck, sleeves, and back seam, in contrast to the hitatare's silk cords. The overly long and slightly awkward trousers drag on the floor behind the wearer, emphasizing his status as a member of the upper class. Such matched outfits are used in Kyōgen plays for the roles of daimyo or other high-ranking characters.

This suō ensemble is stencil-resist dyed with a motif of swallow-tail butterflies in two sizes. To make it, thick paper stencils reinforced with persimmon tannin were placed alternately on the length of woven cloth and coated one by one with a rice-starch paste that penetrated only the pattern areas. When all the butterflies had been coated, the cloth was dyed. The starch paste was washed off, leaving the pasted areas reserved in the original white of the fabric. Finally, the garment would have been cut and stitched into the finished jacket and trousers.

Through carefully orchestrated placement of the two stencils in the various panels, the artist has avoided visual repetition in this garment and given the butterflies a random, scattered appearance. —MR

front view

1. Kirihata Ken, "Kyōgen Costumes: The Fascinating World of Dyed Textiles," in Sharon Takeda, ed., *Miracles and Mischief: Noh and Kyōgen Theater in Japan* (Los Angeles: Los Angeles County Museum of Art, 2002), 161.

149 ▲

浜松文素袍

KYŌGEN COSTUME, SUŌ JACKET

with design of pines on the shore

Japan; Edo period (1615–1868), approx. 1800–1840

Hemp tabby with ink and freehand paste-resist dyeing (*yūzenzome*)

L. 78.5 cm x W. 212.6 cm

Eisei-Bunko Museum, 2846

Unlike Noh costumes, Kyōgen garments are commonly made of bast fibers such as hemp or ramie and have patterns that are surface-dyed rather than woven into the material. Their designs are drawn from every aspect of life, from classical motifs to depictions of lowly quotidian articles.

This *suō* jacket incorporates imagery found in woven or dyed textiles of much higher rank, giving it a quasi-sophisticated feel. Using the natural buff, a pale indigo, and an inky black to create overlapping color sections with dramatically undulating edges, the artist combined the visually similar motifs of tree-lined sandbars (*suhama*) with mist (*kasumi*), a familiar device in classical painting. Piney shores across Japan are the subjects of numerous poetic references, conjuring up a variety of geographic associations. The motif's evocative literary connotations are pleasantly offset by three crests across the back bearing the slightly incongruous standard Kyōgen motif of dandelions inside snowflakes (see also cat. no. 150).

This robe does not have extant matching long trousers (*nagabakama*); instead, it may have been worn over shorter ankle-length trousers for roles such as that of a wealthy farmer traveling to the capital. Such usage might take advantage of the various locales alluded to by the motif. —MR

150 ▶

黄茶地葡萄文肩衣

KYŌGEN COSTUME KATAGINU VEST

with design of grapes

Japan; Edo period (1615–1868)

18th century

Hemp tabby with ink and freehand paste-resist dyeing (*yūzenzome*)

L. 93 cm x W. 136.0 cm

Eisei-Bunko Museum, 8249

The textile scholar Kirihata Ken finds that the *kataginu* best conveys the quintessential charm of Kyōgen costumes.[1] Generally worn over a kimonolike *kosode* robe of checked silk (*noshime*) tucked into floor-length *hakama* trousers, the vest is secured with a sash (*koshiobi*) that ties in the front and bisects the visual canvas of the back side into upper and lower registers.

This saffron-colored garment's design of fruit-laden grapevines winding over a broken lattice of bamboo culms is arranged to show primarily in the upper section: only tendrils extend below the waist. The center back displays the stock Kyōgen costume crest of dandelions within a lozenge-shaped snowflake. This may represent an early sign of spring; or perhaps it is a visual metaphor for the hourglass shoulder drum (*kotsuzumi*) used in Noh and sometimes in Kyōgen performances.[2]

Executed in a combination of freehand paste-resist dyeing and supplementary surface application of ink and dyes, the design typifies the casual, informal nature of Kyōgen costumes. —MR

1. Kirihata Ken, "Kyōgen Costumes: The Fascinating World of Dyed Textiles," in Sharon Takeda, ed., *Miracles and Mischief: Noh and Kyōgen Theater in Japan* (Los Angeles: Los Angeles County Museum of Art, 2002), 171.
2. The sound of the word for dandelion (*tanpopo*) echoes the sound of a drum; also, when placed in water, a dandelion's stem curls up to resemble the kotsuzumi's flared shape. Ibid, 175, note 1.

151

赤茶地笹に帆柱文肩衣

KYŌGEN COSTUME, KATAGINU VEST

with design of bamboo leaves and masts
Japan; Edo period (1615–1868), 18th century
Hemp tabby with ink and freehand paste-resist dyeing (*yūzenzome*)
L. 84.5 cm x W. 132.0 cm
Eisei-Bunko Museum, 8256

The *kataginu* is worn most often in the Kyōgen theater by the frequently appearing character Tarō Kaja. The mishaps of this good-hearted but weak-willed manservant protagonist provide much of the comic-dramatic irony in Kyōgen plays. Though the types of costume worn to play particular roles in Kyōgen, including Tarō Kaja, are usually fixed, the actors themselves decide which garment to wear for a given performance. A costume may be chosen more for visual effect than for its symbolic or metaphorical relationship to the script; however, the costume's bold, often freehand design can subtly enhance the comic or dramatic strength of the actor's performance.

This kataginu is dyed in freehand paste resist with small additional applications of ink and colors. A design of masts amid waves and interlocking hexagons (perhaps representing stylized gabions—large baskets holding rocks to prevent riverside erosion) appears on the garment's upper back, and waterside reeds primarily in the lower part. These motifs would seem to conjure literary associations; however, their effectiveness on stage may have come more from the strong visual statement made by their organic simplicity. —MR

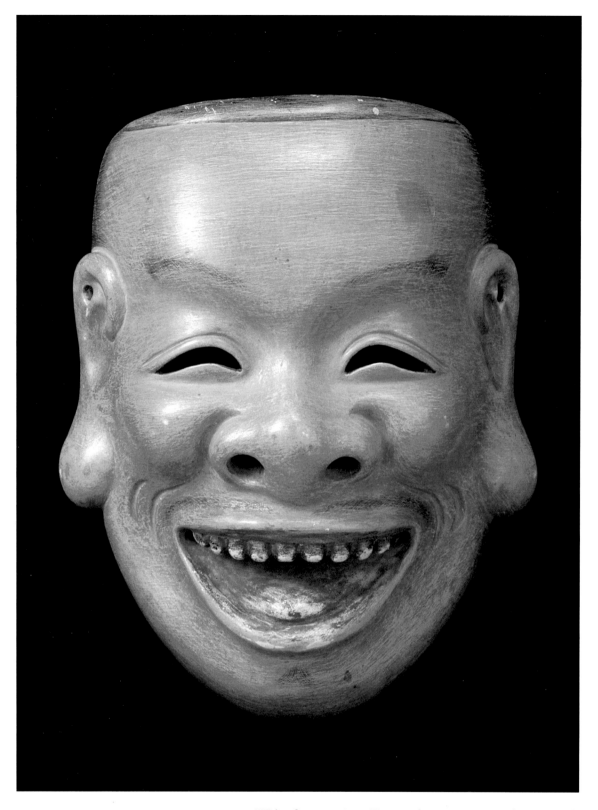

152

狂言面　恵比寿

KYŌGEN MASK, EBISU

Japan; Edo period (1615–1868)

approx. 1800–1840

Ink and colors on wood

H. 19.4 cm x W. 16.0 cm

Eisei-Bunko Museum, 2838

With a few exceptions, Kyōgen plays use masks for the roles of living human characters less frequently than do Noh plays. Kyōgen masks are more likely to represent deities, demons, animals, or the spirits of insects, animals, or plants.

This mask represents Ebisu, one of the Seven Gods of Good Luck (Ebisu, Daikokuten, Bishamonten, Hotei, Fukurokuju, Jurōjin, Benzaiten), who appears paired with other deities from this group in such Kyōgen plays as *Ebisu Daikoku* and *Ebisu Bishamon*.

Ebisu is an indigenous Japanese god dating to the medieval period. Often shown carrying a fishing pole and a large sea bream, he has traditionally been worshiped by commoners, especially fishermen and merchants, and is associated with prosperity and the good life. In this mask, he is depicted with a broad smiling face and oversized earlobes signifying happiness and good fortune.

—MR

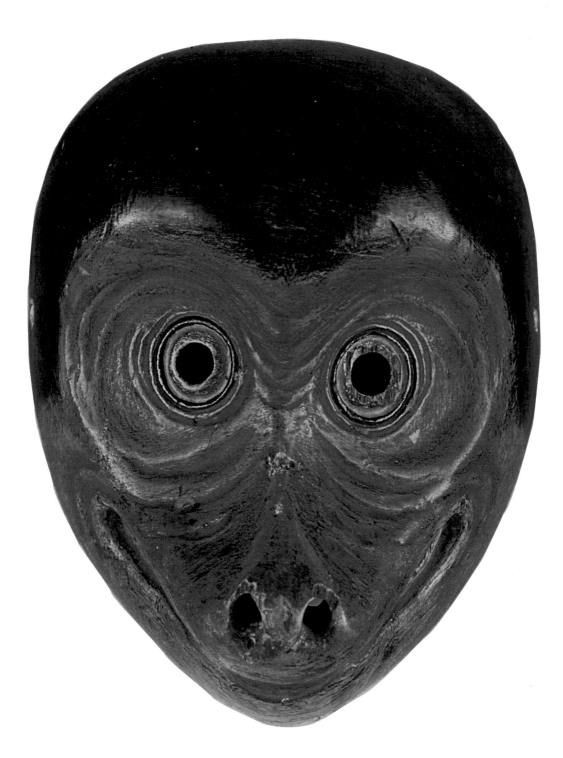

153

狂言面　さる

KYŌGEN MASK, SARU
(MONKEY)

Japan; Edo period (1615–1868)
18th century
Ink and colors on wood
H. 17.6 cm x W. 14.6 cm
Eisei-Bunko Museum, 2816

The three main animal masks used in Kyōgen are Kitsune (Fox), Tanuki (Racoon Dog), and Saru (Monkey). Saru masks can represent monkeys of different sizes and ages and facial expressions and are used in a variety of plays. In one of these, *Saru muko* (The Monkey Groom), the entire cast is composed of monkey characters who chatter nothing but the monkey-like sounds "*kyakya.*" The old saying "Begin with the monkey, finish with the fox" reflects the fact that many Kyōgen actors debut on the stage in the child's role of the monkey in *Utsubozaru* (The Monkey-Skin Quiver) and may play the old fox in *Tsurigitsune* (Trapping of the Fox) at the height of maturity.

This Saru mask is carved on the back with the name Deme and a cipher, telling us it was made by one of the two branches of the twelve-generation Deme families of mask carvers based in Echizen province (present-day Fukui prefecture) and active from the late Muromachi (1392–1573) through Meiji (1868–1912) periods. —MR

154 ▲

細川護貞絵付　鍋島焼　姫ひまわり絵皿

DISH WITH CUCUMBER-LEAF SUNFLOWER
DESIGN

Nabeshima ware

Design painted by Hosokawa Morisada (1912–2005)

Japan; Showa period (1926–1989), 1966

Porcelain with underglaze blue and overglaze enamels

H. 6.0 cm x Diam. 27.0 cm; Diam. 13.2 cm (foot)

Eisei-Bunko Museum, H1

155 ▲

細川護貞絵付　染付徳利　一対

SAKE BOTTLES WITH DECORATION
Design painted by Hosokawa Morisada (1912–2005)
Japan; Showa period (1926–1989), 1964
Two bottles; porcelain with underglaze blue
H. 13.3 cm x Diam. 7.5 cm; Diam. 1.9 cm (mouth)
Eisei-Bunko Museum, H2

156 ▼

細川護貞絵付　倣豆彩小杯　六口

SAKE CUPS
with Chinese *doucai*-style decoration
Design painted by Hosokawa Morisada (1912–2005)
Japan; Showa period (1926–1989), 1967
Six cups; porcelain with underglaze blue and overglaze enamels
(Each) H. 4.2 cm x Diam. 6.9 cm
Diam. 3.6 cm (foot)
Eisei-Bunko Museum, H3

157
細川護熙作　長次郎倣い獅子
LION
after Raku Chōjirō (?–1589)
By Hosokawa Morihiro (born 1938)
Japan; Heisei period (1989–), 2001
Glazed stoneware
H. 16.7 cm
Collection of the artist, H12

158

細川護熙作　唐津鉄釉水指

FRESH-WATER JAR (MIZUSASHI)
Karatsu ware
By Hosokawa Morihiro (born 1938)
Japan; Heisei period (1989–), 2007
Stoneware with iron glaze (jar), wood with lacquer and gold leaf (lid)
H. 18 cm x W. 17.5 cm
Collection of the artist, H5

159 ◄

細川護熙作　赤茶碗

TEABOWL

Red Raku ware

By Hosokawa Morihiro (born 1938)

Japan; Heisei period (1989–), 2004

Glazed earthenware

H. 8.5 cm x Diam. 11.3 cm

Collection of the artist, H6

160 ►

細川護熙作　赤茶碗

TEABOWL

Red Raku ware

By Hosokawa Morihiro (born 1938)

Japan; Heisei period (1989–), 2003

Glazed earthenware

H. 7.8 cm x Diam. 11.8 cm

Japan; Heisei period (1989–)

Collection of the artist, H7

161 ◄

細川護熙作　柿の蔕茶碗

TEABOWL

Kakinoheta type

By Hosokawa Morihiro (born 1938)

Japan; Heisei period (1989–), 2006

Stoneware

H. 7.5 cm x Diam. 14.4 cm

Collection of the artist, H25

162
細川護煕作　信楽花入
FLOWER VASE
Shigaraki ware
By Hosokawa Morihiro
(born 1938)
Japan; Heisei period
(1989–), 2005
Stoneware
H. 25.7 cm x Diam. 10.4 cm
Collection of the artist, H84

163
細川護熙作　信楽四方皿
SQUARE PLATE
Shigaraki ware
By Hosokawa Morihiro (born 1938)
Japan; Heisei period (1989–), 2004
Stoneware, partially glazed
H. 4.2 cm x W. 27.4 cm
Collection of the artist, H91

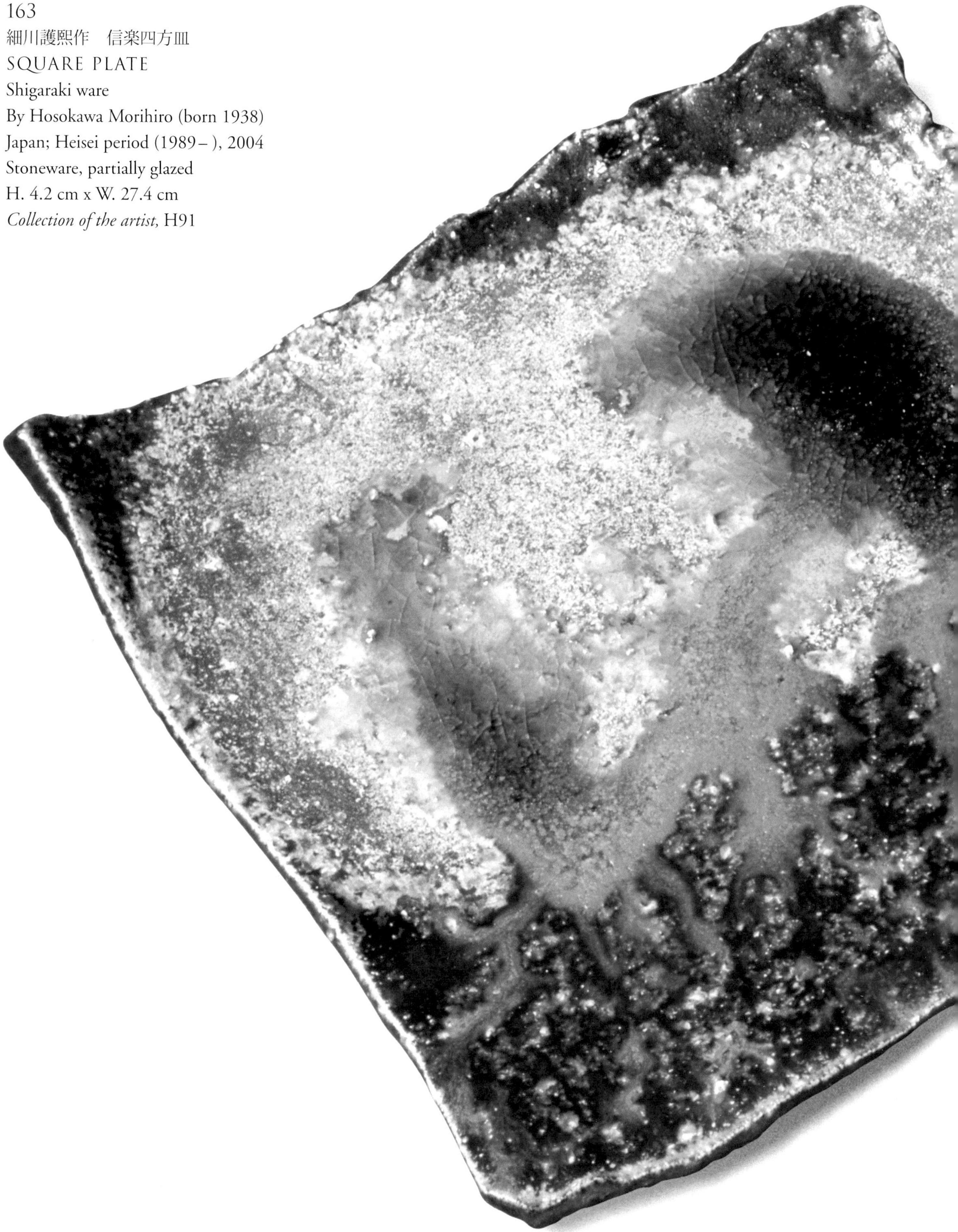

164 ▲
細川護熙作　黒茶碗
TEABOWL
Black Raku ware
By Hosokawa Morihiro (born 1938)
Japan; Heisei period (1989–), 2007
Glazed earthenware
H. 8.2 cm x Diam. 12.6 cm
Collection of the artist, H2

165 ▶
細川護熙作　志野茶碗
TEABOWL
Shino ware
By Hosokawa Morihiro (born 1938)
Japan; Heisei period (1989–), 2007
Glazed stoneware
H. 8.3 cm x Diam. 13.6 cm (mouth)
Collection of the artist, H63

215

166
細川護煕作　唐津掛花入
HANGING FLOWER VASE
Karatsu ware
By Hosokawa Morihiro (born 1938)
Japan; Heisei period (1989–), 2004
Stoneware
H. 23.9 cm x Diam. 11.8 cm
Collection of the artist, H59

HOSOKAWA FAMILY TREE

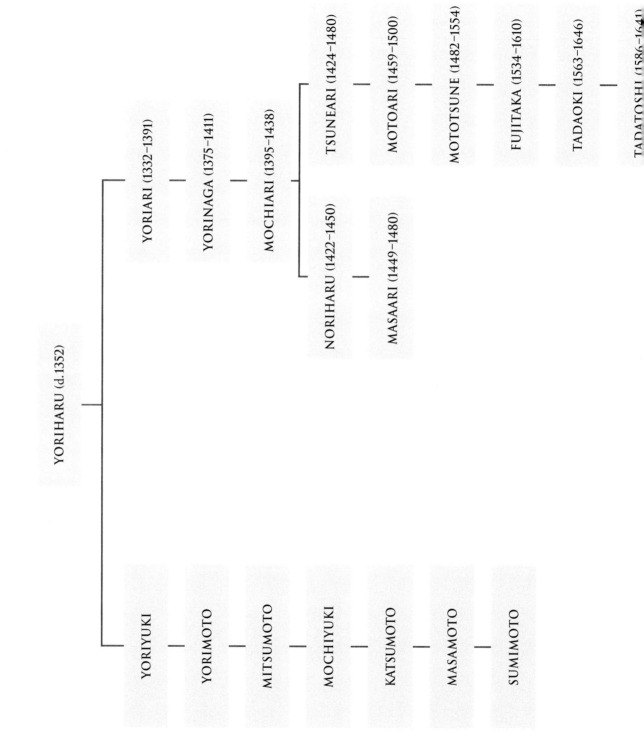

YORIHARU (d.1352)

YORIYUKI

YORIMOTO

MITSUMOTO

MOCHIYUKI

KATSUMOTO

MASAMOTO

SUMIMOTO

YORIARI (1332–1391)

YORINAGA (1375–1411)

MOCHIARI (1395–1438)

NORIHARU (1422–1450)

MASAARI (1449–1480)

TSUNEARI (1424–1480)

MOTOARI (1459–1500)

MOTOTSUNE (1482–1554)

FUJITAKA (1534–1610)

TADAOKI (1563–1646)

TADATOSHI (1586–1641)

MITSUNAO (1617–164?)

TSUNATOSHI (1643–1714)

NOBUNORI (1676–1732)

MUNETAKA (1718–1747)

SHIGEKATA (1720–1785)

HARUTOSHI (1759–1787)

NARISHIGE (1759–1836)

NARITATSU (1789–1826)

NARIMORI (1804–1860)

MORIHISA (1839–1893)

YOSHIKUNI (1835–1876)

MORITATSU (1883–1970)

MORISHIGE (1868–1914)

MORISADA (1912–2005)

MORIHIRO (B. 1938)

HISTORY

The Cambridge History of Japan: Volume 4, Early Modern Japan. Edited by John Whitney Hall and James L. McClain. Cambridge: Cambridge University Press, 1991.

The Cambridge History of Japan: Volume 5, The Nineteenth Century. Edited by Marius B. Jansen. Cambridge: Cambridge University Press, 1989.

Eisenstadt, S. N. *Japanese Civilization: A Comparative View.* Chicago & London: University of Chicago Press, 1996.

Sansom, George B. *Japan: A Short Cultural History.* Revised edition. Englewood Cliffs, New Jersey, 1962 (&c.).

Sources of Japanese Tradition: Volume One, From Earliest Times to 1600. Compiled by Wm. Theodore de Bary, Donald Keene, George Tanabe and Paul Varley. Second edition. New York: Columbia University Press, 2001.

Turnbull, Stephen R. *The Samurai: A Military History.* New York: MacMillan Publishing Co., 1977.

———. *Samurai Sourcebook.* London: Cassell & Co., distributed in the U.S.A. by Sterling Publishing Co. Inc. , 1998.

———. *The Samurai Swordsman: Master of War.* North Clarendon, Vt.: Tuttle Pub., 2008.

———. *Warriors of Medieval Japan.* Oxford & New York: Osprey Press, 2005.

Varley, Paul. *Japanese Culture.* 4th edition, revised and expanded. Honolulu: University of Hawaii Press, 2000.

Warlords, Artists, and Commoners: Japan in the Sixteenth Century. Edited by George Elison and Bardwell L. Smith. Honolulu: University of Hawaii Press, 1981.

ART, GENERAL

Eisei Bunko: Hosokawa-ke no meihō (永青文庫：細川家の名宝) = *Arts Treasured by the Hosokawa Clan: Selections from the Eisei Bunko Museum Collection.* Shigaraki: Miho Museum, 2002.

Gerhart, Karen. *The Eyes of Power: Art and Early Tokugawa Authority.* Honolulu: University of Hawaii Press, 1999.

Hisamatsu, Shin'ichi. *Zen and the Fine Arts.* Translated by Gishin Tokiwa. Tokyo & Palo Alto; Kodansha International, 1971.

Hosokawa sandai: Dai junikai Eisei Bunko ten (細川三大：第十二回永青文庫展). Kumamoto-shi: Kumamoto Kenritsu Bijutsukan, 1982.

Japan: The Shaping of Daimyo Culture, 1185–1868. Edited by Yoshiaki Shimizu. Washington: National Gallery of Art, 1988.

Mason, Penelope. *History of Japanese Art.* 2nd edition. Revised by Donald Dinwiddie. Upper Saddle River, New Jersey ; Pearson, Prentice Hall, 2004.

Singer, Robert T. *Edo: Art in Japan, 1615–1868.* With John T. Carpenter, Hollis Goddall, Victor Harris, Matthew McKelway, Herman Ooms, Nicole Coolidge Rousmaniere, Henry D. Smith III, Sharon S. Takeda, Melinda Takeuchi. Washington, DC: The National Gallery of Art, The Agency for Cultural Affairs, Japan, The Japan Foundation, 1998.

Stanley-Baker, Joan. *Japanese Art.* London & New York: Thames and Hudson, 1984, 2000.

Suzuki, Daisetsu Teitaro. *Zen and Japanese Culture.* Bollingen Series 64. New York: Pantheon Books in cooperation with the Bollingen Foundation, 1959.

Traditional Japanese Arts and Culture: An Illustrated Sourcebook. Edited by Stephen Addiss, Gerald Groemer, J. Thomas Rimer. Honolulu: University of Hawaii Press, 2006.

THE WAY OF TEA

Cha no bijutsu: Yōhen tenmoku to meibutsu cha hin (茶の美術：曜変天目と名物茶品). Tokyo: Seikadō Bunko Bijutsukan, 1994.

Cha no geijutsu: Daimyō cha no meihō: Hosokawa-ke daidai, Eisei Bunko korekushon (茶の芸術：大名茶の名宝 ―細川家代々永青文庫コレクション). Fukuyama-shi, Hiroshima-ken: Fukuyama Bijutsukan, 2005.

Daimyō chajin Matsudaira fumai ten (大名茶人松平不昧展). Henshu: Shimane Kenritsu Bijutsukan, NHK Puromoshon. Matsue: Shimane Kenritsu Bijutsukan, 2001.

Hayashiya, Seizo. *Chanoyu: Japanese Tea Ceremony.* Foreward by Grand Master Sen Soshitsu, Preface by Goto Noboru. Catalogue adapted and translated by Emily J. Sano. New York: Japan Society, 1979.

Okakura, Kakuzo. *The Book of Tea.* Edited and introduced by Everett F. Bleiler. New York: Dover Publications, 1964.

Sasaki, Sanmi. *Chado: The Way of Tea: A Japanese Tea Master's Almanac.* Translated from the Japanese by Shaun McCabe and Iwasaki Satoko. Foreward by Sen Soshitsu XV. Boston, Rutland, Vermont, Tokyo: Tuttle Publishing, 2005.

Sen, Soshitsu. *Chado: The Japanese Way of Tea.* New York, Tokyo, Kyoto: Weatherhill, 1979.

Tanaka, Sen'o. *The Tea Ceremony.* Foreward by Edwin O. Reischauer, preface by Yasushi Inoue, photography by Takeshi Nishikawa. Tokyo, New York & San Francisco: Kodansha International, 1973.

Tea in Japan: Essays on the History of Chanoyu. Edited by Paul H. Varley and Kumakura Isao. Honolulu: University of Hawai'i Press, 1989.

CALLIGRAPHY AND PAINTING

Addiss, Stephen. *The Art of Zen: Paintings and Calligraphy by Japanese Monks, 1600–1925.* New York: Harry N. Abrams, 1989.

Akiyama, Terukazu. *Japanese Painting.* Series: Treasures of Asia. Skira, 1961.

Art of Japan: Paintings, Prints and Screens: Selected Articles from Orientations 1984–2002. Hong Kong: Orientations Magazine, 2002.

Awakawa, Yasuichi. *Zen Painting.* Translated by John Bester. Tokyo & Palo Alto, Kodansha International, 1970.

Brinker, Helmut & Hiroshi Kanazawa. *Zen: Masters of Meditation in Images and Writings.* Translated by Andreas Leisinger. Artibus Asiae, Supplementum 40. Zurich: Artibus Asiae Publishers, 1996.

Boudonnat, Louise & Harumi Kushizaki. *Traces of the Brush: The Art of Japanese Calligraphy.* San Francisco: Chronicle Books, 2003.

Eisei Bunko no byobu-e: Dai jūyōnkai Eisei Bunko ten (永青文庫の屏風江：第十四回永青文庫展). Kumamoto-shi: Kumamoto Kenritsu Bijutsukan, 1984.

Matsushita, Takaaki. *Ink Painting.* Translated and adapted by Martin Collcutt. Series: Arts of Japan. New York & Tokyo ; Weatherhill & Shibundo, 1974.

Miyajima, Shin'ichi. *Buke no shōzō* (部家の肖像). Series: Nihon no bijutsu, No. 385. Tokyo: Shibundō, 1998.

Nakata, Yujiro. *The Art of Japanese Calligraphy.* Translated by Alan Woodhull in collaboration with Armins Nikovskis. Series: The Heibonsha Survey of Japanese Art. New York, Tokyo: Weatherhill/Heibonsha, 1973.

Shimizu, Yoshiaki and John M. Rosenfield. *Masters of Japanese Calligraphy, 18th–19th Century.* New York: The Asia Society Galleries and The Japan House Gallery, 1984.

CERAMICS

Genshoku tōki daijiten (原色陶器大辞典)。Henshū: Katō Tōkurō. Tokyo: Tankōsha, 1972.

Jenyns, Soame. *Japanese Pottery.* New York, Washington: Praeger Publishers, 1971.

Hosokawa Morihiro no sakutō: Go shū-nen kinen (細川護煕の作陶：五周年記念). Henshū: Chadō Shiryōkan. Kyoto: Chadō Shiryōkan, 2005.

Kadokawa Nihon tōki daijiten (角川日本陶器大辞典). Henshū daihyō: Yabe Yoshiaki. Tokyo: Kadokawa Shoten, 2002.

Mikami, Tsugio. *The Art of Japanese Ceramics.* Translated by Ann Herring. Series: The Heibonsha Survey of Japanese Art. Tokyo, New York: Weatherhill/Heibonsha, 1972.

Miller, Roy Andrew. *Japanese Ceramics*. Rutland, Vermont & Tokyo: Toto Shuppan Co. distributed by Charles E. Tuttle, Co., 1960.

Wilson, Richard L. *Inside Japanese Ceramics: A Primer of Materials, Techniques, and Traditions*. Tokyo, New York: Weatherhill, 1995.

Yanagi, Koichi. *Beyond Politics: Recent Works of Art by Japan's Former Primier*. New York: Koichi Yanagi Oriental Fine Arts, 2007.

ARMS AND ARMOR

Arai, Hakuseki. *The Sword Book in Honcho Gunkiko and the Book of Same: Ko Hi Sei Gi of Inaba Tsurio*. [translated and edited by Joly, Henri L. & Hogitaro Inada]. A reprint of the edition published in 1913. London ; Holland Press, 1962.

Bottomley, I. and A. P. Hopson. *Arms and Armor of the Samurai: The History of Weaponry in Ancient Japan*. New York: Crescent Books, 1988.

Kapp, Leon, Hiroko Kapp, Yoshindo Yoshihara. *The Craft of the Sword*. with photographs by Tom Kishida. Tokyo, New York ; Kodansha International, Ltd., 1987.

Robinson, H. Russell. *Japanese Arms and Armor*. New York: Crown Books, 1969.

Sakakibara, Kozan. *The Manufacture of Armour and Helmets in Sixteenth Century Japan (Chukokatchu Seisakuben)*. Translated by T. Wakameda, revised by A. J. Koop, B. A. and Hogitaro Inada, revised and edited by H. Russell Robinson. Rutland & Tokyo: Charles E. Tuttle Co., 1963.

Sato, Kanzan. *The Japanese Sword*. translated and adapted by Joe Earle. Series: Japanese Arts Library. Tokyo, New York ; Kodansha International, Ltd. & Shibundo, 1983.

Sinclaire, Clive. *Samurai: The Weapons and Spirit of the Japanese Warrior*. Guilford, Connecticut: Lyons Press, 2004.

Yumoto, John M. *The Samurai Sword: A Handbook*. Rutland & Tokyo: Charles E. Tuttle, Co., 1958.

BUSHIDŌ AND THE ART OF WAR

Cleary, Thomas. *Code of the Samurai: A Modern Translation of the Bushido Shoshinshu*. Illustrated by Oscar Ratti. Boston, Rutland, Tokyo: Tuttle Publishing, 1999.

———. *Samurai Wisdom: Lessons from Japan's Warrior Culture*. Rutland, Vermont & Singapore: Tuttle Publishing, 2009.

———. *Soul of the Samurai*. Tokyo, Rutland, Vermont & Singapore: Tuttle Publishing, 2005.

Miyamoto, Musashi. *The Book of Five Rings*. Translated by Victor Harris. Woodstock, NY.: The Overlook Press, 1974.

Musashi: Bujin gaka to kengō no sekai ten (武蔵：武人画家と剣豪の世界展). Henshū: NHK, NHK Puromoshon. Tokyo: NHK, NHK Puromoshon, 2003.

Nitobe, Inazo. *Bushido, The Soul of Japan: An Exposition of Japanese Thought*. With an introduction by William Elliot Griffiths. New York: G. P. Putnam's Sons, 1905.

Soho, Takuan. *The Unfettered Mind: Writings from a Zen Master to a Master Swordsman*. Translated by William Scott Wilson. Tokyo, New York & London: Kodansha International, 2002.

Yamamoto, Tsunetomo. *Hagakure: The Book of the Samurai*. Translated by William Scott Wilson. Tokyo, New York & London: Kodansha International, 2002.

LACQUER

Eisei Bunko no shikkōgei: Dai jusankai Eisei Bunko Ten (永青文庫の漆工芸：大十三回永青文庫展). Kumamoto-shi: Kumamoto Kenritsu Bijutsukan, 1983.

Haino Akio. *Shikkō (Kinsei hen)* (漆工[近世編]). Series: *Nihon no bijutsu*, No. 231. Tokyo: Shibundō, 1985.

Jahss, Melvin and Betty Jahss. *Inro and Other Miniature Forms of Japanese Lacquer Art*. Rutland, Vermont & Tokyo: Charles E. Tuttle, Co., 1971.

Maki-e: Tokubetsu Tenrankai, Shikkoku to Kogane no Nihon Bi (蒔絵：特別展覧会、漆黒と黄金の日本美). Kyoto: Kyoto Kokuritsu Hakubutsukan, 1995.

Okada, Barbara Teri. *Symbol & Substance in Japanese Lacquer: Lacquer Boxes from the Collection of Elaine Ehrenkranz*. New York, Tokyo: Weatherhill, 1995.

Pekarik, Andrew J. *Japanese Lacquer, 1600–1900: Selections from the Charles A. GreenField Collection*. New York: The Metropolitan Museum of Art, 1980.

Von Rague, Beatrix. *A History of Japanese Lacquerwork*. Translated from the German by Annie R. De Wassermann. Toronto: University of Toronto Press, 1976.

Yonemura, Ann. *Japanese Lacquer*. Washington: The Freer Gallery of Art, Smithsonian Institution, 1979.

KIMONO

Dalby, Liza Crihfield. Kimono: *Fashioning Culture*. New Haven & London: Yale University Press, 1994.

Four Centuries of Fashion: Classical Kimono from the Kyoto National Museum. San Francisco: Asian Art Museum of San Francisco, Kyoto National Museum, The Agency for Cultural Affairs, 1997.

Izutsu Gafu. *Genshoku Nihon fushoku shi* (原色日本服飾史). Kyoto: Kōrinsha, 1982.

Kennedy, Alan. *Japanese Costume: History and Tradition*. Paris: Editions Adam Biro, 1990.

Maruyama Nobuhiko. *Buke no fukushoku* (武家の服飾). Series: Nihon no bijutsu, No. 340. Tokyo: Shibundo, 1994.